THE PSYCHOLOGY OF CONSPIRACY

- Why did the third World Trade Center building (WTC7) collapse on September 11th, even though it was not struck by any aircraft?
- Why did Princess Diana's "drunk" driver look sober as he climbed into the car minutes before their deadly accident?
- Could a slender birch tree really have caused the plane crash that killed the president of Poland in 2010?

"Conspiracy thinking" – the search for explanations of significant global events in clandestine plots, suppressed knowledge, and the secret actions of elite groups – provides simple and logical answers to the social doubts and uncertainties that occur at times of major national and international crises. Contemporary social psychology seeks to explain the human motivation to create, share, and receive conspiracy theories and to shed light on the consequences of these theories for people's social and political functioning.

This important collection, written by leading researchers in the field, is the first to apply quantitative empirical findings to the subject of conspiracy theorizing. The first section of the book explores conspiracy theories in the context of group perception and intergroup relations, paying particular attention to anti-Semitic conspiracy stereotypes. It then goes on to examine the relationship between an individual's political ideology and the degree to which he or she engages in conspiracy thinking. The concluding part of the book considers the explanatory power of conspiracy, focusing on the link between social paranoia and digital media and highlighting the social, political, and environmental consequences of conspiracy theories.

The Psychology of Conspiracy will be of great interest to academics and researchers in social and political psychology and be a valuable resource to those in the fields of social policy, anthropology, political science, and cultural studies.

Michal Bilewicz is Associate Professor in the Faculty of Psychology, University of Warsaw, Poland.

Aleksandra Cichocka is Lecturer in the School of Psychology, University of Kent, UK.

Wiktor Soral is a PhD Candidate at the Robert B. Zajonc Institute for Social Studies, University of Warsaw, Poland.

THE PSYCHOLOGY OF CONSPIRACY

A *Festschrift* for Mirosław Kofta

Edited by Michal Bilewicz,
Aleksandra Cichocka, and
Wiktor Soral

Routledge
Taylor & Francis Group
LONDON AND NEW YORK

First published 2015
by Routledge
27 Church Road, Hove, East Sussex BN3 2FA

and by Routledge
711 Third Avenue, New York, NY 10017

Routledge is an imprint of the Taylor & Francis Group, an informa business

British Library Cataloguing in Publication Data
A catalogue record for this book is available from the British Library

Library of Congress Cataloging-in-Publication Data
The psychology of conspiracy : a festschrift for Mirosław Kofta /
    edited by Michal Bilewicz, Aleksandra Cichocka, Wiktor Soral.
        pages cm
    1. Conspiracies—Psychological aspects.   2. Conspiracy theories—
Psychological aspects.   I. Bilewicz, Michal.   II. Cichocka, Aleksandra.
III. Soral, Wiktor.   IV. Kofta, Miroslaw
    HV6275.P79 2015
    001.9—dc23
    2014049724

ISBN: 978-1-138-81520-9 (hbk)
ISBN: 978-1-138-81523-0 (pbk)
ISBN: 978-1-315-74683-8 (ebk)

Typeset in Bembo
by Apex CoVantage, LLC

Chapters 1, 2, 3, 7, 9 and 10 are based on the work conducted within
the framework of COST Action IS1205 "Social psychological dynamics
of historical representations in the enlarged European Union"

Index editor: Marta Beneda

CONTENTS

CONTRIBUTORS

Michal Bilewicz, Faculty of Psychology, University of Warsaw, Poland

Marcin Bukowski, Institute of Psychology, Jagiellonian University, Poland

Aleksandra Cichocka, School of Psychology, University of Kent, UK

Karen M. Douglas, School of Psychology, University of Kent, UK

Agnieszka Golec de Zavala, Department of Psychology, Goldsmiths, University of London, UK

Monika Grzesiak-Feldman, Faculty of Psychology, University of Warsaw, Poland

Roland Imhoff, Faculty of Human Sciences, University of Cologne, Germany

Daniel Jolley, School of Psychology, University of Kent, UK

Mikhail Kissine, Université Libre de Bruxelles, Belgium

Olivier Klein, Université Libre de Bruxelles, Belgium

Małgorzata Kossowska, Institute of Psychology, Jagiellonian University, Poland

Péter Krekó, ELTE University, Hungary

André P. M. Krouwel, VU University Amsterdam, Department of Communication Science and Kieskompas (Election Compass) Amsterdam, the Netherlands

Marta Marchlewska, Institute for Social Studies, University of Warsaw, Poland

Mateusz Olechowski, Faculty of Psychology, University of Warsaw, Poland

Myrto Pantazi, Université Libre de Bruxelles, Belgium

Grzegorz Sedek, Faculty of Psychology, University of Social Sciences and Humanities, Poland

Wiktor Soral, Institute for Social Studies, University of Warsaw, Poland

Robbie M. Sutton, School of Psychology, University of Kent, UK

Nicolas Van der Linden, Université Libre de Bruxelles, Belgium

Jan-Willem van Prooijen, VU University Amsterdam, Department of Social and Organizational Psychology and the Netherlands Institute for the Study of Crime and Law Enforcement (NSCR), the Netherlands

Mikolaj Winiewski, Faculty of Psychology, University of Warsaw, Poland

Michael J. Wood, School of Psychology, University of Kent, UK

PREFACE

Why did the third World Trade Center building collapse, although no plane had hit it? Why did Princess Diana's drunk driver look sober when he was entering the car minutes before the deadly accident? Could a 17-inch-thick birch tree have caused the airplane catastrophe in which the Polish president died? Similar questions arise in almost all social and political events that focus public attention and inspire complex theorizing among lay people. Conspiracy theories – looking for causes of such events in clandestine plots, suppressed knowledge, and secret actions – provide simple and logical answers to people's doubts and uncertainties.

Although the term "conspiracy theory" was popularized by philosopher Karl Raimund Popper in 1949, the interest of psychologists in people's reasoning about the hidden nature of social processes and secret intentions of certain groups remained quite limited until the 1980s, when the first publications on the topic of conspiracies started to appear (Groh, 1987; McCauley & Jacques, 1979; Moscovici, 1987). The first edited volume on conspiracy mentality (Graumann & Moscovici, 1987) included theoretical investigations of the topic and historical analyses of anecdotal evidence. Yet, the empirical work about conspiracy theorizing remained scarce.

In the late 1980s, much of the contemporary world underwent rapid transformation. The societies living in the area between the Elbe River in Germany and the Kamchatka Peninsula in Siberia switched from the communist political system to various forms of liberal democracy, and economies changed from state controlled to capitalist free market. People living in this region needed explanations of the extremely dynamic processes that they witnessed. Thus, the post-communist societies became a natural soil in which conspiracy theories could flourish. A Polish social psychologist, Mirosław Kofta, decided to explore the function of such theories and the consequences they have with respect to perception of social groups. During the first democratic elections in Poland, Kofta – together with

Grzegorz Sedek – observed the activation of the belief in a Jewish conspiracy during times of political mobilization and found that such beliefs become a core predictor of intergroup attitudes in Poland (Kofta & Sedek, 1992, 2005). What is more, they showed that the perception of certain groups cannot be described in a traditional social-psychological way, as a trait-laden stereotype (i.e., a social schema of a prototypical group member having certain traits). They claimed that conspiracy theories are not only lay explanations of social processes (Clarke, 2002), but also a specific form of intergroup cognition – representations of certain groups as entities. Subsequently, research on essentialism and entitativity confirmed the unique features of such perceptions (Yzerbyt, Judd, & Corneille, 2004).

In the years that followed, conspiracy theories became a common topic of studies in social psychology. Important advancements have been made by psychologists who took an individual difference approach in analyzing the extent to which an individual endorses conspiracy theories of specific events, facts, and groups. These efforts included exploring the "conspiracy mentality" (Bruder, Haffke, Neave, Nouripanah, & Imhoff, 2013; Imhoff, this volume), creating inventories of conspiracy theory (Swami, Chamorro-Premuzic, & Furnham, 2010), conspiracy belief scales (Grzesiak-Feldman, 2013), and conspiracy stereotype measures (Kofta & Sedek, 2005; Bilewicz, Winiewski, Kofta, & Wójcik, 2013). This progress in the measurement of people's willingness to interpret reality with conspiracy theories also allowed researchers to better explain the mechanisms underlying such theorizing.

While it still remains difficult to identify one common mechanism responsible for construing and maintaining conspiracy beliefs, we can distinguish at least three broad approaches to studying conspiracy thinking. Each of these approaches puts weight on a different set of mechanisms. The first approach places the source of belief in conspiracies within traits and characteristics of the individual. Thus, scholars who pursue this area of study focus on personality and individual differences, as well as political attitudes, that predispose people to conspiracy theorizing. Studies in this area suggest that people who believe in various conspiracy theories tend to be less neurotic but less open to new experiences (Furnham, 2013) and have lower self-esteem but are more agreeable (Swami & Furnham, 2012). Moreover, belief in conspiracy theories is linked to cognitive style, specifically lower analytic thinking, and open-mindedness and higher intuitive thinking (Swami, Voracek, Stieger, Tran, & Furnham, 2014). Interestingly, according to studies by Douglas and Sutton (2011), those who follow conspiracy theories are also more willing to conspire in their personal life.

Psychologists have also extensively explored the links between political attitudes and conspiracy beliefs. According to Abalakina-Paap, Stephan, Craig, and Gregory (1999), one could seek sources of conspiracy theorizing in feelings of alienation, powerlessness, hostility, and being disadvantaged. Grzesiak-Feldman and Irzycka (2009) proved that high right-wing authoritarianism is related to conspiracy stereotypes of Jews, Arabs, Germans, and Russians (for a more detailed description, see Chapter 6 by Monika Grzesiak-Feldman). Aside from studies that link conspiracy thinking to specific political orientations (such as right-wing views), recent evidence points to a more general notion of conspiracy thinking as a monological belief system (Clarke, 2002; Wood, Douglas, & Sutton, 2012). This approach to conspiracy mentality is presented in more detail in Chapter 7 by Roland Imhoff. On the other hand, Jan-Willem van Prooijen and André Krouwel argue in Chapter 5 that conspiracy theories are not characteristic to political left vs. right views but rather to political extremism.

Rather than seeking the sources of belief in conspiracies in certain characteristics of the individual, the second approach focuses on characteristics of human nature. Such an approach tries to explain conspiracy thinking in terms of universal cognitive schemes and attributional biases. Authors of this perspective argue that people have a tendency to perceive any body of evidence as supportive of their position, which ultimately leads to attitude polarization (see, for example, McHoskey, 1995). Moreover, it seems that the probability of even a single piece of evidence is judged to be more likely if it is presented along with some other evidence, thus forming a conjunction fallacy (Ahn & Bailenson, 1996); this phenomenon could explain the irrationality of conspiracy narratives that frequently include mutually contradictory evidences. Indeed, studies by Brotherton and French (2014) showed that people who endorse conspiracy theories are also more susceptible to the conjunction fallacy. Thus, certain characteristics of human cognition lead to adherence to conspiracy explanations of certain events. Also, the more the event is perceived as grave and important, the more people will be prone to perceive its causes as equally serious (Leman & Cinnirella, 2007; van Prooijen & Dijk, 2014). The role of cognitive processing that promotes the endorsement of conspiracy theories is presented in greater detail in Chapter 9 by Olivier Klein, Nicolas Van der Linden, Myrto Pantazi, and Mikhail Kissine. A different approach is taken by Mikolaj Winiewski, Wiktor Soral, and Michal Bilewicz in Chapter 2, in which the authors identify specific cognitive schemas and stereotype content that are related to perceiving out-groups as conspiring against the in-group.

Finally, the third approach tries to identify the motivational roots of biased social cognition leading to conspiracy beliefs, as well as particular situational and system-related cues that trigger such motivations. The motivation of special importance that is probably the most often linked to conspirational, as well as paranormal, beliefs is the control motivation. In their famous studies, Whitson and Galinsky (2008) showed that situations that evoke feelings of a lack of control increase illusory pattern perceptions, including a belief in conspiracies and superstitions. The authors argue that "when individuals are unable to gain a sense of control objectively, they will try to gain it perceptually" (p. 115). Similar conclusions about the role of motivation to gain control, certainty, and a sense of meaning in fostering conspiracy theorizing flow from the large body of studies conducted in diverse social and cultural contexts (e.g., Bukowski, de Lemus, Rodriguez-Bailón, & Willis, 2014; Grzesiak-Feldman, 2013; Kofta & Sedek, 2005; Newheiser, Farias, & Tausch, 2011; Sullivan, Landau, & Rothschild, 2010; van Prooijen & Jostmann, 2013). Chapter 8 by Małgorzata Kossowska and Marcin Bukowski provides an overview of such literature. Control deprivation likely increases in the harsh times of economic crisis and social change. A particular kind of conspiracy theory is likely to develop under such conditions. So-called conspiracy stereotypes blame certain group for poor living conditions. Their socio-psychological antecedents and consequences are discussed in Chapter 1 by Michal Bilewicz and Grzegorz Sedek. However, being disadvantaged (be it a result of an economic crisis or a discriminatory system) is not only an individual but also a collective experience. Research by Crocker, Luhtanen, Broadnax, and Blaine (1999) shows an example of how endorsing theories of the U.S. government conspiring against Blacks is associated with blaming the problems of Black Americans on prejudice and discrimination. Collective narcissism is a type of in-group positivity linked to such threatened identity and group defensiveness (Golec de Zavala, Cichocka, Eidelson, & Jayawickreme, 2009). The evidence for the links between conspiracy beliefs and collective narcissism is presented in Chapter 3 by Aleksandra Cichocka, Agnieszka Golec de Zavala, Marta Marchlewska, and Mateusz Olechowski. In general, one could say that conspiracy theories are a particular form of collective motivated cognition, an idea presented in Chapter 4 by Péter Krekó.

A full understanding of the psychology of conspiracy beliefs requires not only identifying their antecedents, but also examining their consequences. Most recent work on conspiracy theories seeks to understand what happens when people are exposed to conspiratorial ideas. For example, research by Lewandowsky, Oberauer, & Gignac (2013) shows that conspiratorial thinking predicts a rejection of scientific evidence in the context of genetically modified foods, vaccinations, and climate science. An overview of the advancements in the study of consequences of conspiracies is presented in Chapter 10 by Karen Douglas, Robbie Sutton, Daniel Jolley, and Michael Wood.

Overall, the current volume is the first to thoroughly present the application of the quantitative empirical findings of social-psychological research (including experimental work, cross-sectional studies, surveys, and archival studies) to the context of conspiracy theorizing. It is the first edited volume that collects chapters written by leading scholars in the social psychology of conspiracies. As such, it offers a state-of-the-art account of the field. We dedicate this volume to our teacher, Mirosław Kofta, whose research on conspiracy stereotypes was one of the first psychological attempts to understand the complex nature and explanatory power of conspiracy theories in politics and social life.

Mirosław Kofta received his graduate training under the supervision of Professor Andrzej Lewicki at Adam Mickiewicz University in Poznań – a school of empirically oriented clinical psychology. Soon after, he moved to Warsaw where he started his fruitful career in experimental social psychology. His own research focused on the topic of cognitive control – still one of his major research interests. Together with his doctoral student, Grzegorz Sedek, he developed an informational model of learned helplessness (Kofta, 1993; Kofta & Sedek, 1989a, 1998, 1999; Sedek & Kofta, 1990). The model proposed that the state of learned helplessness is caused by irreducible uncertainty (informational chaos) rather than just

Professor Mirosław Kofta

Photo: Tadeusz Późniak/Polityka

by the process of repeated failures. Kofta and Sedek (1989a) questioned the dominant paradigm in learned helplessness research and performed several experiments using their novel procedure: the informative helplessness training. Their research on this topic, published in top psychological journals (*Journal of Personality and Social Psychology, Journal of Experimental Psychology: General, European Journal of Social Psychology*), received a great deal of attention in the field and led to several polemics on the nature of learned helplessness (e.g., Snyder & Frankel, 1989; Kofta & Sedek, 1989b). The informative helplessness training developed by Kofta and Sedek has been used in various areas of psychology, such as in research on the effects of control deprivation on cognitive processes (Ric, 1997; Ric & Scharnitzky, 2003), on the ability to achieve cognitive structure (Otten & Bar-Tal, 2002), or on cognitive exhaustion in decision making (Sedek, Kofta, & Tyszka, 1993).

In the 1990s, after exploring the phenomenon of conspiracy stereotypes, Mirosław Kofta extended his research interest to a new field in social psychology: intergroup relations. He was probably the first researcher in Eastern Europe who employed experimental methods to the study of intergroup relations. He worked intensively on the processes of dehumanization and infrahumanization (see a review of this research in Kofta, Baran, & Tarnowska, 2013), collective moral emotions of guilt and shame (Kofta & Slawuta, 2013), and, more generally, the ways in which people cope with threats to their social identity (Bilewicz & Kofta, 2011; Cichocka, Golec de Zavala, Kofta, & Rozum, 2013).

After moving from basic experimental social cognition research to the study of intergroup relations, Kofta remained not only a prolific author and researcher, but also a very active organizer of scientific life. He organized several conferences, among them several European Association of Social Psychology meetings: on shared reality construction in 2002, on dehumanization and infrahumanization in 2008, and on control and power in intergroup relations in 2012 (all of them organized in his beloved town of Kazimierz Dolny). He is also very active in the local life of Polish social psychology, as co-founder of the Polish Society of Social Psychology and frequent contributor to Polish psychological journals and volumes. He edited several important handbooks that are widely used to educate the future generations of social psychologists: "Złudzenia które pozwalają żyć" ("Illusions that help us to live: Essays in social psychology," with Teresa Szustrowa, 1991), "Psychologia poznania społecznego" ("The psychology of social cognition," with Małgorzata Kossowska, 2009), "Myślenie stereotypowe i uprzedzenia" ("Stereotypes and prejudice," with sociologist Aleksandra Jasinska-Kania, 2001), "Wobec Obcych: Zagrożenia psychologiczne a stosunki międzygrupowe" ("Toward 'them': Psychological threat and intergroup relations," with Michal Bilewicz, 2011), and most recently, "Poza stereotypy" ("Beyond stereotyping," with Marek Drogosz & Michal Bilewicz, 2012).

Mirek Kofta is passionate about his own research, as well as the work of his students. He has always stressed the importance of good theorizing, well-designed experiments, and good replications. These habits are especially worth noting in times when social psychology suffers from a flow of atheoretical, nonreplicated, "flashy" research results. Mirek spent long hours teaching his students proper experimental procedures during individual tutorials. His discussions during seminars and conferences often changed into lengthy yet vibrant theoretical debates. For Mirek, doing social psychology means contributing to the theory and questioning the existing theoretical mainstream. At the same time, he is always committed to the field of social psychology – publishing his work internationally, presenting research findings at major conferences, and being engaged in lively discussions with top American and European psychologists. Such international careers were not so frequent in Polish psychology or, more broadly, in East European social science. His example was followed by his former and current students, who work both in the fields of experimental social cognition and the social psychology of intergroup relations.

This volume includes contributions of Mirek's current and former students, friends, and colleagues. With this *Festschrift*, we would like to express our gratitude for years of inspiration and fantastic collaboration and wish him even more future discoveries and theoretical advances in social psychology.

Michal Bilewicz
Aleksandra Cichocka
Wiktor Soral

References

Abalakina-Paap, M., Stephan, W. G., Craig, T., & Gregory, W. L. (1999). Beliefs in conspiracies. *Political Psychology, 20*(3), 637–647.

Ahn, W. K., & Bailenson, J. (1996). Causal attribution as a search for underlying mechanisms: An explanation of the conjunction fallacy and the discounting principle. *Cognitive Psychology, 31*(1), 82–123.

Bilewicz, M., & Kofta, M. (2011). Less biased under threat? Self-verificatory reactions to social identity threat among groups with negative self-stereotypes. *Journal of Applied Social Psychology, 41*(9), 2249–2267.

Bilewicz, M., Winiewski, M., Kofta, M., & Wójcik, A. (2013). Harmful ideas, the structure and consequences of anti-Semitic beliefs in Poland. *Political Psychology, 34*(6), 821–839.

Brotherton, R., & French, C. C. (2014). Belief in conspiracy theories and susceptibility to the conjunction fallacy. *Applied Cognitive Psychology, 28*(2), 238–248.

Bruder, M., Haffke, P., Neave, N., Nouripanah, N., & Imhoff, R. (2013). Measuring individual differences in generic beliefs in conspiracy theories across cultures: The generic conspiracist beliefs scale. *Frontiers in Psychology, 4*, 279.

Bukowski, M., de Lemus, S., Rodriguez-Bailón, R., & Willis, G. B. (2014). *Who's to blame? Causal attributions of the economic crisis and personal control.* Manuscript in preparation.

Cichocka, A., Golec de Zavala, A., Kofta, M., & Rozum, J. (2013). Threats to feminist identity and reactions to gender discrimination. *Sex Roles, 68*(9–10), 605–619.

Clarke, S. (2002). Conspiracy theories and conspiracy theorizing. *Philosophy of the Social Sciences, 32*(2), 131–150.

Crocker, J., Luhtanen, R., Broadnax, S., & Blaine, B. E. (1999). Belief in U.S. government conspiracies against Blacks among Black and White college students: Powerlessness or system blame? *Personality and Social Psychology Bulletin, 25*(8), 941–953.

Douglas, K. M., & Sutton, R. M. (2011). Does it take one to know one? Endorsement of conspiracy theories is influenced by personal willingness to conspire. *British Journal of Social Psychology, 50*(3), 544–552.

Furnham, A. (2013). Commercial conspiracy theories: A pilot study. *Frontiers in Psychology, 4*, 379.

Golec de Zavala, A., Cichocka, A., Eidelson, R., & Jayawickreme, N. (2009). Collective narcissism and its social consequences. *Journal of Personality and Social Psychology, 97*(6), 1074–1096.

Graumann, C. F., & Moscovici, S. (Eds.). (1987). *Changing conceptions of conspiracy.* New York: Springer.

Groh, D. (1987). The temptation of conspiracy theory, or: Why do bad things happen to good people? In C. F. Graumann & S. Moscovici (Eds.), *Changing conceptions of conspiracy* (pp. 1–37). New York: Springer.

Grzesiak-Feldman, M. (2013). The effect of high-anxiety situations on conspiracy thinking. *Current Psychology, 32*(1), 100–118.

Grzesiak-Feldman, M., & Irzycka, M. (2009). Right-wing authoritarianism and conspiracy thinking in a Polish sample. *Psychological Reports, 105*(2), 389–393.

Kofta, M. (Ed.). (1993). *Psychologia aktywności: zaangażowanie, sprawstwo, bezradność* [The psychology of activity: Personal involvement, agency, helplessness]. Poznan: Nakom.

Kofta, M., Baran, T., & Tarnowska, M. (2013). Dehumanization as a denial of human potentials: The naïve theory of humanity perspective. In P. G. Bain, J. Vaes, & J-Ph. Leyens (Eds.), *Advances in Understanding Humanness and Dehumanization* (pp. 256–275). New York: Psychology Press.

Kofta, M., & Sedek, G. (1989a). Repeated failure: A source of helplessness or a factor irrelevant to its emergence? *Journal of Experimental Psychology: General, 118*(1), 3–12.

Kofta, M., & Sedek, G. (1989b). Egotism versus generalization-of-uncontrollability explanations of helplessness: Reply to Snyder and Frankel (1989). *Journal of Experimental Psychology: General, 118*(4), 413–416.

Kofta, M., & Sedek, G. (1992). *Struktura poznawcza stereotypu etnicznego: Bliskość wyborów parlamentarnych a przejawy antysemityzmu* [Cognitive structure of ethnic stereotype, proximity of parliamentary elections, and anti-Semitism]. In Z. Chlewiński & L. Kurcz (Eds.), *Stereotypy i uprzedzenia, Kolokwia Psychologiczne* [Stereotypes and prejudice. Colloquia Psychologica] (Vol. 1, pp. 67–86). Warsaw: Polish Academy of Sciences, Institute of Psychology Press.

Kofta, M., & Sedek, G. (1998). Uncontrollability as a source of cognitive exhaustion: Implications for helplessness and depression. In M. Kofta, G. Weary, & G. Sedek (Eds.), *Personal control in action: Cognitive and motivational mechanisms* (pp. 391–418). New York: Plenum Press.

Kofta, M., & Sedek, G. (1999). Uncontrollability as irreducible uncertainty. *European Journal of Social Psychology, 29*(5–6), 577–590.

Kofta, M., & Sedek, G. (2005). Conspiracy stereotypes of Jews during systemic transformation in Poland. *International Journal of Sociology, 35*(1), 40–64.

Kofta, M., & Slawuta, P. (2013). Thou shall not kill . . . your brother: Victim–perpetrator cultural closeness and moral disapproval of polish atrocities against Jews after the Holocaust. *Journal of Social Issues, 69*(1), 54–73.

Leman, P. J., & Cinnirella, M. (2007). A major event has a major cause: Evidence for the role of heuristics in reasoning about conspiracy theories. *Social Psychological Review, 9*(2), 18–28.

Lewandowsky, S., Oberauer, K., & Gignac, G. E. (2013). NASA faked the moon landing – Therefore (climate) science is a hoax: An anatomy of the motivated rejection of science. *Psychological Science, 24*(5), 622–633.

McCauley, C., & Jacques, S. (1979). The popularity of conspiracy theories of presidential assassination: A Bayesian analysis. *Journal of Personality and Social Psychology, 37*(5), 637–644.

McHoskey, J. W. (1995). Case closed? On the John F. Kennedy assassination: Biased assimilation of evidence and attitude polarization. *Basic and Applied Social Psychology, 17*(3), 395–409.

Moscovici, S. (1987). The conspiracy mentality. In C. F. Graumann & S. Moscovici (Eds.), *Changing conceptions of conspiracy* (pp. 1–37). New York: Springer.

Newheiser, A.-K., Farias, M., & Tausch, N. (2011). The functioning nature of conspiracy beliefs: Examining the underpinnings of beliefs in the Da Vinci Code conspiracy. *Personality and Individual Differences, 51*(8), 1007–1011.

Otten, S., & Bar-Tal, Y. (2002). Self-anchoring in the minimal group paradigm: The impact of need and ability to achieve cognitive structure. *Group Processes & Intergroup Relations, 5*(4), 267–284.

Ric, F. (1997). Effects of control deprivation on subsequent use of stereotypes. *Journal of Social Psychology, 137*(3), 333–342.

Ric, F., & Scharnitzky, P. (2003). Effects of control deprivation on effort expenditure and accuracy performance. *European Journal of Social Psychology, 33*(1), 103–118.

Sedek, G., & Kofta, M. (1990). When cognitive exertion does not yield cognitive gain: Toward an informational explanation of learned helplessness. *Journal of Personality and Social Psychology, 58*(4), 729–743.

Sedek, G., Kofta, M., & Tyszka, T. (1993). Effects of uncontrollability on subsequent decision making: Testing the cognitive exhaustion hypothesis. *Journal of Personality and Social Psychology, 65*(6), 1270–1281.

Snyder, M. L., & Frankel, A. (1989). Egotism versus learned helplessness as an explanation for the unsolvable problem effect: Comment on Kofta and Sédek. *Journal of Experimental Psychology: General, 118*(4), 409–412.

Sullivan, D., Landau, M. J., & Rothschild, Z. K. (2010). An existential function of enemyship: Evidence that people attribute influence to personal and political enemies to compensate for threats to control. *Journal of Personality and Social Psychology, 98*(3), 434–449.

Swami, V., Chamorro-Premuzic, T., & Furnham, A. (2010). Unanswered questions: A preliminary investigation of personality and individual difference predictors of 9/11 conspiracist beliefs. *Applied Cognitive Psychology, 24*(6), 749–761.

Swami, V., & Furnham, A. (2012). Examining conspiracist beliefs about the disappearance of Amelia Earhart. *Journal of General Psychology, 139*(4), 244–259.

Swami, V., Voracek, M., Stieger, S., Tran, U. S., & Furnham, A. (2014). Analytic thinking reduces belief in conspiracy theories. *Cognition, 133*(3), 572–585.

van Prooijen, J.-W., & Jostmann, N. B. (2013). Belief in conspiracy theories: The influence of uncertainty and perceived morality. *European Journal of Social Psychology, 43*(1), 109–115.

van Prooijen, J.-W., & van Dijk, E. (2014). When consequence size predicts belief in conspiracy theories: The moderating role of perspective taking. *Journal of Experimental Social Psychology, 55*, 63–73. doi:10.1016/j.jesp.2014.06.006

Whitson, J. A., & Galinsky, A. D. (2008). Lacking control increases illusory pattern perception. *Science, 322*(5898), 115–117.

Wood, M. J., Douglas, K. M., & Sutton, R. M. (2012). Dead and alive: Beliefs in contradictory conspiracy theories. *Social Psychological and Personality Science, 3*(6), 767–773.

Yzerbyt, V., Judd, C. M., & Corneille, O. (Eds.). (2004). *The psychology of group perception: Perceived variability, entitativity, and essentialism.* London: Psychology Press.

PART I
Conspiracy theories in group perception

1

CONSPIRACY STEREOTYPES

Their sociopsychological antecedents and consequences

Michal Bilewicz and Grzegorz Sedek

"Judeosoc: the Jewish socialists. This is the most dangerous formation of the socialist, our most worst enemy. They are competent and intelligent. Adam Michnik, TVN television, *Gazeta Wyborcza* daily – this is where they are hidden. They hate me sincerely," said newly elected Polish member of the European Parliament, Janusz Korwin-Mikke in an interview with *Newsweek* magazine (Krzymowski, 2014). His declaration represents a specific genre of political communication in which specific ethnic minority is presented as omnipotent, powerful, and realizing its hidden agenda.

Similar statements could be heard in other political campaigns in Poland, making conspiracy theories pronounced within public discourse (Bilewicz, Winiewski, & Radzik, 2012). In this chapter, we would like to explain this mobilizing role of conspiracy theories in times of political change, focusing mainly on the conspiracy stereotypes of Jews that portray this minority as powerful and engaged in evil plots. At the same time, we propose that conspiracy stereotypes are activated in specific situations, although most of the time they remain dormant. We aim at understanding the popularity of conspiracy stereotypes among different social groups – people who are economically deprived and senior citizens – who tend to be most committed to such theories in times of political mobilization. We propose that conspiracy stereotypes respond to particular needs among such groups – they serve explanatory functions and respond to threatened cognitive motivations.

The belief in Jewish conspiracy as a stereotype

Most of the literature on stereotyping focuses on the cognitive character of this process. Thus, stereotypes are social schemas that organize the knowledge about groups and allow the application of such knowledge in the process of categorization (Hamilton, 1981). Stereotypes lead to several cognitive biases in person perception – in information selection, biased attention to stereotype-confirming information, and selective memory (Fiske, 1998; Snyder, 1981). At the same time, stereotypes serve explanatory functions, justifying intergroup inequalities and legitimizing groups' existence and treatment of specific group members (McGarty, Yzerbyt, & Spears, 2002).

This description applies well to trait-laden stereotypes – social schemas of prototypical group members. At the same time, people often hold representations of certain groups as a whole that differ from the stereotype of a prototypical group member. Such group-level stereotypes often have a form of lay theories, presenting groups as existing entities (Haslam, Rothschild, & Ernst, 2000). Members of entitative groups are perceived as interchangeable individuals bonded with an underlying essence. Such groups become natural kinds, similar to chemical particles, physical elements, or biological species (Keller, 2005). Most psychological research reflects on the biological forms of essentialism (Haslam et al., 2000; Keller, 2005). Research by Kofta and Sedek (1992; 2005) on the stereotype of a group as a whole, later named "conspiracy stereotypes," is an attempt to study social forms of essentialism, in which group essence is ascribed not as a biological metaphor, but rather as a social lay theory. Although such stereotypes do not offer a schema of individuals, they are often applied in processing information about groups. Conspiracy stereotypes also serve an explanatory role, allowing the creation of lay theories about the social world and offering an interpretation of political events and conflicts.

The original research on conspiracy stereotypes was conducted in the context of the stereotypical perception of Jews in Poland (Kofta & Sedek, 1992; 1995; 1999a; 2005). Such stereotypes form a causal, holistic theory of an ethnic group. It points to alleged collective goals of a group (i.e., striving for power and dominance over other ethnic groups), secret character of collective behavior (i.e., plots, conspiracies, secret agreements), and high levels of group egoism (i.e., support for fellow in-group members combined with a lack of interest in the well-being of other groups). Group members become merely executors of the collective intentions of the group as a whole (Kofta & Sedek, 2005).

The belief in Jewish conspiracy is a part of the modern anti-Semitic imagery, although its sources can be traced back to the social position of Jews in premodern societies. It has been observed in areas populated by sizeable Jewish minorities, such as Britain (Billig, 1987) or Ukraine (Bilewicz & Krzeminski, 2010), and in countries where large Jewish communities existed in the past, such as Poland (Bilewicz et al., 2012), but also in countries where almost no Jews ever lived, such as Malaysia (Swami, 2012). The existence of conspiracy stereotype of Jews in countries where the target of stereotype is virtually absent raises an important question about the sources of this stereotype, as well as its function in contemporary society. In this chapter, we present a model that aims to explain the antecedents and consequences of conspiracy stereotypes (Figure 1.1). The model suggests that both individual characteristics and objective situational circumstances are

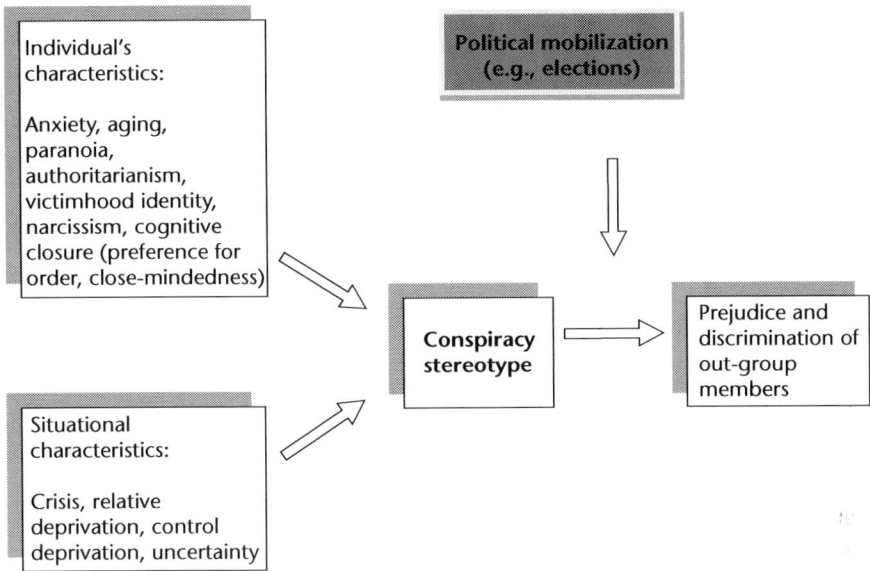

FIGURE 1.1 The model of conspiracy stereotyping: antecedents and consequences.

responsible for people's endorsement of conspiracy beliefs. At the same time, we argue that such beliefs are activated by a specific trigger: namely, the situation of political mobilization. Such a situation allows people to translate a conspiracy stereotype into collective action, discriminatory behavior, or prejudice.

Trait antecedents of conspiracy stereotypes: Between personality and cognition

People who believe in conspiracy are often accused of possessing a paranoid cognitive style and other mild forms of psychopathology. The authors of original research on authoritarian personality cautiously observed: "there is . . . evidence that can be interpreted as in accord with the possibility of paranoid trends in our subjects extremely high on anti-Semitism" (Frenkel-Brunswik & Sanford, 1945, p. 280). Further research provided mixed evidence about the impact of paranoia (in its clinical sense) on belief in Jewish conspiracies, although certainly the relation of politicized forms of paranoia and belief in Jewish conspiracy is a well-established fact (Korzeniowski, 2009; 2010). In his rigorous studies on the topic, Krzysztof Korzeniowski (2010) found that the link between political paranoia and the belief in Jewish conspiracy holds even after controlling for general social distance towards Jews. People with political paranoia believe in Jewish control over the economy; they perceive Jews as aiming to dominate the world and contracting secret plots. Political paranoia and conspiracy stereotypes have similar correlates: political alienation and authoritarianism (Bilewicz et al., 2012; Korzeniowski, 2009; Swami, 2012). What links paranoid style in political thinking

spiracy stereotyping is the general perception of threats in one's social
..onment.

Early theorizing by Allport (1954) perceived anxiety, insecurity, and fearfulness
as a core of the prejudiced personality. Evidence from the studies on intergroup
anxiety, as well as on intergroup threat theory, confirms that many of the negative intergroup attitudes are based on fears of either symbolic or realistic character
(Stephan & Stephan, 1985; 2000). Conspiracy stereotypes of Jews – forming the
grounds for anti-Semitic attitudes – were often linked with anxiety and sense of
threat (Ackerman & Jahoda, 1950; Frenkel-Brunswik & Sanford, 1945).

In a recent study of this issue, Monika Grzesiak-Feldman (2013) analyzed the
influence of anxiety on conspiracy stereotypes of several ethnic out-groups (Jews,
Germans, and Arabs). She found systematic positive correlations between anxiety
(both state and trait anxiety) and conspiracy stereotypes of all three ethnic groups.
Trait anxiety was particularly linked with beliefs in Arab conspiracy, whereas state
anxiety was particularly linked with a belief in Jewish conspiracy. Her subsequent
studies (Grzesiak-Feldman, 2013, Studies 2 and 3) confirmed this observation:
threatening situations, such as pre-examination stress, increased people's endorsement of a conspiracy stereotype of Jews. This points to the situational antecedents
of conspiracy stereotypes – such as relative deprivation or crises – as potential
determinants of state anxiety. Anxiety is also an essential part of an authoritarian
personality. Authoritarians believe that the social world is dangerous and threatening (Altemeyer, 1998; Duckitt, 2008). In his integrative model of personality,
ideology, and prejudice, Duckitt (2008) showed that high authoritarians express
a motivational goal of establishing stability that helps them regain security in a
threatening and dangerous social world. Group membership forms a buffer against
such threats (see also Fritsche et al., 2013). This leads to out-group prejudice and
the maintenance of stereotypes, among them conspiracy stereotypes.

The main aim of the original research on authoritarian personality (Adorno,
Frenkel-Brunswik, Levinson, & Sanford, 1950; Frenkel-Brunswik & Sanford,
1945) was to analyze the psychological bases of support for fascism and anti-Semitic
ideologies. Several studies found that authoritarianism, as well as its more modern
form of right-wing authoritarianism (Altemeyer, 1998), is a crucial antecedent of
conspiracy stereotypes, particularly the belief in Jewish conspiracy (Abalakina-
Paap, Stephan, Craig, & Gregory, 1999; Bilewicz et al., 2012; Grzesiak-Feldman &
Irzycka, 2009; Korzeniowski, 2010). The influence of authoritarianism on conspiracy beliefs is further discussed by Grzesiak-Feldman and Imhoff (this volume).

The least researched of the individual-difference antecedents of conspiracy
stereotypes are the cognitive and motivational influences on judgmental processes across the adult life span. Early survey findings based on a national sample
of Polish adults (Polish General Social Survey, 1992) indicated a relatively strong
correlation ($r = .26$) between the age of respondents and conspiracy stereotypes
of Jews (see Kofta & Sedek, 1999a, Table 1). Interestingly, a social survey conducted in the United States, the Chicago Area Survey from 1992, in the same
year, indicated that both the age of respondents and their level of conspiracy

stereotype of Jews were significant predictors of negative attitudes towar icans of Jewish origin, when partialling out the significant roles of edu political conservatism (Kofta & Sedek, 1999a, Table 4). The more recent stuai̇cs also indicate that beliefs in Jewish conspiracy are often found to be related with age – senior people are more committed to conspiracy stereotypes than younger cohorts (Bilewicz, Winiewski, Kofta, & Wójcik, 2013; Krzeminski, 2002; Zick, Küpper, & Hövermann, 2011).

This leads to a conclusion that there might be some cognitive and motivational factors responsible for older adults' endorsement of conspiracy stereotypes. In recent years, researchers have demonstrated that older adults are more likely to stereotype a variety of social groups than younger adults (for a recent review, see Radvansky, Copeland, & von Hippel, 2010; Stewart, von Hippel, & Radvansky, 2009). One of the common explanations for this finding is that older adults find greater difficulty than do younger adults in inhibiting stereotypic thoughts because of a decline in the inhibitory function (e.g., Hasher, Zacks, & May, 1999; von Hippel & Dunlop, 2005; von Hippel, Silver, & Lynch, 2000). Another set of explanations asserts that aging-related limitations in other cognitive functions involved in social information processing (e.g., limitations in mental speed, working memory, or flexibility) constrain the amount and type of information used in constructing judgments (Henry, von Hippel, & Baynes, 2009; Hess, 2000). This reduced utilization of cognitive resources among older adults results in the use of schematic representations, biased judgments about others, and greater social inappropriateness. The recent research (Czarnek, Kossowska, & Sedek, in press) extends previous research by examining both the cognitive and motivational aspects of deficient flexibility, which might be responsible for stereotypic inferences about out-group members among older adults. We hypothesized and found that the motivational mediator between age and the tendency to draw stereotypical inferences about out-groups is the need for closure (NFC) (Kruglanski, 1989). NFC is defined as a need to have *any* answer on a given topic in order to avoid further ambiguity about that topic. It is well established that a high NFC is associated with a schematic processing style, in which attitudes and judgments are based on schema-related cues rather than on thoughtful consideration. In contrast, low NFC is associated with a systematic processing style, in which attitudes and judgments are based on careful scrutiny and the elaboration of information. We suggested that this motivation, exhibited as a tendency to preserve available resources and engage in activities that minimize any drain on these resources (Kossowska, 2007; Sedek, Kossowska, & Rydzewska, 2014), may play a crucial role in how information is processed in older versus younger adults.

In a recent study, we found substantial support for the predicted mediating role of the need for cognitive closure on the relationship between aging and the level of accepting the conspiracy stereotypes. In this online study, we measured belief in Jewish conspiracy and the need for cognitive closure in a sample of 571 adult Poles from two age groups: 18–25 years old and 50–60 years old. We found that senior Poles express significantly higher levels of conspiracy stereotype than do young

Poles. Additionally, we performed a set of mediation analyses in order to test for indirect effects of age on conspiracy stereotypes through different components of need for cognitive closure. The findings of this study support the prediction that the effect of age on conspiracy stereotype is significantly mediated by four subscales of NFC (preference for order, predictability, discomfort with ambiguity, and closed-mindedness).

Overall, these findings might be interpreted in motivational terms (see Czarnek et al., in press; Hess, 2014; Hess & Queen, 2014). According to this motivational account, aging is related to increasing costs of engagement in effortful cognitive activities. As aging proceeds, more resources are necessary to achieve a particular level of performance in an effortful task. Furthermore, perception of costs results in the lack of intrinsic motivation to commit resources to cognitively demanding tasks, and that in turn is reflected in the selection processes of directing and energizing. Hence, older adults tend to invest their very limited cognitive resources in tasks that are important to them and relate to their everyday activities. Older adults may conserve resources by simplifying their interactions with the environment and limiting both the quantity and complexity of information to which they attend. This tendency to conserve resources may be expressed as a reliance on highly routinized and schematic cognitive patterns, rather than the construction of new, and perhaps more adaptive, cognitive patterns on the spot (see Hess, 2014; Sedek et al., 2014).

Applying this rationale to the current discussion on the antecedents of conspiracy beliefs, it could be hypothesized that the tendency of older adults to conserve resources may be expressed as a reliance on schematic conspiracy explanations of economic and social events rather than on the construction of novel and mentally demanding causal mechanisms.

Situational antecedents of conspiracy stereotypes: Relative deprivation, experience of victimization, and loss of control

Already the classic formulation of the scapegoat theory of prejudice (Zawadzki, 1948) suggested that the situation of deprivation might be an important source of racial hatred, as well as stereotyping. Social psychologists used the scapegoat model in order to explain different acts of discrimination, conflicts, and genocide (Glick, 2002; Green, Glaser, & Rich, 1998). According to the ideological model of scapegoating proposed by Peter Glick (2002), widespread frustration motivates people to seek an explanation of their difficult life condition. The popularity of conspiracy stereotypes in times of economic or political crises might be attributed to the broader desire for explanation among deprived societies. Anti-Semitic ideology that provides such an explanation seems to satisfy that desire very well. Glick (2002) suggests that successful ideology has to portray certain minority groups (Jews in the Weimar Republic, Armenians in the Young Turk Movement, Tutsis in Habyarimana-era Rwanda) as having a high level of competence and negative intentions towards the in-group ("envious prejudice," according to the authors of the stereotype-content model [Fiske, Xu, Cuddy, & Glick, 1999; Glick & Fiske, 2001]). The concept of envious prejudice highly resembles conspiracy stereotype; thus, one could argue that similar situations (economic crises, shared frustrations) could be a basis for the popularity of conspiracy stereotypes (see Winiewski, Soral, & Bilewicz, this volume).

Although situational factors, such as economic deprivation, have a relatively smaller impact on conspiracy stereotypes of Jews than do personality traits (Bergman, 2008; Gibson & Howard, 2007), the scapegoating model of prejudice was still worth empirical examination, as it focused not on economic conditions themselves, but rather on people's subjective experiences of external difficulties, operationalized as relative deprivation. Relative deprivation is known to affect ethnic prejudice and out-group discrimination, especially if it is experienced on a collective level (Pettigrew et al., 2008). Bilewicz and Krzeminski (2010) expected that the effects of relative deprivation on out-group discrimination should be mediated by the endorsement of conspiracy stereotypes. In line with the theoretical model of Glick (2002), relative deprivation should breed prejudice towards groups perceived as responsible for one's difficult living conditions. Thus, relative deprivation increases conspiracy stereotypes of Jews, which in turn leads to higher intentions to discriminate against Jews. The nationwide study on a representative sample of Polish participants supported this prediction: people who suffered relative deprivation were more supportive of discriminatory policies against Jews, such as restrictions in buying land and establishing companies in Poland. What is more, this effect was mediated by the endorsement of conspiracy stereotypes of Jews (Bilewicz & Krzeminski, 2010). This finding was supported by further research that found relative deprivation to be one of the three main antecedents of the conspiracy stereotypes of Jews in Poland (Bilewicz et al., 2012; Bilewicz et al., 2013) – the other two being authoritarian personality and victimhood-based identity.

Collective victimhood was conceptualized in social psychology as competitive victimhood (Noor, Shnabel, Halabi, & Nadler, 2012), victimhood consciousness (Vollhardt & Bilali, 2014), victimhood-based identity (Bilewicz & Stefaniak, 2013), or perpetual in-group victimhood orientation (Klar, Schori-Eyal, & Klar, 2013). All of these concepts consider victimhood as individual construal or even trait, rather than as an experience of group members. In the abovementioned studies, victimhood – when defined in an exclusive and competitive way – was largely responsible for negative intergroup relations, stereotyping, and prejudice observed in various contexts – Israel, Poland, Congo, Rwanda, Burundi, and Northern Ireland. People who are considered to be members of a victimized group tend to derogate all other groups that also possess a victim status.

Here, we would like to analyze the influence of victimhood on conspiracy stereotyping as a situational factor contributing to conspiracy mentality rather than as an individual difference. We believe that people's collective experiences of victimization – regardless of subjective construals – can make them more prone to conspiracy stereotypes. After experiencing collectively acts of discrimination, disadvantage, or crimes, people can develop a naïve theory about other groups conspiring against the in-group. Several lines of research support such a claim.

In a nationwide study performed in Poland, we found that two forms of victimhood could be distinguished: an absolute victimhood (belief that the victimhood is an essence of an in-group's identity) and a relative victimhood (belief that one's in-group was more victimized than was another ethnic group [Bilewicz & Stefaniak, 2013]). In this study, we analyzed how these two forms of victimhood affect beliefs in Jewish excessive power – an important component of conspiracy stereotype. We found that even after partialling out the well-known influence of absolute victimhood on exaggerated beliefs about Jewish power, the relative aspect of victimhood still positively predicted this dependent variable (Bilewicz & Stefaniak, 2013, Study 1). This suggests that even apart from individual construals of in-group identity, there is some influence of more specific and situational experiences, such as unrecognized victimization or competition with other ethnic groups over victim status.

More direct insight into this issue comes from a study on African Americans' perceptions of race-based conspiracies (Nelson, Adams, Branscombe, & Schmitt, 2010). It found that groups with a long history of mistreatment (i.e., African Americans) believe more often in current conspiracies against their group compared to the groups without such history (i.e., European Americans). More importantly, these effects were mediated by a larger awareness of anti-Black victimhood among African Americans, as compared to European Americans (Nelson et al., 2010, Study 1). Building on these findings, we developed a more general framework of understanding how past victimization affects contemporary conspiracy beliefs. We suggest that people are "learning from the past," as negative historical experiences of ancestors shape negative expectations of contemporaries – such as beliefs in out-group conspiracy against the in-group. In a set of studies performed in Poland and Greece, we found that knowledge about historical in-group victimization led to conspiracy theories about current events, such as the Smolensk aviation catastrophe, in which the Polish president died, and the Greek economic crisis, as well as to the endorsement of conspiracy stereotypes about Jews (Pantazi, Bilewicz, Klein, & Witkowska, in press). Thus, we suppose that situational experiences – also historically distant ones – might affect current tendencies to use conspiracy stereotypes.

One of the specific aspects of victimization that might directly lead to conspiracy stereotyping is control deprivation. Control deprivation has been differently conceptualized in the literature, as irreducible uncertainty in cognitive tasks (Kofta & Sedek, 1999b) or as general loss of influence over important domains of life (Fritsche et al., 2013).

Both conceptualizations of control deprivation are used interchangeably in a series of six experiments by Whitson and Galinsky (2008; see also Wang, Whitson, & Menon, 2012), who study the relation of such deprivation with conspiracy beliefs. The authors of these experiments conclude that lack of control leads to illusory pattern perception (e.g., seeing images in a random noise), the development of superstitions, and the perceiving of conspiracies. Their reasoning points to the fact that people have a desire to combat uncertainty and maintain control, so the perception of patterns (such as of conspiracies instead of accidental events) is a cognitive way to regain control over the environment. However, Whitson and Galinsky (2008) seem to confound the two essentially different forms of control deprivation: cognitive and behavioral control. When the researchers manipulate cognitive control, they systematically find effects on pattern perception (Whitson & Galinsky, 2008, Studies 1 and 2), but when they manipulate behavioral control, they find effects on superstitions and conspiracy perceptions (Studies 4 and 5). The manipulations are clearly different: the first being a cognitive task of completing an unsolvable task, whereas the latter being a recall task in which participants are reminded about uncontrollable and threatening situations in their life. In the latter respect, Whitson and Galinsky's (2008) manipulation is similar to the one used in the studies of focal enemyship (Sullivan, Landau, & Rothschild, 2010), in which participants had to assess how much control they have over various issues in their life, or in the studies of uncertainty (van Prooijen & Jostmann, 2013), in which participants who recalled the events in their life that made them uncertain endorsed more conspiratorial beliefs about immoral political figures. All of these studies focused on a very general sense of control and certainty (control over life, certainty about life, etc.), most of them employing recall techniques rather than actually putting people in uncontrollable situations.

To the extent of our knowledge, there is no evidence that control, understood as cognitive certainty about one's environment, decreases conspiracy beliefs, as there are no studies showing the direct impact of uncontrollable situations (such as the one generated in informational helplessness tasks [Sedek & Kofta, 1990]) on conspiracy theorizing.

In a closely related study of the scapegoating process, Rothschild, Landau, Sullivan, and Keefer (2012) found that control deprivation (priming the concept of climate change being caused by unknown sources) increased willingness to perceive oil companies as conspiring, and that this effect was mediated by the general sense of personal control. But again, the climate change issues are an ideological concept rather than everyday uncertainty. It seems that the effects of cognitive control deprivation on conspiracy stereotypes still need to be explored.

The additional link that deserves further research is the striking similarities between the motivational constrains of older adults that were described in previous sections and the state of cognitive exhaustion produced by contact with unsolvable problems (Sedek & Kofta, 1990; Kofta & Sedek, 1998; von Hecker & Sedek, 1999). This cognitive exhaustion model assumes that some of the cognitive impairments observed after uncontrollability preexposure (and in depression) can be explained in terms of experiences of unsolvable situations, leading to uncertainty. Such experiences may stem from past, irreversible life events, from subsequent rumination, or from counterfactual thinking. It is hypothesized that uncontrollability and, in particular, ruminating thoughts about uncontrollable conditions can lead to a depletion of these cognitive resources that support flexible, novel thinking. Although constructive thinking may be initiated by individuals with uncontrollability preexposure (as well as by depressed individuals), this state of cognitive exhaustion will impair the quality of new, integrative constructions or mental models related to a particular episode, a class of situations, or in more severe cases about numerous aspects of life (cf. von Hecker, McIntosh, & Sedek, in press). Further, this may cause broader deficits given the central role of mental model construction for cognition in general (see Brewer, 1987; Garnham, 1997).

Therefore, in similar vein as observed among older adults' increased costs of mental effort (Hess, 2014), cognitive exhaustion after uncontrollability experience could also be the psychological mechanisms related to the approval of schematic conspiracy explanations instead of the building of mental models of societal and political events.

Discriminatory consequences

Conspiracy stereotypes are not only a structure of cognitive processing, but also an important process in intergroup relations. As in any form of stereotyping, conspiracy stereotypes have crucial impact on the way people treat others, who in this case are allegedly made responsible for designing evil plots and concocting secret plans.

Stereotyping has traditionally been considered to be a proximal cause of prejudice and discrimination (Allport, 1954; Fiske, 2000). The stereotype–discrimination link can have several potential underlying mechanisms, one of which is a process of behavioral confirmation: the perceiver categorizes targets using stereotypes, making the perceiver behave in a biased fashion and ultimately leading to stereotype-confirming behavior of the target itself (Fiske, 2000; Snyder, 1981). Alternatively, automatic stereotyping can lead to implicit prejudice, which is known to cause avoidance and discriminatory nonverbal behavior (Dovidio, Kawakami, & Gaertner, 2002). Finally, stereotyping might justify existing inequalities – it can lead to the perception of the disadvantaged as deserving their situation (Kay & Jost, 2003). In that respect, stereotyping might lead to greater systemic justification, thus reinforcing the structural discrimination. The debate over the stereotype-discrimination link shows that stereotyping can be both a cause and a consequence of discrimination. This is also true about the more general discussion of the attitude-behavior link.

The ability to predict behavior (such as discrimination, in the case of prejudice or stereotyping) is a crucial aspect of any attitude (Eagly & Chaiken, 1993). Although behaviors can be predicted by attitudes, their predictive power is rather weak (Wicker, 1969). Similar observations were made in the literature on prejudice and discrimination. Meta-analyses suggest that the influence of prejudice on discrimination is relatively weak and is qualified by several moderators;

moreover, it depends strongly on the method of measurement (Schütz & Six, 1996). The implicit and subtle measures of prejudice were predicting discriminatory behavior more strongly than explicit prejudice (Dovidio, Kawakami, Smoak, & Gaertner, 2009).

In order to test whether conspiracy stereotypes allow the prediction of behavior towards a group that is allegedly responsibly for conspiring, we performed two studies using nationally representative samples (Bilewicz et al., 2013). In these studies, we wanted to compare conspiracy stereotypes about Jews with two other forms of anti-Semitic stereotypes: traditional anti-Judaic stereotypes that portray Jews as responsible for the death of Jesus (Langmuir, 1990) and secondary anti-Semitic stereotypes that present Jews as responsible for their fate and as abusing their victim status (Frindte, 2006; Imhoff, 2010). The main aim was to examine the predictive power of conspiracy stereotypes on different forms of discrimination. Consistently, we found that people who hold a conspiracy stereotype support the legal discrimination of Jews (e.g., they favor policies that prevent Jews from buying Polish land, real estate, and companies), more often accept discrimination in material restitution (e.g., they accept claims to property historically owned by Poles, but not to the ones owned by Jews), and express higher degrees of social distance (e.g., avoidance of Jewish people in their environment). In all of these cases, conspiracy stereotyping was a stronger predictor of discriminatory intentions than traditional and secondary anti-Semitism. A second study also included a monetary allocation task: participants could distribute money between different charity institutions. We found that holders of a conspiracy stereotype of Jews were less willing to donate to a Jewish cultural organization than to a Polish cultural organization. In this case, other forms of anti-Semitism were also significantly predictive, although one could speculate whether such a money allocation task is in fact a form of discrimination or just a mere in-group preference. Anyway, the studies allowed us to establish a clear link between conspiracy stereotypes and discrimination: people who believe in Jewish conspiracy are more inclined to support discriminatory policies against Jews, as well as to discriminate against Jews in their behavior.

Interestingly, belief in Jewish conspiracy is linked to prejudice towards other ethnic groups. Polish studies (Kofta & Sedek, 2005) found that conspiracy stereotypes of Jews were strongly predicting prejudice towards German and Russian targets, as well as towards Poles of German and Russian origin. In a study on Malaysian samples, Swami (2012) showed that belief in Jewish conspiracy predicted negative attitudes towards Chinese people. In that context, conspiracy beliefs are mobilizing political efforts against current political enemies. Imhoff and Bruder (2014) show that conspiracy mentality predicts prejudice against groups that are perceived as strong and powerful. This regulatory function of conspiracy beliefs as a generator of intergroup attitudes and biases shows that conspiracy stereotypes are not only stereotypes, but a core mindset that defines the enemies and mobilizes political action against them.

Political mobilization: A trigger of conspiracy stereotyping

Conspiracy theories cannot be viewed only as forms of stereotypes or explanations of intergroup relations. They are also important components of political reasoning and reflect people's willingness to understand complex political realities. Carl Raimund Popper, who coined the term "conspiracy theory" in his paper from 1949, suggests that conspiracy beliefs are political world views derived from secularized religious imageries in which gods are replaced by imperialists, monopolists, or secret plots. In Popper's view, naïve understandings of Marxism as well as vulgarized versions of other social schools of thought become highly popular because of their potential to define the world conflicts in a conspiracy-theory manner (Popper, 1949; see also Sapountzis & Condor, 2013). This could lead to a conclusion that conspiracy theories have a particularly strong potential in political mobilization, like religions had in the premodern world. The role of conspiracy beliefs in political mobilization has been studied by social psychologists in several geographical contexts, and the results of social-psychological research in this area seem contradictory.

One approach to the problem suggests that conspiracy theories serve a demobilizing role in times of political campaigns. Jolley and Douglas (2014) showed that British university students exposed to conspiracy theories expressed lower political engagement (e.g., voting in elections, contributing money to candidates, supporting parties) than students who were exposed to an anticonspiracy message. This effect was mediated by the sense of political powerlessness among students who were exposed to conspiracy theories, which seems to correspond with other lines of research indicating that belief in conspiracy theories is associated with political anomie (Abalakina-Paap, Stephan, Craig, & Gregory, 1999; Goertzel, 1994; Swami et al., 2010).

On the other hand, a large body of evidence points to the mobilizing role of conspiracy beliefs in political life. Conspiracy believers engage in political actions to undermine perceived conspiracies (Imhoff & Bruder, 2014). People engaged in conspiracy theorizing are not passive individuals lost in reality. Instead, strong evidence suggest that conspiracy theorists are people who themselves tend to conspire (Douglas & Sutton, 2011). The profile of a typical person who endorses conspiracy theory is a Machiavellist who is personally willing to participate in conspiracies. This would link conspiracy to political activism rather than passivity.

Although rarely used during election campaigns in an overt way, conspiracy stereotypes are often activated by subtle suggestions and remarks made by politicians. We suppose that political mobilization – in times of ruptures, election campaigns, crises, or wars – can become a trigger of conspiracy-motivated prejudice, aggression, and discrimination. This reasoning can be traced back to early discoveries in aggression literature showing that aggressive cues (such as the presence of weapons, symbols of aggression, or even acts of aggression in one's environment) moderate the impact of frustration on aggressive behavior (Berkowitz, 1974; Huesmann & Kirwil, 2007). It is only after a person faces such cues that the frustration translates into aggression. Political campaigns, which are full of accusations towards people and groups, raising uncertainty about the future but also mobilizing political thinking, can also allow for the expression of hatred among people who already have a predisposition for conspiracy thinking.

This strongly justifies the need to study the effects of elections on the regulatory potential of conspiracy beliefs. If election times activate the structure of conspiracy beliefs, political mobilization should then lead to an increase in the predictive power of such beliefs. The first study addressing the role of political elections in the activation of conspiracy stereotypes was performed before the 1991 parliamentary elections in Poland (Kofta & Sedek, 1992), the first free parliamentary elections in this country after World War II. Participants were approached twice, first in a time when there was no election campaign (June 1991) and then during the election campaign, before the elections (September–October 1991). The study found increases in prejudice just before the elections and a strong influence of conspiracy stereotypes about Jews on attitudes towards the out-group as a whole (higher social distance to Jews, lower willingness to cooperate with Israel, etc.). Another study was performed on a sample of Polish high school students before the parliamentary elections (two sessions: five weeks before the elections and in the middle of the election campaign) and after the parliamentary elections (two sessions: two weeks after the elections and four weeks later, Kofta & Sedek, 1995). The study found that conspiracy stereotypes were significant predictors of prejudice (social distance towards Jews, attitudes towards Israel) before the elections, but were unrelated to prejudice after the elections, when no political mobilization appeared. Such temporal effects were not observed for traditional, trait-laden stereotypes.

These studies suggest that an intensive election campaign is in fact a trigger of conspiracy stereotyping. Times of elections clearly activate the conspiracy theories about Jews, as they are times when political life becomes brutalized and politicians often raise different conspiracy theories. On the other hand, these times can also raise a sense of uncertainty among large sections of society – a process known to generate conspiracy thinking.

Our most recent study examined these effects on a larger, nationally representative sample of Poles. We aimed at examining the influence of conspiracy stereotypes (i.e., belief in Jewish conspiracy) on attitudes towards different ethnic groups in an election year (2009: the study was performed in the middle of the European Parliament elections campaign) and in a nonelection year (2013). We found that the impact of conspiracy stereotypes (belief in Jewish conspiracy) on prejudice towards Jews and Germans (measured with social distance scales) was significantly moderated by the year of study. The effects of conspiracy stereotypes on prejudice were stronger in 2009 (when the EU parliament elections took place) than in 2013 (Figure 1.2). What is more, we found that increased endorsement of the belief in Jewish conspiracy in election times also predicts prejudice towards an unrelated national group (Germans). This study further supports our predictions about political mobilization being a trigger of conspiracy stereotyping.

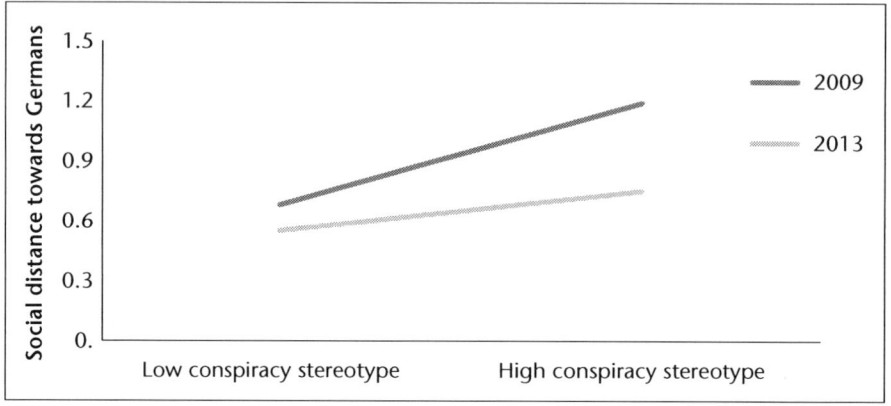

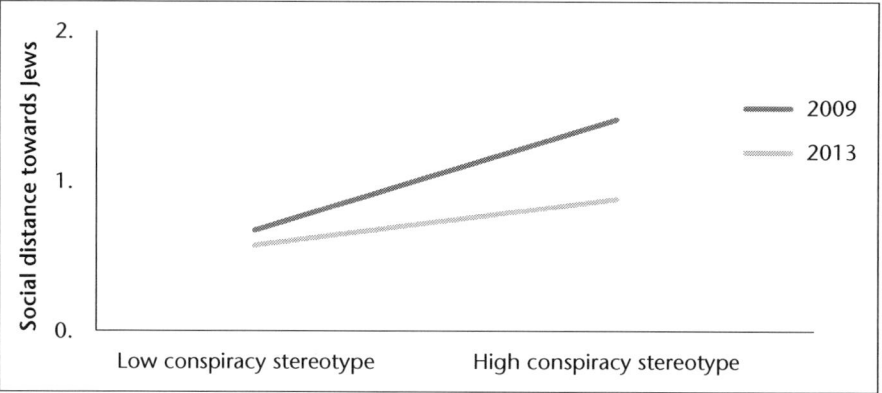

FIGURE 1.2 The influence of conspiracy stereotypes of Jews on social distance (towards Germans [upper panel] and Jews [lower panel]) in an election year (2009) and in a nonelection year (2013).

Summary

The concept of conspiracy stereotype, developed by Kofta and Sedek (1995; 1999a; 2005), provides an important extension of the existing literature on stereotyping and prejudice. Although conspiracy stereotype is not a typical social schema – as it also includes attributional structure (known as "diabolic causality"), essentialist perception of a group, and metaphorical representation of a group – it is still worth considering it a stereotype because it serves a similar function: justifying discrimination and prejudice. We also found that, in several cases, conspiracy stereotypes are better predictors of discriminatory behavior and discriminatory intentions than other forms of stereotypes or prejudicial beliefs.

Research on conspiracy stereotyping informs not only social psychological work, but can also be applied in sociological, anthropological, and historical contexts. It allows a better understanding of prejudice against groups that are ostensibly considered of high status. We presented a vast body of evidence specifically about the belief in Jewish conspiracy in Eastern Europe and other regions, but historically many other groups were portrayed using conspiracy stereotypes, for example Armenians in the Ottoman Empire or Tutsis in pregenocide Rwanda (Bilewicz & Vollhardt, 2012). The concept of conspiracy stereotype can also be utilized in political science to explain increases of prejudice in times of political mobilization. Such periods (times of elections or crises) make conspiracy stereotypes salient and activate their influence on behavior. Conspiracy stereotypes give lay explanations of the political world to people in times of political and social unrest seems to be the reason for their popularity. Finally, conspiracy stereotypes simplify the world and respond to the epistemic motivations particularly pronounced among older and more authoritarian people.

The overall model of conspiracy stereotyping presented in previous sections seeks to explain the dynamics, antecedents, and activation of conspiracy stereotypes. We believe that further research will expand on this model and aid in an understanding of how conspiracy stereotypes become pronounced in times of political unrest. In that respect, we hope that the psychological findings will serve as immunization for the crisis-torn societies in which conspiracy stereotypes lead to acts of discrimination and scapegoating of ethnic, religious, and cultural minorities.

Author note

Michal Bilewicz, Faculty of Psychology, University of Warsaw. Preparation of this chapter was supported by Polish Ministry of Science and Higher Education Iuventus Plus Grant IP2014 002273 to the first author. Grzegorz Sedek, Faculty of Psychology, University of Social Sciences and Humanities. Correspondence regarding this chapter should be directed to Michal Bilewicz, University of Warsaw, Faculty of Psychology, Stawki 5/7, Warsaw (Poland). E-mail: bilewicz@psych.uw.edu.pl

References

Abalakina-Paap, M., Stephan, W. G., Craig, T., & Gregory, W. L. (1999). Beliefs in conspiracies. *Political Psychology, 20*(3), 637–647.

Ackerman, N. W., & Jahoda, M. (1950). *Anti-Semitism and emotional disorder; a psychoanalytic interpretation.* New York: Harper.

Adorno, T. W., Frenkel-Brunswik, E., Levinson, D. J., & Sanford, R. N. (1950). *The authoritarian personality.* New York: Harper & Row.

Allport, G. W. (1954). *The nature of prejudice.* Reading, MA: Addison-Wesley.

Altemeyer, B. (1998). The other "authoritarian personality." *Advances in Experimental Social Psychology, 30,* 47–92.

Bergman, M. M. (2008). The straw men of the qualitative-quantitative divide and their influence on mixed methods research. In M. M. Bergman (Ed.), *Advances in mixed methods research: Theories and applications* (pp. 11–21). New York: Sage.

Berkowitz, L. (1974). Some determinants of impulsive aggression: Role of mediated associations with reinforcements for aggression. *Psychological Review, 81,* 165–176.

Bilewicz, M., & Krzeminski, I. (2010). Anti-Semitism in Poland and Ukraine: The belief in Jewish control as a mechanism of scapegoating. *International Journal of Conflict and Violence, 4*(2), 234–243.

Bilewicz, M., & Stefaniak, A. (2013). Can a victim be responsible? Antisemitic consequences of victimhood-based identity and competitive victimhood in Poland. In B. Bokus (Ed.), *Responsibility: An Interdisciplinary Perspective* (pp. 69–80). Warszawa: LEXEM.

Bilewicz, M., & Vollhardt, J. R. (2012). Evil transformations: Psychological processes underlying genocide and mass killing. In A. Golec de Zavala & A. Cichocka (Eds.), *Social psychology of social problems. The intergroup context* (pp. 280–307). New York: Palgrave Macmillan.

Bilewicz, M., Winiewski, M., Kofta, M., & Wójcik, A. (2013). Harmful Ideas, the structure and consequences of anti-Semitic beliefs in Poland. *Political Psychology, 34*(6), 821–839.

Bilewicz, M., Winiewski, M., & Radzik, Z. (2012). Antisemitism in current Poland: Psychological, religious and historical aspects. *Journal for the Study of Antisemitism, 4*, 801–820.

Billig, M. (1987). Anti-Semitic themes and the British far Left: Some social-psychological observations on indirect aspects of the conspiracy tradition. In C. F. Graumann & S. Moscovici (Eds.), *Changing conceptions of conspiracy* (pp. 115–136). New York: Springer.

Brewer, W. F. (1987). Schemas versus mental models in human memory. In P. Morris (Ed.), *Modelling cognition* (pp. 187–197). Chichester, England: Wiley.

Czarnek, G., Kossowska, M., & Sedek, G. (in press). The influence of aging on outgroup stereotypes: The mediating role of cognitive and motivational facets of deficient flexibility. *Experimental Aging Research.*

Douglas, K. M., & Sutton, R. M. (2011). Does it take one to know one? Endorsement of conspiracy theories is influenced by personal willingness to conspire. *British Journal of Social Psychology, 50*(3), 544–552.

Dovidio, J. F., Kawakami, K., & Gaertner, S. L. (2002). Implicit and explicit prejudice and interracial interaction. *Journal of Personality and Social Psychology, 82*(1), 62–68.

Dovidio, J. F., Kawakami, K., Smoak, N., & Gaertner, S. L. (2009). The roles of implicit and explicit processes in contemporary prejudice. In R. E. Petty, R. H. Fazio, & P. Brinol (Eds.), *Attitudes: Insights from the new implicit measures* (pp. 165–192). New York: Psychology Press.

Duckitt, J. (2008). Personality and prejudice. In J. F. Dovidio, P. Glick, & L. A. Rudman (Eds.), *On the nature of prejudice: Fifty years after Allport* (pp. 395–412). Malden, MA: Blackwell.

Eagly, A. H., & Chaiken, S. (1993). *The psychology of attitudes.* Fort Worth, TX: Harcourt Brace Jovanovich.

Fiske, S. T. (1998). Stereotyping, prejudice, and discrimination. In D. T. Gilbert, S. T. Fiske, & G. Lindzey (Eds.), *Handbook of social psychology* (4th ed., pp. 357–411). New York: McGraw-Hill.

Fiske, S. T. (2000). Stereotyping, prejudice, and discrimination at the seam between the centuries: Evolution, culture, mind, and brain. *European Journal of Social Psychology, 30*(3), 299–322.

Fiske, S. T., Xu, J., Cuddy, A. C., & Glick, P. (1999). (Dis) respecting versus (dis) liking: Status and interdependence predict ambivalent stereotypes of competence and warmth. *Journal of Social Issues, 55*(3), 473–489.

Frenkel-Brunswik, E., & Sanford, R. N. (1945). Some personality factors in anti-Semitism. *Journal of Psychology, 20*(2), 271–291.

Frindte, W. (2006). *Inszenierter Anti-Semitismus: Eine Streitschrift.* Wiesbaden: Vieweg.

Fritsche, I., Jonas, E., Ablasser, C., Beyer, M., Kuban, J., Manger, A.-M., & Schultz, M. (2013). The power of we: Evidence for group-based control restoration. *Journal of Experimental Social Psychology, 49*(1), 19–32.

Garnham, A. (1997). Representing information in mental models. In M. A. Conway (Ed.), *Cognitive models of memory* (pp. 149–172). Cambridge, MA: MIT Press.

Gibson, J. L., & Howard, M. M. (2007). Russian antisemitism and the scapegoating of Jews. *British Journal of Political Science, 37,* 193–223.

Glick, P. (2002). Sacrificial lambs dressed in wolves' clothing: Envious prejudice, ideology, and the scapegoating of Jews. In L. S. Newman & R. Erber (Eds.), *Understanding genocide: The social psychology of the Holocaust* (pp. 113–142). London: Oxford University Press.

Glick, P., & Fiske, S. T. (2001). Ambivalent stereotypes as legitimizing ideologies: Differentiating paternalistic and envious prejudice. In J. T. Jost & B. Major (Eds.), *The psychology of legitimacy: Emerging perspectives on ideology, justice, and intergroup relations* (pp. 278–306). New York: Cambridge University Press.

Goertzel, T. (1994). Belief in conspiracy theories. *Political Psychology, 15,* 731–742.

Green, D. P., Glaser, J., & Rich, A. (1998). From lynching to gay bashing: The elusive connection between economic conditions and hate crime. *Journal of Personality and Social Psychology, 75*(1), 82.

Grzesiak-Feldman, M. (2013). The effect of high-anxiety situations on conspiracy thinking. *Current Psychology, 32*(1), 100–118.

Grzesiak-Feldman, M., & Irzycka, M. (2009). Right-wing authoritarianism and conspiracy thinking in a Polish sample. *Psychological Reports, 105*(2), 389–393.

Hamilton, D. L. (1981). Stereotyping and intergroup behavior: Some thoughts on the cognitive approach. In D. L. Hamilton (Ed.), *Cognitive processes in stereotyping and intergroup behaviour* (pp. 333–353). Hillsdale, NJ: Erlbaum.

Hasher, L., Zacks, R. T., & May, C. P. (1999). Inhibitory control, circadian arousal, and age. In D. Gopher & A. Koriat (Eds.), *Attention & Performance, XVII, Cognitive regulation of performance: Interaction of theory and application* (pp. 653–675). Cambridge, MA: MIT Press.

Haslam, N., Rothschild, L., & Ernst, D. (2000). Essentialist beliefs about social categories. *British Journal of Social Psychology, 39*(1), 113–127.

Henry, J. D., von Hippel, W. V., & Baynes, K. (2009). Social inappropriateness, executive control and aging. *Psychology and Aging, 24,* 239–244.

Hess, T. M. (2000). Aging-related constraints and adaptations in social information processing. In U. von Hecker, S. Dutke, & G. Sedek (Eds.), *Generative mental processes and cognitive resources: Integrative research on adaptation and control* (pp. 129–155). Dordrecht, Netherlands: Kluwer.

Hess, T. M. (2014). Selective engagement of cognitive resources: Motivational influences on older adults' cognitive functioning. *Perspectives on Psychological Science, 9,* 388–407.

Hess, T. M., & Queen, T. L. (2014). Aging influences on judgment and decision processes: Interactions between ability and experience. In P. Verhaeghen & C. Hertzog (Eds.), *The Oxford handbook of emotion, social cognition, and problem solving in adulthood* (pp. 238–255). Oxford: Oxford University Press.

Huesmann, L. R., & Kirwil, L. (2007). Why observing violence increases the risk of violent behavior in the observer. In D. J. Flannery, A. T. Vazsonyi, & I. D. Waldman (Eds.), *The Cambridge handbook of violent behavior and aggression* (pp. 545–570). Cambridge: Cambridge University Press.

Imhoff, R. (2010). Zwei Formen des modernen Antisemitismus? Eine Skala zur Messung primären und sekundären Antisemitismus. *Conflict and Communication Online, 9.*

Imhoff, R., & Bruder, M. (2014). Speaking (un-)truth to power: Conspiracy mentality as a generalised political attitude. *European Journal of Personality, 28*(1), 25–43.

Jolley, D., & Douglas, K. M. (2014). The social consequences of conspiracism: Exposure to conspiracy theories decreases the intention to engage in politics and to reduce one's carbon footprint. *British Journal of Psychology, 105*(1), 35–56.

Kay, A. C., & Jost, J. T. (2003). Complementary justice: Effects of "poor but happy" and "poor but honest" stereotype exemplars on system justification and implicit activation of the justice motive. *Journal of Personality and Social Psychology, 85*(5), 823.

Keller, J. (2005). In genes we trust: The biological component of psychological essentialism and its relationship to mechanisms of motivated social cognition. *Journal of Personality and Social Psychology, 88*, 686–702.

Klar, Y., Schori-Eyal, N., & Klar, Y. (2013). The "never again" state of Israel: The emergence of the Holocaust as a core feature of Israeli identity and its four incongruent voices. *Journal of Social Issues, 69*(1), 125–143.

Kofta, M., & Sedek, G. (1992). Struktura poznawcza stereotypu etnicznego, bliskość wyborów parlamentarnych a przejawy uprzedzen antysemickich. In Z. Chlewiński and I. Kurcz (Eds.), *Stereotypy i uprzedzenia* (pp. 67–86). Warszawa: Wydawnictwo Instytutu Psychologii PAN.

Kofta, M., & Sedek, G. (1995). Stereotyp "duszy grupowej," wybory parlamentarne, a postawy wobec osób pochodzenia żydowskiego. In B. Wojciszke (Ed.), *Jacy są Polacy? Badania opinii społecznej jako źródło wiedzy psychologicznej* (pp. 55–72). Warszawa: Wydawnictwo Instytutu Psychologii PAN.

Kofta, M., & Sedek, G. (1998). Uncontrollability as a source of cognitive exhaustion: Implications for helplessness and depression. In M. Kofta, G. Weary, & G. Sedek (Eds.), *Personal control in action: Cognitive and motivational mechanisms* (pp. 391–418). New York: Plenum Press.

Kofta, M., & Sedek, G. (1999a). Stereotypy duszy grupowej a postawy wobec obcych: Wyniki badań sondażowych. In B. Wojciszke and M. Jarymowicz (Eds.), *Psychologia zjawisk społecznych* (pp. 173–207). Warszawa: PWN.

Kofta, M., & Sedek, G. (1999b). Uncontrollability as irreducible uncertainty. *European Journal of Social Psychology, 29*, 577–590.

Kofta, M., & Sedek, G. (2005). Conspiracy stereotypes of Jews during systemic transformation in Poland. *International Journal of Sociology, 35*(1), 40–64.

Korzeniowski, K. (2009). O dwóch psychologicznych przesłankach myślenia spiskowego. Alienacja czy autorytaryzm. *Psychologia społeczna, 4*, 144–154.

Korzeniowski, K. (2010). Paranoja polityczna. Charakterystyka zjawiska i metody jego pomiaru. *Przegląd Psychologiczny, 52*, 145–162.

Kossowska, M. (2007). Motivation toward closure and cognitive processes: An individual differences approach. *Personality and Individual Differences, 43*, 2149–2158.

Kruglanski, A. W. (1989). *Lay epistemics and human knowledge: Cognitive and motivational bases*. New York: Plenum Press.

Krzeminski, I. (2002). Polish-Jewish relations, anti-Semitism and national identity. *Polish Sociological Review, 137*, 25–51.

Krzymowski, M. (2014, June 2). Korwin-Mikke: Żydowscy socjaliści to nasz wróg. *Newsweek*. Retrieved from http://polska.newsweek.pl/korwin-mikke-zydowscy-socjalisci-to-nasz-wrog-newsweek-pl,artykuly,287355,1.html

Langmuir, G. L. (1990). *History, religion, and anti-Semitism*. Berkeley: University of California Press.

McGarty, C., Yzerbyt, V. Y., & Spears, R. (Eds.). (2002). *Stereotypes as explanations: The formation of meaningful beliefs about social groups*. Cambridge: Cambridge University Press.

Nelson, J., Adams, G., Branscombe, N., & Schmitt, M. (2010). The role of historical knowledge in the perception of race-based conspiracies. *Race and Social Problems, 2*, 69–80.

Noor, M., Shnabel, N., Halabi, S., & Nadler, A. (2012). When suffering begets suffering: The psychology of competitive victimhood between adversarial groups in violent conflicts. *Personality and Social Psychology Review, 16*(4), 351–374.

Pantazi, M., Bilewicz, M., Klein, M., & Witkowska, M. (in press). Victimhood and beliefs in conspiracies – evidence from two countries. Unpublished research.

Pettigrew, T. F., Christ, O., Wagner, U., Meertens, R. W., Van Dick, R., & Zick, A. (2008). Relative deprivation and intergroup prejudice. *Journal of Social Issues, 64*(2), 385–401.

Popper, K. R. (1949). Prediction and prophesy and their significance for social theory. In E. W. Beth, H. J. Pos, & J. H. A. Hollack (Eds.), *Proceedings of the Tenth International Congress of Philosophy* (pp. 82–91). Amsterdam: North-Holland.

Radvansky, G., Copeland, D. E., & von Hippel, W. (2010). Stereotype activation, inhibition, and aging. *Journal of Experimental Social Psychology, 46*, 51–60.

Rothschild, Z. K., Landau, M. J., Sullivan, D., & Keefer, L. A. (2012). A dual-motive model of the motives underlying scapegoating: Displacing blame to reduce guilt or increase control. *Journal of Personality and Social Psychology, 102*, 1148–1163.

Sapountzis, A., & Condor, S. (2013). Conspiracy accounts as intergroup theories: Challenging dominant understandings of social power and political legitimacy. *Political Psychology, 34*(5), 731–752.

Schütz, H., & Six, B. (1996). How strong is the relationship between prejudice and discrimination? A meta-analytic answer. *International Journal of Intercultural Relations, 20*, 441–462.

Sedek, G., & Kofta, M. (1990). When cognitive exertion does not yield cognitive gain: Toward an informational explanation of learned helplessness. *Journal of Personality and Social Psychology, 58*, 729–743.

Sedek, G., Kossowska, M., & Rydzewska, K. (2014). The importance of adult life-span perspective in explaining variations in political ideology. *Behavioral and Brain Sciences, 37*(3), 329–330.

Snyder, M. (1981). On the self-perpetuating nature of social stereotypes. In D. L. Hamilton (Ed.), *Cognitive processes in stereotyping and intergroup behavior* (pp. 183–212). Hillsdale, NJ: Lawrence Erlbaum.

Stephan, W. G., & Stephan, C. W. (1985). Intergroup anxiety. *Journal of Social Issues, 41*(3), 157–175.

Stephan, W. G., & Stephan, C. W. (2000). An integrated threat theory of prejudice. In S. Oskamp (Ed.), *Reducing prejudice and discrimination* (pp. 23–46). Hillsdale, NJ: Lawrence Erlbaum.

Stewart, B. D., von Hippel, W., & Radvansky, G. (2009). Age, race, and implicit prejudice: Using process dissociation to separate the underlying components. *Psychological Science, 20*(2), 164–168.

Sullivan, D., Landau, M. J., & Rothschild, Z. K. (2010). An existential function of enemyship: Evidence that people attribute influence to personal and political enemies to compensate for threats to control. *Journal of Personality and Social Psychology, 98*(3), 434–449.

Swami, V. (2012). Social psychological origins of conspiracy theories: The case of the Jewish conspiracy theory in Malaysia. *Frontiers in Psychology, 3*, 280.

Swami, V., Frederick, D. A., Aavik, T., Alcalay, L., Allik, J., Anderson, D., & Shashidharan, S. (2010). The attractive female body weight and female body dissatisfaction in 26 countries across 10 world regions: Results of the International Body Project I. *Personality and Social Psychology Bulletin, 36*(3), 309–325.

van Prooijen, J.-W., & Jostmann, N. B. (2013). Belief in conspiracy theories: The influence of uncertainty and perceived morality. *European Journal of Social Psychology, 43*(1), 109–115.

Vollhardt, J. R., & Bilali, R. (2014). The role of inclusive and exclusive victim consciousness in predicting intergroup attitudes: Findings from Rwanda, Burundi, and DRC. *Political Psychology*, online first.

von Hecker, U., McIntosh, D. N., & Sedek, G. (in press). Mental model construction, not just memory, is a central component of cognitive change in psychotherapy. *Behavioral and Brain Sciences.*

von Hecker, U., & Sedek, G. (1999). Uncontrollability, depression, and the construction of mental models. *Journal of Personality and Social Psychology, 77,* 833–850.

von Hippel, W., & Dunlop, S. M. (2005). Aging, inhibition, and social inappropriateness. *Psychology and Aging, 20,* 519–523.

von Hippel, W., Silver, L. A., & Lynch, M. E. (2000). Stereotyping against your will: The role of inhibitory ability in stereotyping and prejudice among the elderly. *Personality and Social Psychology Bulletin, 26,* 523–532.

Wang, C. S., Whitson, J. A., & Menon, T. (2012). Culture, control, and illusory pattern perception. *Social Psychological and Personality Science, 3*(5), 630–638.

Whitson, J. A., & Galinsky, A. D. (2008). Lacking control increases illusory pattern perception. *Science, 322,* 115–117.

Wicker, A. W. (1969). Attitudes versus actions: The relationship of verbal and overt behavioral responses to attitude objects. *Journal of Social Issues, 25*(4), 41–78.

Zawadzki, B. (1948). Limitations of the scapegoat theory of prejudice. *Journal of Abnormal and Social Psychology, 43*(2), 127–141.

Zick, A., Küpper, B., & Hövermann, A. (2011). Intolerance, prejudice and discrimination: A European report. Berlin: Friedrich-Ebert-Stiftung Forum Berlin.

2

CONSPIRACY THEORIES ON THE MAP OF STEREOTYPE CONTENT

Survey and historical evidence

Mikolaj Winiewski, Wiktor Soral, and Michal Bilewicz

About 10 years ago, Professor Hasan Bolkhari, a cultural advisor to the Iranian Ministry of Education, delivered a lecture about the implicit message ostensibly hidden in Tom and Jerry cartoons. In this lecture, Bolkhari argued, "If you study European history, you will see who was the main power in hoarding money and wealth in the 19th century. In most cases, it is the Jews. . . . The mouse is very clever and smart. Everything he does is so cute. He kicks the poor cat's ass. Yet this cruelty does not make you despise the mouse. He looks so nice, and he is so clever" (Kressel, 2012, p. 44). Bolkhari suggested that the filmmakers of Jewish descent aim at changing the perception of Jews by modifying the dominant perception of mice. This lecture is a typical example of anti-Semitic conspiracy theory: it uses two dominant stereotypical traits attributed to Jews by anti-Semites: competence ("very clever and smart") and hostile intentions ("cruelty"), at the same time suggesting that these intentions are hidden and covert ("he looks so nice").

In this chapter, we will try to place the concept of conspiracy stereotypes – particularly belief in Jewish conspiracy as one of the most often endorsed of the conspiracy stereotypes (Kofta & Sedek, 2005) – in a more general framework of stereotype content models (Fiske, Cuddy, Glick, & Xu, 2002; Judd, James-Hawkins, Yzerbyt, & Kashima, 2005; Phalet & Poppe, 1997). In the first part of the chapter, we will elaborate on several theoretical models of stereotypes, their implications and functions. In the second part, we will present several secondary analyses of survey data that support the theoretical connection between the constructs of conspiracy stereotypes and two-dimensional models of social perception. We will also present preliminary findings from the content analysis of archival materials (i.e., Nazi propaganda). Results show that the stereotypical presentation of Jewish characters in terms of stereotype content model dimensions – as being of low warmth and highly competent – and in terms of conspiracy stereotype – as conspiring representatives of a "global Jewish community" – is related. The same results also show that the dynamics of those two types of presentations are different and therefore could serve distinct purposes.

Belief in Jewish conspiracy: Conspiracy stereotypes

According to Kofta and Sedek (2005), conspiracy stereotypes are qualitatively different from trait-laden stereotypes. While the latter pertain to (positive or negative) evaluations of an individual group member, the former determine attitudes towards the group as a whole. Thus, people holding conspiracy stereotypes tend to personalize groups, viewing them as collective agents with ill intentions towards their in-group. More important, conspiracy stereotypes are causal (vs. merely descriptive) theories, which ascribe to its targets "(1) a collective goal – a permanent, obsessive striving for power and dominance over other groups in general (and the observer's in-group in particular), (2) collective behavior – a secret way of acting (e.g., engagement in plots, deception, subversive activities, acting in disguise), and (3) a high degree of group egoism and solidarity (high supportiveness for in-groupers combined with complete disregard for out-groupers' well-being)" (Kofta & Sedek, 2005, p. 42).

A similar perspective can also be found in work outside the field of social psychology. Historians, especially those interested in anti-Semitism and Holocaust studies, have been pointing to the role of conspiracy mentality and ideologies in forming the historical relations between Jews and other groups (see Poliakov, 2003; Cohn, 1967). However, Kofta and Sedek's (2005) perspective additionally emphasize the role of belief in Jewish conspiracy as satisfying several sociopsychological motives of the in-group members. First of all, such beliefs have the potential to explain negative events that affect the entire group, such as military defeats or economic crises, or its individual members, such as unemployment and worsening life conditions. The beliefs allow people to detect potential threats to the in-group and to mobilize individual and collective actions against supposed threats from out-groups. Conspiracy theories can also simplify and explain complex events, allowing for easy interpretation and explanation of history, as well as making predictions about future events. Finally, they provide moral justification for immoral actions such as discrimination or cruelty towards allegedly conspiring out-group members.

Another important distinction between trait-laden and conspiracy stereotypes refers to the particular role of the target. While the two-dimensional models assume that the content of the perception is well-generalizable to self, other people, in-group, and out-group (see, for example, Wojciszke, Baryla, Parzuchowski, Szymkow, & Abele, 2011), the concept of conspiracy stereotypes is heavily grounded within the theory of natural categories (Rosch, 1973; 1975). Within this approach, one can distinguish the group conspiring par excellence: The target of the conspiracy stereotypes is rather a stored prototype, an abstract notion without any cognitive visual representation, yet full of informational content. While several groups may be the target of conspiracy stereotyping (depending on the geopolitical context, they might be Russians, Chinese, or Americans), it seems that the group that takes the central place, as the prototype, in the broad category of conspiring groups are Jews.

Despite some differences between trait-laden and conspiracy stereotypes, we would like to argue that both forms of out-group attitudes are strictly related. A certain pattern of ascribed (ambivalent) traits causes one group to become a target of envious prejudice. In time, this form of prejudice becomes part of a superior beliefs system: the ideology in which a scapegoated group takes the central place as responsible for conspiring against the in-group. Thus, as we will argue further, trait-laden stereotypes – placed along two fundamental dimensions of warmth and competence – play a role both of the primal cause and the supporting factor of the conspiracy stereotypes.

Stereotype content models

A vast majority of contemporary scholars adhere to the position that stereotypes are more than a mere simplification of the social world. Instead, they seem to pursue the functional perspective within which stereotypes operate as monitors and indicators of intergroup relations (Allport, 1954). One example of such an approach can be found within the framework of group image theory (Alexander, Brewer, & Herrmann, 1999; Brewer & Alexander, 2002). Group image is the product of three features of the relations between groups: goal compatibility (cooperation vs. competition), relative power (stronger vs. weaker), and cultural status (superior vs. inferior). Consequently, groups/countries representations can portray negative (e.g., enemy, barbarian, imperialist, colonial, rogue) or positive images (e.g., ally or father). These images tell group members what they should expect and how to behave during interaction with the out-group (e.g., cooperate with the ally, rely on the father, feel threatened by the barbarian or imperialist). The ideological imagery of Jews in current Iranian social sciences – as presented in the introductory part of this chapter – is a good example of such a group image. In this case, the conspiracy stereotype uses metaphorical language and depictions in order to mobilize in times of potential military conflict (Kressel, 2012).

In more general terms, the descriptive meaning of concepts used to characterize individuals and social groups clusters along two fundamental dimensions. Though names given to these dimensions vary widely, the first includes characteristics indicative of human power (agency, competence, dominance) and the second includes characteristics indicative of human benevolence (warmth, communion, nurturance). Considerable evidence suggests that the characteristics indicative of human benevolence are primary: They are judged before characteristics indicative of power and carry more weight in affective and behavioral reactions (Fiske, Cuddy, & Glick, 2006; Wojciszke & Abele, 2008). Traits related to benevolence are "other-relevant" and, as such, they control approach-avoidance processes. In their studies, Wentura, Rothermund, and Bak (2000) found that positive other-relevant words promoted approach-related behavior and interfered with avoidance-related behavior, while negative other-relevant words showed the reverse pattern. These effects were specific to other-relevant and not possessor-relevant words. As suggested by the authors, "this vigilance mechanism seems to operate at a level of preconscious automaticity" (p. 1032).

One should note that benevolence, as "other-profitable," is similar to some conceptualizations of morality (see Haidt & Joseph, 2004). However, out-group members can be seen as warm, friendly, and likeable without being seen as moral people who can be trusted (Leach, Ellemers, & Barreto, 2007). It is therefore important to differentiate out-group trustworthiness from perceptions of sociability, communion, and nurturance.[1] In fact, recent findings suggest that global group evaluations (in the case of the cited study: evaluation of an unfamiliar immigrant group) are predicted by morality rather than by sociability or competence-trait ascriptions (Brambilla, Sacchi, Rusconi, Cherubini, & Yzerbyt, 2012). Furthermore, moral information seems to predict behavioral intentions to interact with a target group over and above competence or sociability (Brambilla, Sacchi, Pagliaro, & Ellemers, 2013). It should be noted that, in the study, the relation between perception of low morality and a desire to avoid the out-group was mediated by a feeling of threat to group safety. Thus, the study shows more evidence that the warmth dimension – especially morality – plays a crucial role in determining approach-avoidance tendencies (Peeters, 2002). The common cultural depictions of immoral Jews, such as the figure of Fagin in Dickens's *Oliver Twist* or Shylock in Shakespeare's *Merchant of Venice*, played a crucial role in the exclusion of Jews from Western society by raising a sense of threat posed by Jews to the autochthons – a process that confronted the Jewish assimilation in the West.

While benevolence predicts the valence of judgments, power predicts the intensity of impressions (Wojciszke, Bazinska, & Jaworski, 1998). In a similar vein, while the former predicts a target's intentions, the latter predicts a target's ability to implement the intentions. Therefore, although judgments of agency and competence are secondary, they may serve a particularly important role when the target is perceived as immoral-unsociable; the competence of an enemy has greater consequences than the competence of a friend (Peeters, 2002). Furthermore, possessing enough capacity and skills seems a necessary component for judgments of intentionality (Guglielmo & Malle, 2010) and, consequently, blame attribution (Malle, Guglielmo, & Monroe, 2014).

Predictive power of the two-dimensional models exceeds beyond the ascription of others' intentions and beyond inferring what one should expect during interaction with an out-group member. Warmth and competence have also been proven to predict behavioral intentions towards certain groups. On the one hand, being judged primarily, warmth predicts active behaviors: active facilitation vs. active harming. In studies conducted by Cuddy, Fiske, and Glick (2007), participants were asked to what degree people in America tend to help and protect (active facilitation) or fight and attack (active harm) several social groups. These behaviors were significantly related to the ascription of traits to the target groups related to warmth but not competence. On the other hand, competence predicts passive behaviors: passive facilitation and passive harm. Intentions to cooperate with, associate with (passive facilitation), or exclude and demean (passive harm) were correlated with the competence dimension, but not the warmth dimension.

Thus, the two fundamental dimensions form a base that links discriminatory behavioral tendencies to the content of group stereotypes, but also allow the prediction of specific emotions evoked by groups perceived as high/low competent and as warm/cold (BIAS map, Cuddy et al., 2007). According to the model, groups stereotyped as competent and warm (e.g., in-group) elicit admiration and pride, whereas groups stereotyped as incompetent and cold elicit contempt and disgust. However, the most common form of group stereotypes emerges from the ambivalent mix of the two dimensions (Fiske et al., 2002): Groups stereotyped as incompetent but warm elicit pity, and groups stereotyped as competent but cold elicit envy.

Envious prejudice

Envy is an unpleasant and painful complex emotion. It is a mixture of feelings of inferiority, hostility, and resentment. Although envy may sometimes increase motivation for self-improvement, it is most often accompanied with ill will towards the advantaged other (Smith, Parrott, Ozer, & Moniz, 1994). Hill, DelPriore, and Vaughan (2011) argue that although aversive, envy is a sociofunctional emotion. Their studies indicate that when envy is activated, people attend to information about social targets and are able to better recall this information. The finding was confirmed at the neurological level by Zhong, Liu, Zhang, Luo, and Chen (2013), who showed that people preferentially attend towards envy-related stimuli (reflected by enhanced P300 amplitudes). These findings may suggest that, specifically in the case of envious stereotypes (high competent, low warmth), the emotional background plays a particularly important role in maintaining hostile beliefs about envied groups. Attitudes towards such a group could be characterized not only by ill will, but also by a higher level of vigilance on information that would justify preexisting prejudices and stereotypes. Thus, one could speculate, envious prejudice would lead to a better performance in coding and recalling information that would support the conspiracy theory of a certain group.

However, one could think also of another explanation of the relation between envious prejudice and conspiracy stereotypes. As pointed out by Glick and Fiske (2001), ambivalent stereotypes serve as the beliefs that legitimize existing ideologies. Indeed, in their studies, Kay and Jost (2003) showed that exposure to complementary stereotypes leads to increased support for the status quo and existing (unjust) social system (see also Cichocka, Winiewski, Bilewicz, Bukowski, & Jost, in press). Such stereotypes may justify discrimination against the nondominant groups – women, Blacks, immigrants, or Jews – as they did in the case of Nazi Germany. In the latter case, envious prejudice seemed to support ideology that held a certain group as responsible (through alleged secret plots and diabolical plans) for the poor condition of the in-group.

Scapegoat theory

Pondering the phenomenon of focusing hostility and hatred on particular groups and minorities, social psychology theorists most often invoke the concept of scape-goating – the act of blaming and often punishing an innocent but weak target for a negative outcome that is due to other causes. In its early conceptualizations, the scapegoat theory was bounded within drive-based models. Within this approach, external frustrating events or internal conflicts resulted in aggressive impulses, the discharge of which was prevented by social norms (the superego). Subsequently, these impulses were supposedly vented through aggression and hostility towards a safe target – a scapegoat – the aggression towards which was not associated with aversive consequences. Unfavorable stereotypes of a target group were then assumed to arise as rationalizations that justify aggression towards the scapegoat; the process denoted as complementary or direct projection (Allport, 1954).

The classical scapegoat theory came in for serious criticism soon after its for-mulation (Allport, 1954; Zawadzki, 1948). Particularly, it failed to explain why aggression is often directed towards powerful groups. For example, although Jews were indeed a vulnerable minority within Germany, German stereotypes of Jews did not characterize them as powerless (see Durante, Volpato, & Fiske, 2010, for depictions of Jews in fascist Italy). Thus, in his reformulation of the scapegoat theory, Peter Glick (2002; 2005) argues that the scapegoated group is not likely to be just any minority that happens to be vulnerable and helpless, but rather a group that (although it may actually be vulnerable) is believed to be powerful, cunning, and dangerous. Within his approach, frustration is not a direct cause of aggressive behavior, but it leads to a commitment to ideology identifying the scapegoat as the cause of shared problems. This ideological commitment in turn is a cause of ideo-logically motivated actions (Glick, 2002; 2005). Thus, envious prejudice (Glick & Fiske, 1999; 2001) plays a crucial role as a mediator of scapegoating. Envious ste-reotypes suggest which group might have the ability and intention to cause the difficulties the in-group is facing. Therefore, in Glick's approach, the content of stereotype plays a particularly important role before any action towards the scape-goat is taken. This approach opposes Allport's (1954) complementary projection model, in which stereotypes were ascribed after the aggressive behavior actually occurred. Moreover, Glick argues specifically that stereotypes of high competence accompanied by low warmth make a particular target a likely scapegoat, in con-trast to the classical approach, which assumes that any unfavorable stereotypes can lead to scapegoating.

Still, similar to the original formulation of scapegoat theory, Glick's ideologi-cal model of scapegoating (Glick, 2002; 2005) points to frustration as an essential cause of the process. However, Rothschild, Landau, Sullivan, and Keefer (2012) suggest other sources of scapegoating. According to these authors, scapegoating can be viewed as a response to a threat to moral values and personal control. In line with this approach, scapegoating serves two meaningfully distinct motives: "(a) maintaining perceived personal moral value by minimizing feelings of guilt over one's responsibility for a negative outcome and (b) maintaining perceived personal control by obtaining a clear explanation for a seemingly inexplicable negative outcome that is otherwise difficult to explain or control" (Rothschild et al., 2012, p. 1148). Furthermore, as threat to control appears to strengthen people's beliefs in the conspiratorial power of political enemies (Sullivan, Landau, & Rothschild, 2010), the scapegoated group's competence and power may even be exaggerated as a means of compensating for perceptions of reduced control over one's environment. This could explain why before World War II, Jews in German society went from being presented as a vulnerable minority to potent and dangerous enemies.

Whether we assume frustration or the lack of personal control as causes of scapegoating, it is clear that the time of crisis and rapid economic changes makes people search for explanations of their problems in the actions of a scapegoat. One example of such a process could be the systemic transition in post-communist Eastern Europe. In Bilewicz and Krzeminski's (2010) work on anti-Semitism in Poland and Ukraine, the authors found a significant relationship between relative deprivation and the strength of belief in Jewish influences in politics, the economy, and media. This belief acted as a mediator between relative deprivation and intentions to discriminate against Jews (although this relation was evident especially in Poland, but not in Ukraine). The authors argued that the scapegoating model "seems to be a good explanation of anti-Semitism only in countries where Jews are still targets of envious stereotypes" (Bilewicz & Krzeminski, 2010, p. 242). Using analytics of Google searches, Bilewicz and Krzeminski (2010) found that over the period from 2004 to 2010, the number of people searching for Jewish-related topics was correlated with the number of people searching for crisis-related topics. This suggests a conceptual relationship of crises and Jews – a blame-placing schema typical for conspiracy theorizing, as well as for the scapegoat model of prejudice.

To sum up, in times of crisis, a need to explain its sources arises and people seek to identify entities that are responsible for the poor living conditions. In such moments, representations of groups and individuals that evoke envy are likely to dominate in the social perception of the disadvantaged group. These entities (perceived as competent but cold) are the target of attack and ostracism, and as "enemies" they consequently become the main target of ideological discourse. This ideology, as a motivated social cognition, builds its narratives on a representation of a dangerous and potent enemy. It serves both explanatory and mobilizing functions: It explains why bad things happen to the in-group and justifies the in-group's actions. Ultimately, the target group starts to appear in the social discourse as an abstract notion rather than something that is visually accessible; that is, it stops having anything to do with reality. Presumably, this process results in accusing the group of engaging in secret plots, deception, and subversive activities as ways of realizing its collective evil goals. In the next section, we will try to demonstrate results of studies that verify these predictions. Specifically, we will present the results of two nationally representative studies conducted in Poland that will shed light on the relation between the stereotype content model and the conspiracy stereotypes.

Conspiracy stereotype on the bias map: Results of survey studies

In order to explore the relation between conspiracy stereotype and the two-dimensional structure of stereotypes, we reanalyzed the existing data from two surveys performed by our research unit – Center for Research on Prejudice. In two recent nationally representative Polish social surveys in 2009 and 2014 (Bilewicz, Winiewski, Kofta, & Wójcik, 2013; Bilewicz, Marchlewska, Soral, & Winiewski, 2014), we measured the conspiracy stereotype (belief in Jewish conspiracy; Kofta & Sedek, 2005), as well as stereotyping on two stereotype content dimensions of sociability and competence (following the methods used in national polls by Cuddy et al., 2007). Additionally, we measured perceived out-group morality as another component of out-group stereotype (Leach et al., 2007). Both studies employed a computer-assisted personal interview method and the samples were drawn using stratified random procedures.

In the reanalysis of survey data, we performed regression models predicting belief in Jewish conspiracy by the three dimensions of stereotype content (two standard dimensions of sociability and competence, and an additional third stereotype dimension of morality), see Table 2.1. Results show a consistent pattern, suggesting that a conspiracy stereotype of Jews is related to a perception of this group as competent but not warm. However, the negative relation of warmth ascription with conspiracy stereotypes was proven to be true for both subdimensions: sociability and morality. These results show that a perception of Jewish conspiracy is related not only to perceiving them as having ill intentions, but independently from that as also being immoral.

TABLE 2.1 Dimensions of stereotype content as a predictor of belief in Jewish conspiracy.

		Study 2009; N = 979	*Study 2014; N = 1007*
	R^2	.14	.11
Sociability		−.27***	−.18***
Competence		.17***	.16***
Morality		−.11*	−.10*

Note: In the table we present standardized regression coefficients. In both models, we controlled for gender, education level, age, and city size.

***p < .001, **p < .01, *p < .05

Researchers frequently pointed out the fact that morality and sociability, as highly correlated, both fall along the more general dimension of warmth and therefore could be treated as one (e.g., Fiske et al., 2002; Phalet & Poppe, 1997; Wojciszke, 1994; for a discussion, see, for example, Leach et al., 2007). Therefore, assuming Glick's ideological model of scapegoating (Glick, 2002; 2005), entering both sociability and morality into a single regression equation should mutually alleviate the impact of these predictors. Why is it then that both morality and sociability explain a significant proportion of variance of the outcome variable?

One plausible explanation points to the more general role of morality judgments, that is, the importance of morality in the out-group perception exceeds the predictions of Glick's model (2002; 2005). According to Leach, Bilali, and Pagliaro (2013), morality is inferentially necessary, that is "[i]f we cannot be sure that a person is trustworthy, we cannot be sure that he or she is genuinely just, kind, or cooperative" (p. 15). Given the general importance of morality in the perception of others, it should be applicable as well to the perception of out-groups. Alternatively, this effect might show an interesting specificity of conspiracy stereotypes. It is possible that conspiracy stereotypes – due to the assumption about hidden, invisible intentions and character of the conspiring group – include all three compositions of sociability and morality: (1) perception of the group as both malicious and immoral; (2) perception of the group as ostensibly moral, but malicious in its real character; and (3) perception of the group as ostensibly nice, but in fact immoral in its real intentions. These three configurations of sociability and morality could lead to independent influence of sociability and morality on conspiracy stereotype. Certainly, more research evidence is needed to support this speculative explanation.

In general, our data support the thesis that conspiracy stereotypes are embedded in the matrix of stereotype content model and seem to be the part of envious prejudice – thus confirming the ideological model of scapegoating (Glick, 2002). However, this conclusion is obviously limited and requires further studies. Aside from their correlational nature, our results do not address one important prediction of ideological model of scapegoating: the crucial role of crisis and lack of control as a source of frustration – both factors that contribute to the endorsement of conspiracy stereotypes. In that sense, the correlational evidence from survey studies (the ones presented above, as well as Bilewicz & Krzeminski, 2010) is clearly ahistorical and overcomes the crucial dynamical aspects of the ideological model of scapegoating, as well as the dynamical effects of conspiracy stereotypes, such as activation in the times of political mobilization (Kofta & Sedek, 2005). Finally, our data cannot explain the specific functionalities of stereotype content, especially in the times of harsh conflict, wars, and genocide. Research findings from the times of peace and stability cannot properly explain the powerful role of envious prejudice and conspiracy stereotypes as mobilizers of war efforts or tools of moral disengagement among criminals (Bandura, 1999). The methodology that could help to resolve these issues – and that recently regained its proper place in the field of social psychology (e.g., Durante et al., 2010; Volpato & Durante, 2009) – is based on the analysis of archival evidence.

Conspiracy stereotypes on the bias map: Archival evidence

In the analysis of historical genocides, Chalk and Jonassohn (1990) suggest that implementation of a belief system, a theory or ideology, is an important aspect of any crime of genocide. In their conceptual framework, the authors distinguish four types of genocidal crimes. In the first type of genocide (like in the case of the Albigensian crusade), the ideology targets an existing group that is accused by the perpetrators of some factual actions (in this case, heresies). In the second type, both the group and the action are invented by the perpetrators (the witch hunt in the Middle Ages is an example of such crime – both witches and their misdeeds were images in the perpetrators' minds). In the third type, an actual group is accused of conspiracies that in fact do not exist. One example of this type is the Armenian genocide, in which the dominant ideology of the perpetrators (Young Turk movement and wartime propaganda) presented Armenians as engaged in a separatist conspiracy and a secret alliance with Russia. Another example of such an ideology could be Stalin's alleged "doctor plot," accusing Jewish physicians of conspiring against the Soviet leader. The fourth type of genocide also involves accusing a group for conspiracy, although in this case an unrelated group is blamed for an actual conspiracy. This scenario is typical for scapegoating. All of these four types (scenarios) of genocide involve conspiracy theories against real plots or alleged plots, and the target groups are often only loosely related to any adverse actions to the dominant in-group.

A careful look of world history shows that in almost all cases of genocide the element of conspiracy and envious prejudice was present. During the Armenian genocide, a motive of the creation of a "fifth column" – an alleged collaboration with the Russian army during World War I – was used by the Turkish propaganda to justify nationalistic ideology in Anatolia, leading ultimately to the destruction of local Armenian population (Levene, 1998). Similar motives could be observed in the genocidal ideology of Hutus, portraying the Tutsi-dominated Rwandan Patriotic Front as a "fifth column" and blaming Tutsi leadership for President Habyarimana's plane crash in 1994 – an event that became a direct trigger of genocide (Lemarchand, 2002). In all of these cases, genocide was fueled by propaganda: leaflets, newspapers, and radio broadcasts that portrayed a specific minority (Armenians in Ottoman Turkey, Tutsis in Hutu-dominated Rwanda) as strong, cunning, and conspiring. In this section, we would like to present the evolution of the conspiracy stereotype and envious prejudice towards Jews in Nazi Germany. We will utilize the example of *Der Stürmer*, a violently anti-Semitic newspaper of the Nazi era, edited by Julius Streicher – one of the chief propagandists of Nazi Germany.

Existing analyses of Nazi propaganda point to the fact that Jews are often portrayed as having highly negative intentions towards Germans. Thus, the genocide becomes only a defense action of the ethnically German majority (Bytwerk, 2005). The propaganda was raising fear of the "Jewish threat" and the alleged Jewish plans to destroy Germany and its population. *Der Stürmer* was instrumental in creating such impression. Here, we would like to show how in *Der Stürmer* the depictions of Jews with respect to the dimensions of warmth and competence were related to conspiracy motives and how these motives evolved in the times of war and genocide.

We would like to stress that both the stereotype content model and conspiracy stereotype are theories developed to describe mechanisms shaping intergroup relations from the perspective of perceivers. Both models deal with how out-group members or out-groups as a whole are perceived by in-group members. While analyzing propaganda, we are focusing on the creations of Nazi ideologists and propagandists that were influencing perceptions of contemporary Germans. The general assumption that lies at the root of this analysis is that Nazi propagandists intuitively used the mechanisms or rules of perceptions in their narratives. Accepting that assumption, we can see whether conspiracy and envious stereotypes of Jews in propaganda were used for the purpose of convincing Germans to adopt the Nazi policy, mobilizing them, and accepting the government actions.

The study presented is a pretest for the larger project[2] with a general aim of exploring the stereotype transition in Nazi propaganda by employing content analysis methodology. The main focus of the coding structure was stereotype content (Figure 2.1) and conspiracy stereotypes (Figure 2.2). Primary materials used in the study were 232 caricatures depicting Jews from *Der Stürmer* magazine that appeared between 1934 and 1945. The material was independently coded by three trained judges. In order

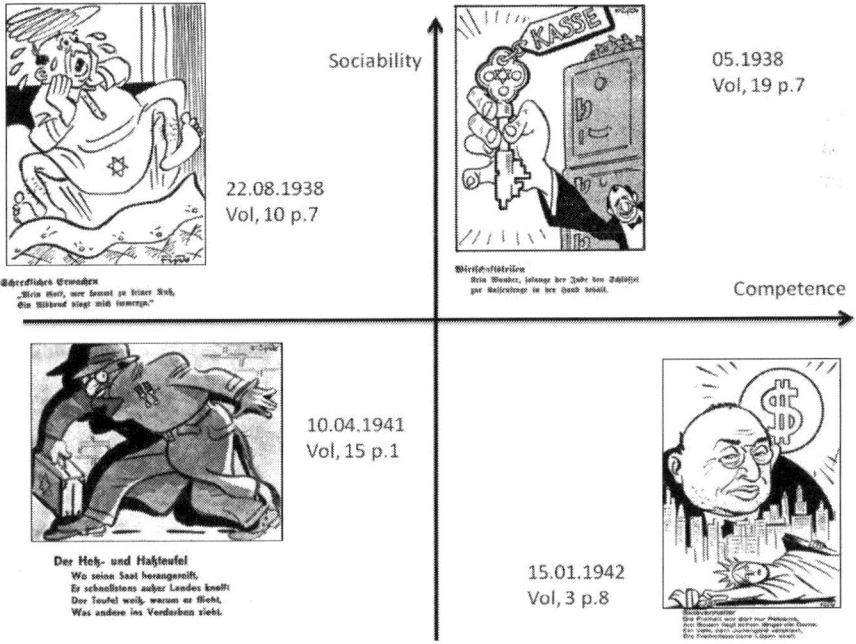

FIGURE 2.1 Examples of coded caricatures depicting Jews coded on the competence and sociability dimensions.

to measure the dimensions of stereotype content, three rating scales (describing whether the person on the picture was portrayed as friendly, moral, and competent) were used. The consistency of ratings were on the acceptable level – intraclass correlation for consistency, average measure was .78 for competence, .69 for morality, and .61 for sociability.

In a similar vein, conspiracy stereotype was coded using 10 binary (yes/no) scales describing situations or elements depicted on the caricature showing Jewish conspiracy (e.g., hiding behind something or conducting in a secret way, acting in the name of all Jews, etc.). Consistencies for pairs of assessments varied between 70% and 99%. For every coder, a single indicator of the conspiracy of a Jewish character was calculated (as a sum of all binary scales); overall consistency of the scale was high (ICC = .76).

The structure of correlations between depicting Jews as conspiring and portraying them on the dimensions of stereotype content is consistent with the findings from our survey data: The portrayal of a Jew on a caricature as conspiring is related positively to attributions of competence ($r = .56$, $p < .001$) and negatively to attributions of sociability ($r = -.43$, $p < .001$) and morality ($r = -.45$, $p < .001$).

In the next step, we attempted to examine the dynamics of stereotypical portrayals of Jews in Nazi propaganda and the functions of conspiracy and envious stereotypes. We compared stereotype dimensions and the portrayal of conspiracy in different time periods in Nazi Germany.[3] Because our sample was relatively small and unequally distributed throughout the years, we have aggregated the time of publishing to three-year intervals for presentation purposes and statistically tested contrasts for specific years that were the turning points.

FIGURE 2.2 Example of caricatures depicting Jews coded for conspiracy.

One of such turning points, which corresponds to Kofta and Sedek's (2005) view of conspiracy stereotype as a mechanism of social mobilization, is the beginning of World War II: 1939. Another important turning point is 1942 – when the genocidal "final solution" plan was designed at the Wannsee conference and its implementation started in the extermination camps located in the General Government. According to the ideological model of scapegoating (Glick, 2002; 2005), this point in time should be of primary interest, as the model suggests that envious stereotypes determine the role of a certain group as a target of aggression and/or justify aggression towards such group when it already occurs.

Analysis shows that the depiction of Jews as conspiring was indeed changing in time. In the beginning of the war in 1939, the caricatures tended to present Jews as more conspiring than in the caricatures printed in previous time points, $F(1, 230) = 6.63$, $p = .028$, $\eta_p^2 = .03$.

Similar analysis for stereotype content model dimensions show that stereotypical presentations of Jews also dynamically changed in response to political events. Similar to a depiction of Jews as conspiring, a stereotypical image during 1934–1939 was relatively stable – high competence and low morality and sociability, with no difference between the latter two. The beginning of the war in 1939 is the first major change that can be noted, but only on the morality dimension, $F(1, 230) = 4.72$, $p = .031$, $\eta_p^2 = .02$. The ascriptions of morality decrease, but this decrease does not influence the relation between all stereotype dimensions.

Focusing on the next turning point (in the year 1942), we observed clear trends in the stereotype content of Jews' depiction: decrease in sociability dimension, $F(1, 230) = 3.41$, $p = .066$, $\eta_p^2 = .02$; increase in competence, $F(1, 230) = 3.64$, $p = .058$, $\eta_p^2 = .02$; and finally, significant decrease of morality, $F(1, 230) = 5.02$, $p = .026$, $\eta_p^2 = .02$ of Jewish characters in caricatures. Interestingly, we observed an interaction of stereotype dimensions and contrasted the year, $F(2, 229) = 4.81$, $p < .001$, $\eta_p^2 = .02$. The difference between competence and both morality and

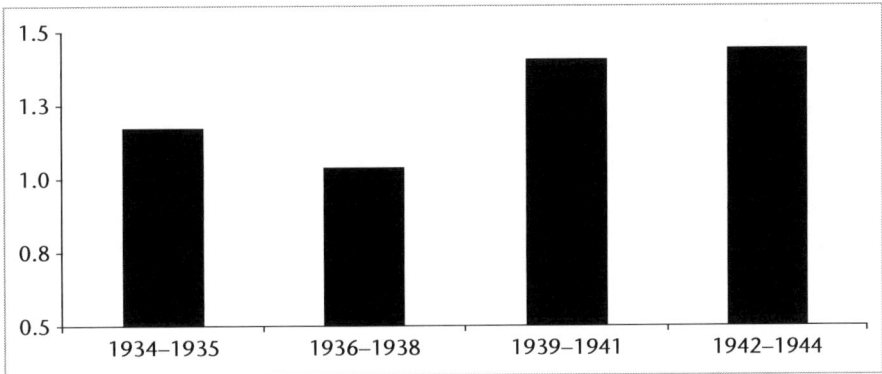

FIGURE 2.3 Jewish conspiracy in *Der Stürmer* caricatures. Bars represent the average composite measure of several attributes related to conspiracy stereotype in three-year intervals.

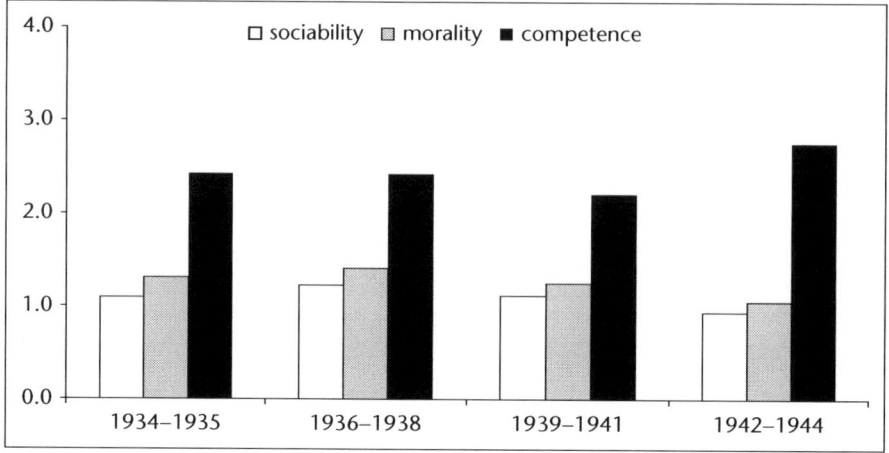

FIGURE 2.4 Average of three stereotype content dimensions of Jewish characters portrayed in *Der Stürmer* caricatures.

sociability became the most extreme during the Holocaust period. Thus, the envious stereotype became more pronounced after 1942, when Nazi Germany implemented its plans of extermination.

Results of the presented study form a very coherent picture of relations between conspiracy stereotype and two dimensions of stereotype content. First, conspiracy image is related to high competence and low warmth in both aspects (morality and sociability). These results are consistent with previous survey data and show that perceptions of conspiracy are definitely related to alleged negative intentions of the stereotyped group members and their high competences. Second, the depiction of Jews in caricatures changes in relation to the ideologically motivated Nazi policy with respect to both conspiracy and trait-laden stereotypes. This implies that functions of both of these components of portraying/perceiving the out-group are closely related to the actual intergroup relations. Finally, the dynamics of those changes in portraying the enemy group by Nazi propagandists are different for both forms and related to different events. Depicting Jews as conspiring is relatively stable until 1938, then it increases significantly and stays relatively high throughout the entire war period. This result is in line with Kofta and Sedek's (2005) results about the politically mobilizing role of the conspiracy stereotype. In terms of the stereotype content model, the same year 1939 brings change only in one dimension: the morality of portrayed Jews. Present findings seem consistent with survey results showing that low morality is an important aspect of beliefs of Jewish conspiracy – although the co-occurrence in time is only a partial evidence of such a claim, the proof of which would require partialling out the effects of potential confounders.

Dynamics of warmth and competence in stereotypical depictions of Jews show that the beginning of World War II is accompanied by only a slight change in the stereotype content of presented Jewish characters. Most notable change takes place in 1942 and at the final stage of the Holocaust. A decrease in perceived morality and sociability and, at the same time, an increase in competence augments the difference between both dimensions. These results seem to be in line with the ideological model of scapegoating (Glick, 2002), suggesting that envious prejudice is a central ideological aspect that allows for identification of a group that will become a scapegoat. Perceived bad intentions and high abilities make the scapegoat an ostensibly powerful enemy that can be blamed for past failures or current bad conditions of the in-group. A powerful, threatening enemy becomes the target of attack in "self-defense" or as a punishment for "misdeeds." This change in the portrayals of Jews – becoming more powerful and more vicious – is linked to acts of collective violence of the majority group towards the powerless minority group.

Summary

The stereotype content model provides a sufficient theoretical framework for understanding most forms of prejudice and biases of modern times. It also explains the affective and behavioral consequences of certain stereotypes, linking group perception with its emotional and behavioral outcomes. In this chapter, we aimed at locating the conspiracy stereotype (Kofta & Sedek, 2005) within the structure of stereotype content model – particularly as related to the envious stereotype of high competence and low warmth (Glick, 2002). To this aim, we used survey research findings and archival analysis of historical data.

The research findings suggest that the dimensions of stereotype content explain more than 10% of the variance of beliefs in Jewish conspiracy, which is a high proportion considering the methodological constraints of large sample survey research (short scales, sources of error, etc.). We found that people who consider Jews to be immoral and hostile but competent are more often perceiving them as conspiring against the in-group. Interestingly, sociability and morality are independent significant predictors of conspiracy beliefs about Jews. A similar pattern of results was obtained in the archival analysis of historical material.

At the same time, archival analysis of Nazi propaganda revealed an interesting difference between envious stereotypes of Jews and conspiracy stereotype. Although both of them seem to be modified by the changing historical and political circumstances, they seem to be related to different kinds of events. The turning point for conspiracy stereotype was the beginning of World War II – a moment when warfare mobilized the whole German society. Conspiracy stereotypes could thus be used to define the focal enemy and to close ranks of the otherwise diverse society. The turning point for the envious stereotype was the Wannsee conference and its direct consequence: rapid extermination of the Jewish population of Europe. In such genocidal crime, the envious prejudice could serve as justification in the process of moral disengagement (Bandura, 1999). Aside from their different functionalities, one should also emphasize the different target of both types of stereotypes. While conspiracy stereotypes seem to target an abstract notion, the mass killing was conducted on living human beings: elders, women, and children – clearly a very different target than Jews portrayed as involved in secret plots and hideous plans against German society. Perhaps this is another reason for differing temporal activation of conspiracy and trait-laden stereotypes.

Our research suggests that although conspiracy stereotypes and envious stereotypes are clearly related, they might serve different societal functions. The first mobilize society and define the enemy, whereas the latter justify crimes and allow for continuous support for genocidal policies. Although in the case of anti-Semitic Nazi propaganda conspiracy stereotypes preceded visible increases in envious prejudice in propaganda, it would be premature to infer any causality or temporal order of these two stereotypes. It is obvious, however, that the treatment of them as identical or synonymous can limit our understanding of the unique character of conspiracy beliefs in times of violent intergroup conflict.

Author note

Mikolaj Winiewski, Faculty of Psychology, University of Warsaw. Wiktor Soral, Institute for Social Studies, University of Warsaw. Michal Bilewicz, Faculty of Psychology, University of Warsaw. The study reported in this chapter was financed by the Foundation for Polish Science FOCUS grant to Michał Bilewicz and the National Science Center (NCN) Opus Grant number .2014/13/B/HS6/04077 to Mikołaj Winiewski. Correspondence regarding this chapter should be directed to Mikolaj Winiewski, University of Warsaw, Faculty of Psychology, Stawki 5/7, Warsaw (Poland). E-mail: mikk@psych.uw.edu.pl

Notes

1 To avoid confusion, for the rest of our chapter – following Leach et al. (2007) – we will use *warmth* as denominating the conjunction of *sociability* and *morality* dimensions. The reader should be cautious that this distinction is quite new in the literature and absent in many previous works. Therefore *warmth* will be used when the intentions of the cited source's author(s) were not clear enough to justify the use of *sociability* and/or *morality*.
2 Conducted together with Johanna Vollhardt, Lucas Mazur, and Mateusz Olechowski.
3 Due to the large range of caricatures frequencies per year (4–52), aggregation was necessary.

References

Alexander, M.G., Brewer, M.B., & Herrmann, R.K. (1999). Images and affect: A functional analysis of out-group stereotypes. *Journal of Personality and Social Psychology, 77*(1), 78–93.
Allport, G.W. (1954). *The nature of prejudice*. Reading, MA: Addison-Wesley.
Bandura, A. (1999). Moral disengagement in the perpetration of inhumanities. *Personality and Social Psychology Review, 3*(3), 193–209.
Bilewicz, M., & Krzeminski, I. (2010). Anti-Semitism in Poland and Ukraine: The belief in Jewish control as a mechanism of scapegoating. *International Journal of Conflict and Violence, 4*(2), 234–243.
Bilewicz, M., Marchlewska, M., Soral, W., & Winiewski, M. (2014). *Mowa nienawisci: Raport z badan sondazowych* [Hate speech: Survey report]. Warsaw: Fundacja im. Stefan Batorego.

Bilewicz, M., Winiewski, M., Kofta, M., & Wójcik, A. (2013). Harmful ideas, the structure and consequences of anti-Semitic beliefs in Poland. *Political Psychology, 34*(6), 821–839.

Brambilla, M., Sacchi, S., Pagliaro, S., & Ellemers, N. (2013). Morality and intergroup relations: Threats to safety and group image predict the desire to interact with outgroup and ingroup members. *Journal of Experimental Social Psychology, 49*(5), 811–821.

Brambilla, M., Sacchi, S., Rusconi, P., Cherubini, P., & Yzerbyt, V. Y. (2012). You want to give a good impression? Be honest! Moral traits dominate group impression formation. *British Journal of Social Psychology, 51*(1), 149–166. doi:10.1111/j.2044-8309.2010.02011.x

Brewer, M. B., & Alexander, M. G. (2002). Intergroup emotions and images. In D. M. Mackie & E. R. Smith (Eds.), *From prejudice to intergroup emotions: Differentiated reactions to social groups* (pp. 209–225). New York: Psychology Press.

Bytwerk, R. L. (2005). The argument for genocide in Nazi propaganda. *Quarterly Journal of Speech, 91*(1), 37–62.

Chalk, F., & Jonassohn, K. (1990). The conceptual framework. In F. Chalk and K. Jonassohn (Eds.), *The history and sociology of genocide: Analyses and case studies* (pp. 2–53). New Haven, CT: Yale University Press.

Cichocka, A., Winiewski, M., Bilewicz, M., Bukowski, M., & Jost, J. T. (in press). Complementary stereotyping of ethnic minorities predicts system justification in Poland. *Group Processes and Intergroup Relations.*

Cohn, N. (1967). *Warrant for genocide.* London: Chatto Heinemann.

Cuddy, A. J., Fiske, S. T., & Glick, P. (2007). The BIAS map: Behaviors from intergroup affect and stereotypes. *Journal of Personality and Social Psychology, 92*(4), 631–648.

Durante, F., Volpato, C., & Fiske, S. T. (2010). Using the stereotype content model to examine group depictions in fascism: An archival approach. *European Journal of Social Psychology, 40*(3), 465–483.

Fiske, S. T., Cuddy, A. J., & Glick, P. (2006). Universal dimensions of social cognition: Warmth and competence. *Trends in Cognitive Sciences, 11*(2), 77–83.

Fiske, S. T., Cuddy, A. J., Glick, P., & Xu, J. (2002). A model of (often mixed) stereotype content: Competence and warmth respectively follow from perceived status and competition. *Journal of Personality and Social Psychology, 82*(6), 878–902.

Glick, P. (2002). Sacrificial lambs dressed in wolves' clothing: Envious prejudice, ideology, and the scapegoating of Jews. In L. S. Newman & R. Erber (Eds.), *Understanding genocide: The social psychology of the Holocaust* (pp. 113–142). London: Oxford University Press.

Glick, P. (2005). Choice of scapegoats. In J. F. Dovidio, P. Glick, & L. A. Rudman (Eds.), *On the nature of prejudice: Fifty years after Allport* (pp. 244–261). Malden, MA: Blackwell.

Glick, P., & Fiske, S. T. (1999). Sexism and other "isms": Independence, status, and the ambivalent content of stereotypes. In W. B. Swa, J. H. Langlois, & L. A. Gilbert (Eds.), *Sexism and stereotypes in modern society: The gender science of Janet Taylor Spence* (pp. 193–221). Washington, DC: American Psychological Association.

Glick, P., & Fiske, S. T. (2001). Ambivalent stereotypes as legitimizing ideologies: Differentiating paternalistic and envious prejudice. In J. T. Jost & B. Major (Eds.), *The psychology of legitimacy: Emerging perspectives on ideology, justice, and intergroup relations* (pp. 278–306). New York: Cambridge University Press.

Guglielmo, S., & Malle, B. F. (2010). Enough skill to kill: Intentionality judgments and the moral valence of action. *Cognition, 117*(2), 139–150.

Haidt, J., & Joseph, C. (2004). Intuitive ethics: How innately prepared intuitions generate culturally variable virtues. *Daedalus, 133*(4), 55–66.

Hill, S. E., DelPriore, D. J., & Vaughan, P. W. (2011). The cognitive consequences of envy: attention, memory, and self-regulatory depletion. *Journal of Personality and Social Psychology, 101*(4), 653–666.

Judd, C. M., James-Hawkins, L., Yzerbyt, V., & Kashima, Y. (2005). Fundamental dimensions of social judgment: Understanding the relations between judgments of competence and warmth. *Journal of Personality and Social Psychology, 89*(6), 899–913.

Kay, A. C., & Jost, J. T. (2003). Complementary justice: Effects of "poor but happy" and "poor but honest" stereotype exemplars on system justification and implicit activation of the justice motive. *Journal of Personality and Social Psychology, 85*(5), 823–837.

Kofta, M., & Sedek, G. (2005). Conspiracy stereotypes of Jews during systemic transformation in Poland. *International Journal of Sociology, 35*(1), 40–64.

Kressel, J. (2012). *The sons of pigs and apes: Muslim antisemitism and the conspiracy of silence.* Sterling, VA: Potomac Books.

Leach, C. W., Bilali, R., & Pagliaro, S. (2013). Groups and morality. In J. Simpson & J. F. Dovidio (Eds.), *APA handbook of personality and social psychology: Interpersonal relationships and group processes* (Vol. 2). Washington, DC: American Psychological Association.

Leach, C. W., Ellemers, N., & Barreto, M. (2007). Group virtue: The importance of morality (vs. competence and sociability) in the positive evaluation of in-groups. *Journal of Personality and Social Psychology, 93*(2), 234–249.

Lemarchand, R. (2002). A history of genocide in Rwanda. *Journal of African History, 43*(02), 307–311.

Levene, M. (1998). Creating a modern "zone of genocide": The impact of nation-and state-formation on eastern Anatolia, 1878–1923. *Holocaust and Genocide Studies, 12*(3), 393–433.

Malle, B. F., Guglielmo, S., & Monroe, A. E. (2014). A theory of blame. *Psychological Inquiry, 25*(2), 147–186.

Peeters, G. (2002). From good and bad to can and must: Subjective necessity of acts associated with positively and negatively valued stimuli. *European Journal of Social Psychology, 31*(1), 125–136.

Phalet, K., & Poppe, E. (1997). Competence and morality dimensions of national and ethnic stereotypes: A study in six eastern-European countries. *European Journal of Social Psychology, 27*(6), 703–723.

Poliakov, L. (2003). *The history of anti-Semitism: Suicidal Europe. 1870–1933.* Philadelphia: University of Pennsylvania Press.

Rosch, E. H. (1973). Natural categories. *Cognitive Psychology, 4*(3), 328–350.

Rosch, E. H. (1975). Cognitive Reference Points. *Cognitive Psychology, 7*(4), 532–547.

Rothschild, Z. K., Landau, M. J., Sullivan, D., & Keefer, L. A. (2012). A dual-motive model of the motives underlying scapegoating: Displacing blame to reduce guilt or increase control. *Journal of Personality and Social Psychology, 102*(6), 1148–1163.

Smith, R. H., Parrott, W. G., Ozer, D., & Moniz, A. (1994). Subjective injustice and inferiority as predictors of hostile and depressive feelings in envy. *Personality and Social Psychology Bulletin, 20*(6), 705–711. doi:10.1177/0146167294206008

Sullivan, D., Landau, M. J., & Rothschild, Z. K. (2010). An existential function of enemyship: Evidence that people attribute influence to personal and political enemies to compensate for threats to control. *Journal of Personality and Social Psychology, 98*(3), 434–449.

Volpato, C., & Durante, F. (2009). Empowering the "Jewish threat": The protocols of the elders of Zion. *Journal of US-China Public Administration, 6*(1), 23–36.

Wentura, D., Rothermund, K., & Bak, P. (2000). Automatic vigilance: The attention-grabbing power of approach- and avoidance-related social information. *Journal of Personality and Social Psychology, 78*(6), 1024–1037.

Wojciszke, B. (1994). Multiple meanings of behavior: Construing actions in terms of competence or morality. *Journal of Personality and Social Psychology, 67*(2), 222–232.

Wojciszke, B., & Abele, A. E. (2008). The primacy of communion over agency and its reversals in evaluations. *European Journal of Social Psychology, 38*(7), 1139–1147.

Wojciszke, B., Baryla, W., Parzuchowski, M., Szymkow, A., & Abele, A. E. (2011). Self-esteem is dominated by agentic over communal information. *European Journal of Social Psychology, 41*(5), 617–627.

Wojciszke, B., Bazinska, R., & Jaworski, M. (1998). On the dominance of moral categories in impression formation. *Personality and Social Psychology Bulletin, 24*(12), 1251–1263.

Zawadzki, B. (1948). Limitations of the scapegoat theory of prejudice. *Journal of Abnormal and Social Psychology, 43*(2), 127–141.

Zhong, J., Liu, Y., Zhang, E., Luo, J., & Chen, J. (2013). Individuals' attentional bias toward an envied target's name: An event-related potential study. *Neuroscience Letters, 550*, 109–114.

3

GRANDIOSE DELUSIONS

Collective narcissism, secure in-group identification, and belief in conspiracies

Aleksandra Cichocka, Agnieszka Golec de Zavala,
Marta Marchlewska, and Mateusz Olechowski

On July 17, 2014, as we were finalizing this chapter, a Malaysian airliner with 295 people on board was shot down close to Donetsk, East Ukraine – an area of ongoing conflict between the Ukrainian government and pro-Russian separatists. Most recent news reports indicate that the crash was a consequence of a missile strike by the pro-Russian separatists. Although at this time it seems almost clear that the plane was shot down by mistake, several conspiracy theories about the incident have emerged (Reidy, 2014). These speculate, for example, that the crash might have been an attempt to conceal the truth about HIV/AIDS (as over 100 passengers were doing research in this area) or that a secret society of the Illuminati was involved (Reidy, 2014). Yet most speculate that the involvement of the Russian government was larger than was suspected and that a civilian plane was targeted intentionally. Some people even seem to believe that it might have been Russians themselves who popularized alternative conspiracy theories to divert attention from the role played by their in-group (Zavadski, 2014).

Whether any of these conspiracy theories turn out to be true will, one hopes, be determined by an official investigation by the Dutch Safety Board (2014). In any case, reactions to the Donetsk plane crash in Poland resemble those that followed the Smolensk plane crash of April 10, 2010, in which a Polish Air Force plane crashed in Russia, killing 96 officials, including the presidential couple. This is illustrated by a comment made by Antoni Macierewicz, a right-wing Polish politician: "it is worth realizing that the tragedy associated with the assassination of the Donetsk began on April 10 over Smolensk. This is the same method of operation, the same perpetrator, and the same cause" ("Antoni Macierewicz," 2014). Similarly, in the case of the Smolensk catastrophe, a relatively short period of shock and intense national mourning was followed by a sudden and steep rise of the conspiracy-based explanation for the crash. The popularity of the Smolensk conspiracy was facilitated by the identification of a specific out-group that could be blamed for this traumatic event. The plane crash happened in Russia, during the anniversary of the Russian massacre of Polish officers during World War II in Katyn. Russians then became an obvious target to be called responsible for the tragedy. Indeed, conspiracy theories of Russian involvement in the crash, popularized especially strongly by right-wing politicians and some radical clergy (Hołub, 2010), spread out quickly among the Polish population.

After the Smolensk crash, Radoslaw Sikorski, the Polish minister of foreign affairs, noted that "some Poles believe that the cause must be proportionate to the effect. Death of the president and 95 other people cannot result from such banal causes such as fog or errors of the pilots" (Nowakowska & Wielowieyska, 2011). This quote illustrates why people find it hard to believe that tragedies such as those in Smolensk and Donetsk were the result of a mistake or a coincidence. The need to find alternative explanations is echoed in studies on motivations behind beliefs in conspiracy theories. Especially in the context of catastrophic events with large consequences, intentional malevolent activities of a hostile group of people are often assumed (Hofstadter, 1996). In this chapter we examine whether the conspiratorial explanations of out-group actions are shaped by what people think and feel about their own in-group.

As argued by van Prooijen and van Lange (2014), conspiracy theories often presume an intergroup dimension. According to these authors, "most conspiracy beliefs can be framed in terms of beliefs about how a powerful and evil out-group meets in secret, designing a plot that is harmful to one's in-group" (pp. 238–239). The out-group can be defined in many ways, including other national out-groups (Kofta & Sedek, 2005), or subgroups and organizations within one's in-group, such as the government or a small international malevolent organization. Such conspiratorial beliefs are especially likely to develop in the context of in-group disadvantage. For instance, one notable example of research on intergroup conspiracies compares conspiracy beliefs between Blacks (the disadvantaged group) and Whites (the advantaged group) in the United States. Crocker, Luhtanen, Broadnax, and Blaine (1999) reported that Black Americans are more likely than White Americans to believe in conspiracies of the U.S. government against their in-group. Simmons and Parsons (2005) further demonstrated that this effect is due to feelings of group, rather than individual, deprivation.

Considering the theoretical proposals and empirical research that link conspiracy beliefs with intergroup context, one could expect that beliefs in conspiracies would be associated with one of the basic dimensions that determine intergroup relations: in-group identification. The more important group membership is to someone, the more they should feel the need for protecting the in-group from potential threats (Leach et al., 2008). Therefore, it is surprising that, as noted by van Prooijen and van Lange (2014), little research reports links between beliefs in conspiracies and in-group identification. One explanation for this scarce evidence could be that the relationship between in-group positivity and a tendency to uphold conspiracy beliefs in an intergroup context is more complex than previously thought. It could be that conspiracy beliefs are only linked to certain types of in-group identification. According to van Prooijen and van Lange (2014), "belief in conspiracy theories is to some extent rooted in the psychological dynamics underlying intergroup threat" (p. 244). This suggests that conspiratorial explanations of intergroup events may be especially compelling when positive identification with an in-group is chronically or situationally threatened.

Recent research suggests that conspiracy beliefs indeed flourish in the context of intergroup threat. A study conducted in Indonesia demonstrated that identification with Islam was positively associated with conspiracy beliefs about Westerners instigating terrorism in Indonesia. However, this link was only significant for those participants who perceived Westerners as a threat to their Islamic identity (Mashuri & Zaduqisti, 2013). In addition, a tendency to hold conspiracy beliefs has been linked to a victimhood-based identity – a form of threatened in-group identity concentrated on protecting one's in-group status as a victim of historical atrocities and even competing with other groups over the magnitude of suffering endured by the in-group (Noor, Brown, & Prentice, 2008; Noor, Schnabel, Halabi, & Nadler, 2012; Vollhardt, 2013). Stressing the importance of one's own in-group victimhood creates a paradoxical psychological situation: It might allow for fostering feelings of in-group power (Noor et al., 2012) while at the same time increasing a sense of the in-group's vulnerable position and, as a consequence, feelings of out-group threat.

Polish national identity is a good example of constructing positive in-group identity around the concept of extraordinary and sacrificial Polish suffering throughout years of the nation's turbulent history. This national narrative, infused with Christian ideology of sacrifice, has become widespread during the 19th century, when Poland was partitioned between Russian, Prussian, and Austro-Hungarian empires (Zubrzycki, 2007). Martyrdom and messianic beliefs about the nation remain an important part of Polish national identity (Skarżyńska, Przybyła, & Wójcik, 2012). Polish victimhood-based identity presumes denial of the unique status of Jews as Holocaust victims and stresses the importance of Polish victimhood (Bilewicz & Stefaniak, 2013). Moreover, in a national representative sample of Polish adults, the beliefs in national victimhood were associated with conspiracy-based anti-Semitism (Bilewicz, Winiewski, Kofta, & Wójcik, 2013), even after accounting for other dispositional factors that can increase intergroup threat sensitivity, such as right-wing authoritarianism and perceived relative deprivation (Bilewicz, Winiewski, & Radzik, 2012).

These examples suggest that a tendency to uphold conspiracy beliefs is indeed linked to in-group identity that is somehow threatened. A conviction that others are constantly conspiring to undermine one's own in-group provides an image protecting explanation of the in-group's misfortunes or disadvantaged position. According to this perspective, the glorified in-group is being disadvantaged because it chooses to play fair but faces dishonest and conspiring opponents. Such beliefs may be particularly appealing when the in-group's positive image is already undermined in some way. This may in turn foster the perception that the in-group is threatened by out-groups, which leads to even higher susceptibility to conspiracy theories in explaining intergroup relations. Thus, there are reasons to believe that acceptance of conspiracy theories in intergroup contexts should be associated with a threatened or defensive form of positive in–group identification. A more secure, nondefensive form of in–group identification should be related to a relatively more objective in–group image and compassionate (rather than idealizing) perception of the in–group. Such secure in–group identification would likely decrease sensitivity to intergroup threats and, thus, predict a rejection of conspiratorial explanations of intergroup relations.

Collective narcissism versus secure in-group identification and conspiracy beliefs

Defensive identification with the in–group can be captured by the concept of collective narcissism (Golec de Zavala, Cichocka, Eidelson, & Jayawickreme, 2009). Collective narcissism is defined as an exaggerated belief in greatness of the in–group contingent on its external validation. It combines a belief in in–group prominence with concerns about others not appropriately recognizing the in–group's worth. Such internal fragility contributes to a collective narcissistic preoccupation with what others think or say about the in–group. Collective narcissism predicts sensitivity to threats to the in–group image (Golec de Zavala & Cichocka, 2012; Golec de Zavala et al., 2009). Real or imagined in–group image threats are punished with retaliatory hostility and aggressiveness directed at the source of threat (Golec de Zavala, Cichocka, & Iskra-Golec, 2013). Collective narcissism is also associated with generalized negativity and suspicion of out-groups, especially if there is a history of mutual grievance and mistrust (Golec de Zavala & Cichocka, 2012). Moreover, empirical evidence indicates that collective narcissism increases when ego is weakened – in response to frustration of need for personal control (Cichocka, Golec de Zavala, Marchlewska, Olechowski, & Bilewicz, 2014). Collective narcissism is a specific form of in–group positivity that is chronically undermined. As such it predicts a tendency to uphold conspiratorial beliefs that serve to save the in–group's overly positive image. Below we review various empirical findings that point to the relationship between collective narcissism and a tendency to seek and uphold conspiracy theories in intergroup contexts.

We also elucidate the role secure, of nonnarcissistic in–group positivity in decreasing a tendency to blame out-groups for the disadvantages and difficulties of the in–group. More specifically, empirical results suggest that when collective narcissism and secure in–group positivity are differentiated by controlling their overlap, secure in–group positivity predicts quite different out-group attitudes than collective narcissism. For example, a series of studies demonstrated that when the variance shared between collective narcissism and in–group identification is accounted for, secure in–group identification becomes a predictor of positive out-group attitudes while the positive relationship between collective narcissism and out-group hostility strengthens (Golec de Zavala, Cichocka & Bilewicz, 2013). In addition, covarying out the defensiveness associated with collective narcissism

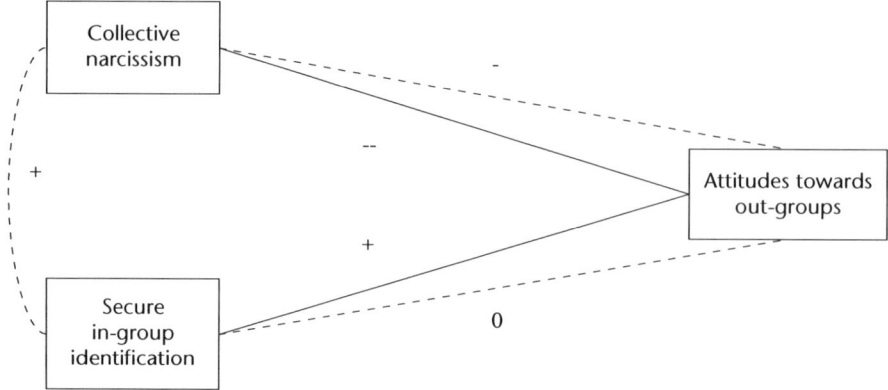

FIGURE 3.1 General model of relationships between collective narcissism versus secure in-group identification and out-group attitudes. Dotted lines represent zero-order relationships, while solid lines represent partial relationships.

allows for demonstrating that secure, nonnarcissistic in-group identification is associated with decreased perception of intergroup threat (Jaworska, Cichocka, & Marchlewska, 2014). The general model of links between collective narcissism versus secure in-group identification and intergroup attitudes is presented in Figure 3.1. Such patterns of relationships suggest that secure in-group positivity may predict decreased support for conspiratorial explanations in intergroup contexts, especially when the overlap between in-group identification and collective narcissism is accounted for.

Collective narcissism and endorsement of conspiracy stereotypes

We first consider studies that show the link between collective narcissism and conspiratorial stereotypes of specific out-groups. Such conspiracy stereotypes "frame an out-group as a dangerous, potent, and deceptive enemy" (Kofta & Sedek, 2005, p. 42), who strives to dominate other groups via highly coordinated, secret actions. Endorsement of conspiracy stereotypes can serve as an explanation for the in-group's alleged underprivileged and underestimated position – any in-group's misfortune could then be attributed to the actions of external enemies, rather than to in-groups' own activities. It is then expected that due to its intergroup threat sensitivity, collective narcissism would be associated with a tendency to embrace conspiracy stereotypes of out-groups, especially if those out-groups had wronged the in-group in some way in the past (Golec de Zavala & Cichocka, 2012).

In a large Polish Internet survey, collective narcissism (but not nonnarcissistic in-group identification measured with Cameron's 2004 Social Identification Scale) was significantly associated with conspiracy stereotypes of three out-groups: Jews, Russians, and Germans (Kofta, 2012). All three out-groups were involved in Polish turbulent history throughout which they frequently posed a threat to Polish realistic and symbolic interests. As such, those groups were likely to create suspicions of continuous malevolent intentions against Poles, and collective narcissism is especially likely to foster a tendency to hold such suspicious beliefs.

Another line of research (Golec de Zavala & Cichocka, 2012) examined the role of belief in conspiracy stereotypes of Jews in fostering anti-Semitism. In a correlational study conducted in Poland, collective narcissism and anti-Semitic attitudes were mediated via conspiracy stereotype of Jews, independently to general perceptions of threat (operationalized as siege mentality; Bar-Tal & Antebi, 1992). No similar effects were found for in-group identification operationalized as the overlap between the in-group and the self (Tropp & Wright, 2001). This pattern of results was replicated in a Polish nationally representative sample (Bilewicz, Bukowski, Cichocka, Winiewski, & Wójcik, 2009). Collective narcissism predicted conspiracy stereotypes of Jews, which in turn predicted greater social distance towards Jews. This mediation pattern was not obtained for secure in-group identification (operationalized as Cameron's 2004 measure, without the variance shared with collective narcissism; see Golec de Zavala, Cichocka, & Bilewicz, 2013): Secure in-group identification was negatively associated with distance towards Jews. However, this effect was not driven by a decreased belief in Jewish conspiracies. These data suggest that collective narcissism, but not secure in-group identification, predicts a tendency to hold stereotypical beliefs about conspiratorial actions and tendencies of specific national out-groups. It is at least plausible that secure in-group identification predicts an unwillingness to stereotype out-groups, regardless of whether the stereotypes are positive or negative. We come back to this issue later.

Collective narcissism and conspiratorial explanations for consequential events

One of major functions of conspiracy beliefs is making sense of events that threaten the social order and bear large consequences for the in-group (Swami & Coles, 2010; van Prooijen & van Dijk, in press). Research shows that collective narcissism is associated not only with chronic stereotyping of out-groups as prone for conspiring (Kofta & Sedek, 2005), but also with conspiratorial explanations of particular events or upheavals that concern the in-group. Collective narcissism should predict blaming others for in-group's misfortunes, and therefore it will likely be associated also with embracing explanations that involve intentional malevolent actions of threatening out-groups. Secure, nonnarcissistic in-group identification, on the other hand, is not related to perceiving excessive threats from conspiracy of out-groups. Rather, it should be associated with the decreased likelihood of accepting conspiratorial explanations of threatening events and, consequently, decreased out-group negativity (see Golec de Zavala, Cichocka, & Bilewicz, 2013). Not distinguishing collective narcissism and secure in-group identification could disguise their divergent relationships with belief in conspiratorial explanations of important societal events.

Such patterns of relationships were demonstrated in two studies conducted in Poland. These studies focused on the role of narcissistic and nonnarcissistic in-group identification in response to two situations that might fuel conspiratorial beliefs: collective trauma and lack of recognition of an in-group's achievements (Cichocka, Marchlewska, Golec de Zavala, & Olechowski, 2014). One study examined reactions to the trauma associated with the presidential plane crash near Smolensk on April 10, 2010, which we discussed above in the introduction. This event inspired the most popular conspiracy theory of recent years in Poland – the belief that the plane crash was an assassination of the Polish president carried out by Russians. Belief in such explanations might have been exacerbated by the feelings of threat accompanying the crash, and could have also served as a moral justification for displays of hostility towards an out-group blamed for the event.

Given that collective narcissism predicts intergroup hostility in the context of intergroup threat, one could expect that the psychological dynamic associated with collective narcissism should be activated after the Smolensk catastrophe. Indeed, a survey study conducted just a few days after the catastrophe among over 200 Polish students showed that national collective narcissism predicted negative feelings and behavioral intentions towards Russians. This effect was mediated by a belief in Russian conspiracy behind the crash of the presidential plane in Smolensk (Cichocka, Golec de Zavala, & Olechowski, 2011). These results suggest that any available convictions that justify collective narcissistic hostility could be embraced. Foreign conspiracy behind the plane crash is a threat to the in-group image that, as demonstrated by previous studies (Golec de Zavala et al., 2013), instigates collective narcissistic retaliatory hostility. Thus, presumably, conspiracy beliefs were used as moral justification for hostility towards Russians – one of the out-groups with which Poland shares a difficult history. Moreover, for collective narcissists an accident would probably seem too trivial a cause for losing a great number of leading national figures – such an explanation would not be in line with the grandiose in-group image cultivated by collective narcissism. A long-lasting, hostile plotting of an out-group seems better fitted to the assumed unparalleled greatness of the in-group.

The survey also explored the effects of nonnarcissistic in-group identification. When in-group identification, measured with Cameron's scale (2004), was considered alone, it did not predict belief in a Russian conspiracy or attitudes towards Russians. However, once collective narcissism was covaried out of positive in-group identification, secure in-group identification was significantly and negatively associated with beliefs in Russian conspiracy. Furthermore, this time the rejection of these conspiracy beliefs served as a mediator between secure in-group identification and more positive attitudes towards Russians, who at the time were working on investigating the cause of the accident. It seems then that, in the context of group traumas, those securely identified with the in-group will be more likely to accept benign explanations for the event and will focus on promoting intergroup cooperation, rather than hostility.

The link between collective narcissism and belief in Russian conspiracy was also found in recent research by Soral, Kofta, and Szymanska (2014). Results of two studies conducted in Poland confirmed that collective narcissism is a predictor of belief in a Smolensk conspiracy. Interestingly, they also revealed a significant interaction between collective narcissism and the need for cognitive closure. Collective narcissism predicted the belief in conspiracy more strongly on lower levels of need for cognitive closure (that is, at higher levels of cognitive openness). According to Soral and colleagues (2014), in the context of constant exposure to diverse conspiratorial explanations for the crash, those who were motivated to look for explanations other than an accident (a tendency perpetuated by collective narcissism) were more likely to embrace conspiracy theories, especially when they were at the same time open to diverse, often contradictory theories of the crash (see also Wood, Douglas, & Sutton, 2012).

Another study considered a different context that can fuel belief in conspiracies: a lack of external recognition of the in-group's achievements. National groups tend to attach collective meaning to specific moments in history that they cherish and celebrate as a source of pride. However, these events might not be perceived in the same way by members of other groups. One such example is the fall of the communist regime in Europe's Eastern Bloc. Poles are proud of their role in initiating the fall of communism in Central and Eastern Europe (Lewicka, 2014). Indeed, the process began with the emergence of the Solidarity movement in Poland in the 1980s, followed by the Round Table negotiations in the spring of 1989, which led to the country's first (partially) free elections on June 4 of the same year. For Polish people, that date demarcates the fall of the communist regime. Nevertheless, for many it was the fall of the Berlin Wall on November 9, 1989, that became the symbol of the end of the communist era. One perception of a competition of Poles with Germans over this historical symbolic moment is expressed in the following Internet comment, "Poles 'lost' with Germans the fight over the consciousness of the Europeans, and the world. In our continent, the symbols of overthrowing communism are neither the Gdansk Shipyard, nor the Round Table, and especially not the Polish elections of June 1989. What is obvious for Poles is not necessarily obvious for other nations. (. . .) It is November 9th 1989 that became a symbol of transitions in Eastern and Central Europe" (Tokarz, 2009).

This comment illustrates how the commemorations of the fall of communism on the anniversary of the fall of the Berlin Wall, rather than on the day of the first free elections in Poland, came to the Poles' attention as evidence for lack of proper acknowledgment for Polish historical contributions. Collective narcissism is related to concern with external recognition of in-group's worth (Golec de Zavala et al., 2009; Golec de Zavala et al., 2013). Thus, not surprisingly, Polish national collective narcissism might foster a tendency to engage into competition over symbolic acknowledgement of alleged contributions with other groups. A survey study conducted in Poland around the 20th anniversary of the fall of the Berlin Wall (Cichocka, Marchlewska et al., 2014) examined attitudes towards the celebrations in Berlin. Specifically, participants were asked to consider whether Germany (rather than Poland) being in the spotlight of these celebrations was a consequence of an anti-Polish conspiracy. Indeed, collective narcissism was linked to accepting conspiratorial explanations for the lack of acknowledgement of the Polish role in fighting communism. For example, collective narcissism predicted agreement with allegations that underestimating Polish achievements is a consequence of malignant international propaganda. Thus, collective narcissism feeds paranoid explanations of intergroup reality.

Importantly, in line with research on the Smolensk conspiracy (Cichocka, Marchlewska et al., 2014; see also Golec de Zavala, Cichocka, & Bilewicz, 2013), when considered separately positive in-group identification (here operationalized as collective self-esteem; Luhtanen & Crocker, 1992) was not significantly associated with belief in intergroup conspiracies. Nevertheless, when included in one model with collective narcissism, secure, nonnarcissistic in-group identification predicted decreased belief in conspiratorial explanations for the presumed lack of acknowledgement of the in-group's achievements. This suggests that mature, well-anchored confidence in the in-group's worth is less susceptible to threat by the potential lack of acknowledgment of the in-group from other groups. In fact, it might be open to sharing the privilege to commemorate the end of communism with other countries, such as Germany.

To sum up, results of several studies conducted in Poland demonstrate that Polish national collective narcissism is associated with a readiness to embrace conspiratorial explanations for negative in-group outcomes. Such explanations involve attributing malevolent intentions to out-groups. Presumably, groups with which the in-group shares a history of grievances would be primary suspects for conspiring against the in-group (Golec de Zavala & Cichocka, 2012). Such readiness to blame out-groups for the in-group's misfortunes may stem from a collective narcissistic need to manage threat and uncertainties regarding a grandiose image of the in-group. Secure in-group positivity, on the other hand, seems to decrease the need to seek external explanations for negative in-group outcomes. It is not related to the narcissistic motivation to protect the in-group's unrealistically positive image.

Collective narcissism and generalized belief in conspiracies

Our review so far has demonstrated that collective narcissism robustly predicts the belief in conspiratorial intentions of out-groups. However, due to the increased sensitivity to threat to the in-group's positive image, collective narcissism also seems to promote a general belief in conspiracies. The same large survey that examined participants' belief in the conspiracies of Jews, Russians, and Germans asked also about general beliefs in national and world politics being influenced by powerful secret organizations. These beliefs were positively associated with collective narcissism and unrelated to positive in-group identification. Moreover, when the common variance of the two forms of in-group positivity was taken into account, the effect of collective narcissism remained significant, while nonnarcissistic in-group positivity became a significant negative predictor of a general belief in political conspiracies (Kofta, 2012). In other words, while collective narcissism promoted a belief that the political world is ruled by powerful secret organizations, secure, nonnarcissistic in-group identification predicted the lesser likelihood of endorsing such beliefs.

A more recent study examined whether collective narcissism also predicts beliefs in *intra*group conspiracies (Cichocka, Marchlewska et al., 2014). Indeed, many conspiracy theories involve beliefs about secret malevolent activities of people's own national governments. For example, one in ten Americans believes that the U.S. government allowed 9/11 to happen (Public Policy Polling, 2013; http://www.publicpolicypolling.com/main/2013/04/conspiracy-theory-poll-results-.html); one in five Americans believes that the U.S. government covered up a UFO crash in Roswell, New Mexico (Public Policy Polling, 2013); and one in four Britons believes that their own intelligence agency, MI6, was involved in Princess Diana's death (Jordan, 2013). Also, among some Poles a belief in the involvement of the Polish government in the Smolensk plane crash seems even stronger than a belief in Russian conspiracy (Fakty TVN, 2012). Because it engenders a generalized lack of intergroup trust, collective narcissism could be related to embracing such theories. At the same time, because of their great preoccupation with the in-group's image, one could suspect that collective narcissists would seek to reject allegations regarding their own government.

These two possibilities were recently tested in an experimental study conducted among American participants (Cichocka, Marchlewska et al., 2014). Participants were asked about the extent to which they endorsed various generic conspiracist beliefs concerning either the American government or foreign governments. Examples, borrowed from Brotherton, French, & Pickering (2013), included suspecting that the governments "are involved in the murder of innocent citizens and/or well-known public figures, and keep this a secret," or that they "routinely carry out experiments involving new drugs or technologies on the public without their knowledge or consent." Secure in-group identification, measured with Leach and colleagues' (2008) identification scale, predicted less likelihood of embracing conspiracy beliefs, regardless of whether they were attributed to one's own or foreign government. Probably, secure in-group identification decreases intergroup mistrust or even promotes general assumptions of benevolence of both in-group and out-group action.

Collective narcissism, on the other hand, was a significant predictor of conspiracy beliefs only in the context of foreign governments condition, but not in the own government conspiracies condition. Thus, it seems that collective narcissism predicts greater readiness to embrace conspiracy beliefs when they pertain to actions of out-groups rather than in-group members, such as one's own government. Of course, these relationships could change if we considered identification at a different level of categorization. For example, belief in conspiracy actions of the American government could be associated with narcissistic identification with groups considered disadvantaged in the American society: for instance, ethnic minority groups (see e.g., Crocker et al., 1999). Similarly, the relationship between national collective narcissism and beliefs in the conspiratorial action of one's own government may depend on whether the government is perceived as representing national or foreign interests.

Why does collective narcissism foster conspiracy beliefs?

Our review demonstrates that collective narcissism is a robust predictor of conspiracy beliefs in intergroup contexts. One explanation of why collective narcissism is associated with conspiracy beliefs about actions of other groups towards the in-group might come from work on antecedents of collective narcissistic attachment to an in-group. Narcissistic in-group identification and belief in conspiracies have both been linked to individual needs for personal control and certainty.

Conspiracy beliefs are thought to help manage the need for control, feelings of powerlessness, and lack of understanding of the sociopolitical reality. Indeed, considerable evidence links a belief in conspiracies to powerlessness, uncertainty, and a low sense of control (Newheiser, Farias, & Tausch, 2011; Sullivan, Landau, & Rothschild, 2010; van Prooijen & Jostmann, 2013; Whitson & Galinsky, 2008), especially sociopolitical control (Imhoff & Bruder, 2014). In fact, belief in conspiracies is robustly predicted by various indices of disillusionment with the political system, including political alienation (Abalakina-Paap, Stephan, Craig, & Gregory, 1999) – a feeling of being estranged from social and political institutions (Seeman, 1959; Citrin, McClosky, Shanks, & Sniderman 1975), anomie (Imhoff & Bruder, 2014; Goertzel, 1994) – a feeling that the world lacks sense or clear rules (McClosky & Shaar, 1965), or political cynicism (Swami, Chamorro-Premuzic, & Furnham, 2010; Swami et al., 2011) – a negative view of human nature and social institutions, accompanied with disregard for societal norms and rules (Leung et al., 2002). Conspiracy theories can be seen as a way of simplifying and explaining otherwise complicated reality (see also Kossowska & Bukowski, this volume).

Another way of dealing with feelings of a lack of control, sense, and predictability can be by developing a defensive attachment to salient social in-groups. Indeed, research demonstrates that collective narcissism (but not secure in-group identification) increases in response to feelings of low personal control (Cichocka, Golec de Zavala et al., 2014). It is then possible that collective narcissism might serve as an additional explanation of the relationship between feelings of uncontrollability and conspiracy beliefs. Although decreased control might directly increase endorsement of conspiracy theories, this effect might be additionally reinforced by increased defensiveness associated with collective narcissism. In order to examine this proposition, we reexamined data from the survey reporting the link between collective narcissism and conspiracy beliefs about the political reality, as well as conspiracy stereotypes of Jews, Russians, and Germans (Kofta, 2012). In this dataset, collective narcissism was positively associated both with political alienation and anomie. In fact, collective narcissism (but not secure, nonnarcissistic in-group identification) mediated between anomie and conspiracy beliefs about the political reality and conspiracy stereotypes of the three out-groups. Similarly, collective narcissism (but not nonnarcissistic in-group identification) mediated between alienation and conspiracy beliefs about the political reality and conspiracy stereotypes of the three out-groups.

The fact that collective narcissism is associated with frustration of personal needs and motives can explain the defensive nature of narcissistic identification, which fosters perceptions of malevolent intentions in the actions of others. Collective narcissism increases the probability of perceiving a threat to the in-group image even when alternative explanations to the undesirable out-group actions are available. The psychological dynamics of threat sensitivity and protectiveness associated with collective narcissism suggest that collective narcissism is likely to foster increased collective paranoia: "collectively held beliefs, either false or exaggerated, that cluster around ideas of being harassed, threatened, harmed, subjugated, persecuted, accused, mistreated, wronged, tormented, disparaged, or vilified by a malevolent out-group or out-groups" (Kramer, 2004, p. 141). Collective paranoia presumes suspicions about others' malevolent actions, excessive preoccupation with others' loyalty, and a reluctance to trust others (Robins & Post, 1997). It is characterized by hypervigilance for potentially threatening information and excessive rumination over threatening interactions, as well as overattributing hostile intentions to others – a phenomenon that has been referred to as the sinister attribution error (Kramer, 1994) or the diabolic causation schema (Kofta, 1995). It is also linked to a biased punctuation of history, which reflects a tendency to create memories of historical events in an in-group-serving fashion (Kramer & Messick, 1998). Such paranoid cognitions inevitably lead to perceptions that other groups secretly conspire to hurt the in-group (Kramer & Messick, 1998).

It is plausible that the psychological dynamics associated with collective paranoia stems from narcissistic in-group identification, which presumes motivation for the protection of the in-group's image. Kramer and colleagues (Kramer, 1998; Kramer & Jost, 2003; Kramer & Messick, 1998) theorized that collective paranoia is linked to categorizing oneself as a member of a distinctive social group that is under evaluative scrutiny. Such a categorization is especially likely in the context of unequal social relations, in which members of disadvantaged groups became self-conscious, paying greater attention to any situations that are potentially diagnostic for intergroup trust. Paranoid beliefs about others can be further exacerbated by uncertainty about one's social standing (Kramer, 1998). All of these factors are characteristic for collective narcissism.

Indeed, there is evidence suggesting that collective narcissism might be an especially good predictor of collective paranoia. Collective narcissism is associated with an exaggerated preoccupation with in-group image. Collective narcissistic positive evaluation of the in-group is contingent on receiving recognition from others (Golec de Zavala et al., 2009). Several empirical studies demonstrate that collective narcissism predicts a tendency to interpret ambiguous actions of an out-group as dangerous, critical, or potentially insulting to the in-group. For example,

Mexican national collective narcissism was linked to perceptions of the construction of the wall at the American border as disrespectful (Golec de Zavala et al., 2009). A similar process was observed even for university-level in-group identification. In a study conducted among psychology students, those who scored high for university peer group collective narcissism perceived criticism from students from another university as threatening (Golec de Zavala et al., 2013).

In addition, collective narcissism fosters a biased perspective on historical events. A new analysis of previously published data (Golec de Zavala et al., 2009; Golec de Zavala & Cichocka, 2012) examined the relationship between Polish national collective narcissism and reactions to a book that presented an unflattering historical and sociological account of Polish anti-Semitism after World War II. A controversial sociohistorical analysis was presented in the book *Fear: Anti-Semitism in Poland after Auschwitz. An Essay in Historical Interpretation*, authored by Jan Thomas Gross (2006). The book has caused many discussions worldwide, provoked critical commentaries on Poland, and has raised controversies within Poland, including strong criticism of the author. The author's ethnicity was brought up as an argument against the book, which was framed by some as a Jewish attack on Poles. A group of right-wing senators even postulated that the author should be prosecuted for "insulting the Polish Nation" (Głuchowski & Kowalski, 2008). However, the prosecutor's office refused to investigate (http://www.rpo.gov.pl/pliki/1202889384.pdf).

Our research demonstrated that Polish national collective narcissism predicted the perception of the book as an insult to Poles and Poland. Moreover, such perceptions further predicted self-reported hatred towards the author of the book and a desire to hurt him. Collective narcissism also predicted open expressions of hostility towards Jews as a result of the criticism of Poles. These relationships were independent of the association between collective narcissism and generalized anti-Semitism. Thus, over and above its relationship with chronic prejudice towards Jews (Golec de Zavala & Cichocka, 2012), Polish national collective narcissism inspired a focused and momentary increase in retaliatory out-group hostility in response to the perceived insult to the in-group.

Similar results were obtained in a more recent nationally representative Polish study, in which we examined participants' reactions to recent movies on Polish-Jewish relations. Some of them, such as *Aftermath*, directed by Pasikowski, were inspired by the 1941 pogrom of Jews in Jedwabne. Collective narcissism was associated with a belief that such movies, portraying Polish anti-Semitism during and after World War II, are full of misrepresentations and can be a consequence of malignant anti-Polish propaganda (Cichocka, Golec de Zavala et al., 2014). These findings suggest that collective narcissism predicts a tendency to make the sinister attribution error characteristic for collective paranoia. It also predicts intergroup hostility in response to such paranoid perceptions (Golec de Zavala et al., 2013).

In summary, empirical results show that collective narcissism is related to being on a constant outlook for affirmation of the in-group greatness and constant vigilance to signs that this greatness may be threatened. The vigilance to signs of disrespect and insult suggests mistrust towards other groups, accompanied by a belief that one's special, extraordinary in-group stands alone against the hostile world (Golec de Zavala & Cichocka, 2012). Presumably, endorsing and even sharing conspiratorial theories helps narcissists justify hostility towards out-groups and fuel the conviction that the in-group is so special that others conspire to bring it down. Furthermore, any evidence against conspiracy is likely to be further interpreted as false or threatening. In consequence, collective narcissism seems to involve a vicious circle of mistrust and suspicion in intergroup contexts.

Why does secure in-group identification decrease conspiracy beliefs?

Given the negative intergroup consequences of conspiracy beliefs (Cichocka et al., 2014; Bilewicz et al., 2013; see also Douglas, Sutton, Jolley, & Wood, this volume), it is important to attempt to decrease exaggerated reliance on conspiratorial explanations of intergroup reality. Our review suggests that one option would be to discourage the mobilization of narcissistic identification with an in-group. Nonnarcissistic in-group identification may increase resilience to in-group image threats and, thus, foster intergroup trust and respect for out-groups. We argue that this is because of the nature of nonnarcissistic in-group identification. Such identification is well-anchored and secure (Cichocka, et al., 2014; Golec de Zavala, Cichocka, & Bilewicz, 2013), and therefore less likely to be undermined by external threats or devaluation. We could see this form of in-group identification as a genuine psychological resource that can decrease appraisals of threat in the actions of others (see also Leach, Rodriguez Mosquera, Vliek, & Hirt, 2010).

Our research shows that nonnarcissistic in-group positivity is either unrelated (Golec de Zavala & Cichocka, 2012) or even negatively related (Cichocka et al., 2014) to support for conspiracy beliefs in the intergroup context. Future research should investigate when these two different patterns of relationships would emerge. For example, it is possible that secure, nonnarcissistic in-group identification does not predict a tendency to stereotype out-groups in general. This would result in its weak and nonsignificant relationship with the endorsement of conspiratorial stereotypes of out-groups. However, in the context of specific events, such as the Smolensk plane crash or the commemorations of the fall of communism, conspiratorial intergroup explanations may become salient. In such contexts, different forms of in-group identification may predict different attitudes towards such explanations. For instance, in the aftermath of the Smolensk crash, various conspiracy theories were so prevalent and widely discussed in the media that any such allegations would require voicing some sort of opinion. In that case, secure in-group identification is likely to promote rejection of conspiracy beliefs and greater concern with encouraging constructive relationships with neighboring countries.

How can the secure, nonnarcissistic in-group identification be increased? One way could be to decrease compensatory, defensive tendencies by satisfying individual and group motives that underlie collective narcissism. There exists evidence that secure in-group identification increases as a consequence of strengthening personal control (Cichocka, Golec de Zavala et al., 2014). Additional processes might take place at the collective level. One way of promoting secure in-group identification could be shaping in-group esteem based on contingent success or praise of the in-group, while defensiveness in-group identification might develop on a basis of noncontingent rewards (see Berglas & Jones, 1978). These possibilities await future empirical validation.

Conclusions and future directions

In this chapter we demonstrated that narcissistic in-group identification is an important predictor of belief in conspiracies against the in-group. Does that mean that people are likely to only endorse theories that explain events directly affecting their in-group? This is not necessarily the case. Recent research by van Prooijen and van Dijk (in press) shows that taking the perspective of the out-group involved in an event that had big (vs. small) consequences for its members increased belief in conspiracies about this event. As argued by van Prooijen and van Dijk (in press), such beliefs help make sense of highly consequential and harmful events. Collective narcissism could moderate this effect. Because collective narcissism predicts intergroup paranoia, it could increase the likelihood of embracing intergroup conspiracies, even on behalf of an out-group. However, it would probably only be the case if the affected out-group is not in any way perceived as threatening or discriminated against by collective narcissists. In that case, taking an out-group perspective would likely be negatively related to collective narcissism. Future research should investigate these interesting possibilities.

We argued that endorsement of conspiracy theories is a defensive response to feelings of threat and uncertainty associated with collective narcissism. Nevertheless, it can also provide a positive feedback loop, in which narcissistic grandiosity is nurtured by the belief that the in-group is important or disturbing enough for other groups to conspire against it. This might be an especially important part of building in-group identity for those groups that have been historically disadvantaged, persecuted, or simply neglected. Creating a conviction that one's group is in some way chosen or special can further nurture defensiveness in intergroup relations.

As we have frequently suggested, being a member of a group that is disadvantaged can breed paranoia and a belief that the dominant out-group conspires against the in-group (Kramer & Jost, 2003). However, it can also sometimes increase trust and reliance on the advantaged out-group (as has been argued by the system justification theory; see e.g., Jost, Banaji, & Nosek, 2004). According to Jost and Kramer (2003), which of these two scenarios is likely to take place depends on the salient motivation to either enhance the in-group or support the overarching system of intergroup relations. Collective narcissism represents especially strong group-enhancement motivation. It should then not be surprising that, among members of disadvantaged groups, high collective narcissism would predict convictions about an out-group's malevolent intentions. Importantly though, such convictions might not always be a sign of exaggerated paranoia. In the case of disadvantaged or victimized groups, narcissistic conviction that other groups have malevolent intentions towards the in-group might be a reflection of reality. As famously noted in the film adaptation of *Catch-22*, "being paranoid does not mean they are not out to get you" (Calley, Ransohoff, & Nichols, 1970).

Author note

Aleksandra Cichocka, School of Psychology, University of Kent, UK. Agnieszka Golec de Zavala, Department of Psychology, Goldsmiths, University of London, UK. Marta Marchlewska, Institute for Social Studies, University of Warsaw, Poland. Mateusz Olechowski, Faculty of Psychology, University of Warsaw, Poland. Preparation of this chapter was supported by funding from the Polish National Science Centre, awarded with the decision number DEC-2011/01/B/HS6/04637 to Aleksandra Cichocka. Correspondence regarding this chapter should be directed to Aleksandra Cichocka, University of Kent, Keynes College, CT2 7NZ, Canterbury, UK. E-mail: a.k.cichocka@kent.ac.uk

References

Abalakina-Paap, M., Stephan, W.G., Craig, T., & Gregory, W.L. (1999). Beliefs in conspiracies. *Political Psychology, 20*(3), 637–647. doi:10.1111/0162-895X.00160

Antoni Macierewicz: Tragedia nad Donieckiem zaczęła się w Smoleńsku. (2014). Retrieved August 26, 2014, from http://wiadomosci.wp.pl/kat,1342,title,Antoni-Macierewicz-tragedia-nad-Donieckiem-zaczela-sie-w-Smolensku,wid,16765739,wiadomosc.html?ticaid=113556

Bar-Tal, D., & Antebi, D. (1992). Siege mentality in Israel. *International Journal of Intercultural Relations, 16*, 251–275. doi:10.1016/0147-1767(92)90052-V

Berglas, S., & Jones, E.E. (1978). Drug choice as a self-handicapping strategy in response to noncontingent success. *Journal of Personality and Social Psychology, 36*, 405–417.

Bilewicz, M., Bukowski, M., Cichocka, A., Winiewski, M., & Wójcik, A. (2009). [Polish Prejudice Survey 2009]. Raw data.

Bilewicz, M., & Stefaniak, A. (2013). Can a victim be responsible? Antisemitic consequences of victimhood-based identity and competitive victimhood in Poland. In B. Bokus (Ed.), *Responsibility: An interdisciplinary perspective.* Warszawa: Lexem.

Bilewicz, M., Winiewski, M., Kofta, M., & Wójcik, A. (2013). Harmful ideas, the structure and consequences of anti-Semitic beliefs in Poland. *Political Psychology, 34*(6), 821–839. doi:10.1111/pops.12024

Bilewicz, M., Winiewski, M., & Radzik, Z. (2012). Antisemitism in current Poland: Psychological, religious and historical aspects. *Journal for the Study of Antisemitism, 4*, 801–820.

Brotherton, R., French, C.C., & Pickering, A.D. (2013). Measuring belief in conspiracy theories: The generic conspiracist beliefs scale. *Frontiers in Psychology, 4*, 1–15. doi:10.3389/fpsyg.2013.00279

Calley, J., & Ransohoff, M. (producers), & Nichols, M. (director). (1970). *Catch-22* [Motion picture]. USA: Paramount Pictures.

Cameron, J. E. (2004). A three-factor model of social identity. *Self and Identity, 3*, 239–262. doi:10.1080/13576500444000047

Cichocka, A., Golec de Zavala, A., Marchlewska, M., Olechowski, M., & Bilewicz, M. (2014). *Personal control decreases collective narcissism but increases secure in-group positivity.* Manuscript submitted for publication.

Cichocka, A., Golec de Zavala, A., Olechowski, M. (2011, July). *Genuine and defensive ingroup identification in the face of collective trauma.* Paper presented at the 16th European Association of Social Psychology General Meeting, Stockholm, Sweden.

Cichocka, A., Marchlewska, M., Golec de Zavala, A., & Olechowski, M. (2014). *"They will not control us": In-group positivity and belief in intergroup conspiracies.* Manuscript submitted for publication.

Citrin, J., McClosky, H., Shanks, J. M., & Sniderman, P. M. (1975). Personal and political sources of political alienation. *British Journal of Political Science, 5*, 1–31. doi:10.1017/S0007123400008024

Crocker, J., Luhtanen, R., Broadnax, S., & Blaine, B. E. (1999). Belief in U.S. government conspiracies against Blacks among Black and White college students: Powerlessness or system blame? *Personality and Social Psychology Bulletin, 25*(8), 941–953. doi:10.1177/01461672992511003

Dutch Safety Board (2014). Investigation on crash MH17, 17 July 2014. Retrieved August 26, 2014, from http://www.onderzoeksraad.nl/en/onderzoek/2049/investigation-crash-mh17-17-july-2014

Fakty TVN. (2012). Interview with Zbigniew Brzeziński. Retrieved from http://www.tvn24.pl/wiadomosci-z-kraju,3/prof-brzezinski-rosji-zalezy-aby-katastrofa-smolenska-dzielila-polakow,287534.html

Głuchowski, P., & Kowalski, M. (2008). Gorączka złota w Treblince [Gold rush in Treblinka]. *Duży Format.* Retrieved from http://wyborcza.pl/duzyformat/1,127291,4811664.html

Goertzel, T. (1994). Belief in conspiracy theories. *Political Psychology, 15*, 731–742.

Golec de Zavala, A., & Cichocka, A. (2012). Collective narcissism and anti-Semitism in Poland. *Group Processes & Intergroup Relations, 15*, 213–229. doi:10.1177/1368430211420891

Golec de Zavala, A., Cichocka, A., & Bilewicz, M. (2013). The paradox of in-group love: Differentiating collective narcissism advances understanding of the relationship between in-group and out-group attitudes. *Journal of Personality, 81*, 16–28. doi:10.1111/j.1467-6494.2012.00779.x

Golec de Zavala, A., Cichocka, A., Eidelson, R., & Jayawickreme, N. (2009). Collective narcissism and its social consequences. *Journal of Personality and Social Psychology, 97*(6), 1074–1096. doi:10.1037/a0016904

Golec de Zavala, A., Cichocka, A., & Iskra-Golec, I. (2013). Collective narcissism moderates the effect of in-group image threat on intergroup hostility. *Journal of Personality and Social Psychology, 104*, 1019–1039. doi:10.1037/a0032215

Gross, J. T. (2006). *Fear: Anti-Semitism in Poland after Auschwitz: An essay in historical interpretation.* New York: Random House.

Hofstadter, R. (1996). *The paranoid style in American politics.* Cambridge, MA: Harvard University Press.

Hołub, J. (2010, April 22). Teorie spiskowe ojca Rydzyka [Conspiracy theories of father Rydzyk]. *Gazeta Wyborcza,* p. 7.

Imhoff, R., & Bruder, M. (2014). Speaking (un-)truth to power: Conspiracy mentality as a generalised political attitude. *European Journal of Personality, 28*, 25–43. doi:10.1002/per.1930

Jaworska, M., Cichocka, A., & Marchlewska, M. (2014). [Collective narcissism and facets of secure in-group identification]. Unpublished raw data.

Jordan, W. (2013, September 17). 38% of Brits think Princess Diana's death "NOT an accident". *yougov.co.uk*. Retrieved from http://yougov.co.uk/news/2013/09/17/38-brits-princess-dianas-death-was-not-accident/

Jost, J. T., Banaji, M. R., & Nosek, B. A. (2004). A decade of system justification theory: Accumulated evidence of conscious and unconscious bolstering of the status quo. *Political Psychology, 25*, 881–919. doi:10.1111/j.1467-9221.2004.00402.x

Jost, J. T., & Kramer, R. M. (2003). The system justification motive in intergroup relations. In D. M. Mackie & E. R. Smith (Eds.), *From prejudice to intergroup emotions: Differentiated reactions to social groups* (pp. 227–246). New York: Taylor & Francis.

Kofta, M. (1995). Stereotype of a group-as-a-whole: The role of diabolic causation schema. *Polish Psychological Bulletin, 26*, 83–96.

Kofta, M. (2012). [Elections panel: Wave 1]. Unpublished data.

Kofta, M., & Sedek, G. (2005). Conspiracy stereotypes of Jews during systemic transformation in Poland. *International Journal of Sociology, 35*(1), 40–64.

Kramer, R. M. (1994). The sinister attribution error: Paranoid cognition and collective distrust in organizations. *Motivation and Emotion, 18*, 199–230. doi:10.1007/BF02249399

Kramer, R. M. (1998). Paranoid cognition in social systems: Thinking and acting in the shadow of doubt. *Personality and Social Psychology Review, 2*, 251–275. doi:10.1207/s15327957pspr0204_3

Kramer, R. M. (2004). Collective paranoia: Distrust between social groups. In R. Hardin (Ed.), *Distrust*. New York: Russell Sage Foundation.

Kramer, R. M., & Jost, J. T. (2003). Close encounters of the suspicious kind: Outgoing paranoia in hierarchical trust dilemmas. In D. M. Mackie & E. R. Smith (Eds.), *From prejudice to intergroup emotions: Differentiated reactions to social groups* (pp. 173–190). New York: Taylor & Francis.

Kramer, R. M., & Messick, D. M. (1998). Getting by with a little help from our enemies: Collective paranoia and its role in intergroup relations. In C. Sedikides, J. Schopler, & C. A. Insko (Eds.), *Intergroup cognition and intergroup behavior* (pp. 233–255). Mahwah, NJ: Lawrence Erlbaum Associates.

Leach, C. W., Rodriguez Mosquera, P. M., Vliek, M. L. W., & Hirt, E. (2010). Group devaluation and group identification. *Journal of Social Issues, 66*, 535–552. doi:10.1111/j.1540-4560.2010.01661.x

Leach, C. W., van Zomeren, M., Zebel, S., Vliek, M. L., Pennekamp, S. F., Doosje, B., . . . & Spears, R. (2008). Group-level self-definition and self-investment: A hierarchical (multicomponent) model of in-group identification. *Journal of Personality and Social Psychology, 95*, 144–165. doi:10.1037/0022-3514.95.1.144

Leung, K., Bond, M. H., de Carrasquel, S. R., Muñoz, C., Hernández, M., Murakami, F., . . . & Singelis, T. M. (2002). Social axioms: The search for universal dimensions of general beliefs about how the world functions. *Journal of Cross-Cultural Psychology, 33*, 286–302. doi:10.1177/0022022102033003005

Lewicka, M. (2014). [Retrieving the lost memory: Role of the social memory of place in identity formation]. Unpublished data.

Luhtanen, R., & Crocker, J. (1992). A collective self-esteem scale: Self-evaluation of one's social identity. *Personality and Social Psychology Bulletin, 18*, 302–318. doi:10.1177/0146167292183006

Mashuri, A., & Zaduqisti, E. (2013). The role of social identification, intergroup threat, and out-group derogation in explaining belief in conspiracy theory about terrorism in Indonesia. *International Journal of Research Studies in Psychology, 3*, 35–50. doi:10.5861/ijrsp.2013.446

McClosky, H., & Shaar, J. H. (1965). Psychological dimensions of anomie. *American Sociological Review, 30*, 14–40.

Newheiser, A.-K., Farias, M., & Tausch, N. (2011). The functional nature of conspiracy beliefs: Examining the underpinnings of belief in the *Da Vinci Code* conspiracy. *Personality and Individual Differences, 51,* 1007–1011. doi:10.1016/j.paid.2011.08.011

Noor, M., Brown, J.R., & Prentice, G. (2008). Precursors and mediators of intergroup reconciliation in Northern Ireland: A new model. *British Journal of Social Psychology, 47,* 481–495. doi:10.1348/014466607X238751

Noor, M., Shnabel, N., Halabi, S., & Nadler, A. (2012). When suffering begets suffering: The psychology of competitive victimhood between adversarial groups in violent conflicts. *Personality and Social Psychology Review, 16,* 351–374. doi:10.1177/1088868312440048

Nowakowska, A., & Wielowieyska, D. (2011, September 30). Polska jak twarz boksera Adamka. *Gazeta Wyborcza.* Retrieved from http:\\www.wyborcza.pl

Public Policy Polling (2013). Conspiracy theory poll results. Retrieved from http://uottawa.ca.libguides.com/content.php?pid=14807&sid=2968021

Reidy, P. (2014, July 22). MH17: Five of the most bizarre conspiracy theories. *theguardian.com.* Retrieved from http://www.theguardian.com

Robins, R.S., & Post, J.M. (1997). *Political paranoia. The psychopolitics of hatred.* New Haven, CT: Yale University Press.

Seeman, M. (1959). On the meaning of alienation. *American Sociological Review, 24,* 783–791.

Simmons, W.P., & Parsons, S. (2005). Beliefs in conspiracy theories among African Americans: A comparison of elites and masses. *Social Science Quarterly, 86,* 582–598. doi:10.1111/j.0038-4941.2005.00319.x

Skarżyńska, K., Przybyła, K., & Wójcik, A. (2012). Grupowa martyrologia: Psychologiczne źródła i konsekwencje. *Psychologia Społeczna, 7,* 335–352.

Soral, W., Kofta, M., & Szymanska, J. (2014, June). *The role of collective narcissism and the need for cognitive closure in acquiring conspiracy beliefs about Smolensk catastrophe.* Paper presented at 5th Annual Tajfel Seminar Social Identities in Conflict in Warsaw, Poland.

Sullivan, D., Landau, M.J., & Rothschild, Z.K. (2010). An existential function of enemyship: Evidence that people attribute influence to personal and political enemies to compensate for threats to control. *Journal of Personality and Social Psychology, 98,* 434–449. doi:10.1037/a0017457

Swami, V., Chamorro-Premuzic, T., & Furnham, A. (2010). Unanswered questions: A preliminary investigation of personality and individual difference predictors of 9/11 conspiracist beliefs. *Applied Cognitive Psychology, 24*(6), 749–761. doi:10.1002/acp.1583

Swami, V., & Coles, R. (2010). The truth is out there: Belief in conspiracy theories. *Psychologist, 23,* 560–563.

Swami, V., Coles, R., Stieger, S., Pietschnig, J., Furnham, A., Rehim, S., & Voracek, M. (2011). Conspiracist ideation in Britain and Austria: Evidence of a monological belief system and associations between individual psychological differences and real-world and fictitious conspiracy theories. *British Journal of Psychology, 102,* 443–463. doi:10.1111/j.2044-8295.2010.02004.x

Tokarz, K. (2009). *Niemcy dali Polakom dobrą szkołę* [Germans gave Poles a lesson]. Retrieved from http://www.de-pl.info/pl/page.php/article/1718

Tropp, L.R., & Wright, S.C. (2001). Ingroup identification as the inclusion of ingroup in the self. *Personality and Social Psychology Bulletin, 27,* 585–600. doi:10.1177/0146167201275007

van Prooijen, J.-W., & Jostmann, N.B. (2013). Belief in conspiracy theories: The influence of uncertainty and perceived morality. *European Journal of Social Psychology, 43*(1), 109–115. doi:10.1002/ejsp.1922

van Prooijen, J.-W., & van Dijk, E. (in press). When consequence size predicts belief in conspiracy theories: The moderating role of perspective taking. *Journal of Experimental Social Psychology.*

van Prooijen, J.-W., & van Lange, P. A. (Eds.). (2014). *Power, politics, and paranoia: Why people are suspicious of their leaders.* Cambridge University Press.

Vollhardt, J. R. (2013). "Crime against humanity" or "crime against Jews"? Acknowledgment in construals of the Holocaust and its importance for intergroup relations. *Journal of Social Issues, 69,* 144–161. doi:10.1111/josi.12008

Whitson, J. A., & Galinsky, A. D. (2008). Lacking control increases illusory pattern perception. *Science, 322,* 115–117. doi:10.1126/science.1159845

Wood, M. J., Douglas, K. M., & Sutton, R. M. (2012). Dead and alive: Beliefs in contradictory conspiracy theories. *Social Psychological and Personality Science, 3,* 767–773. doi:10.1177/1948550611434786

Zavadski, K. (2014, July 17). Russia's Malaysia Airlines conspiracy theory: Ukraine was aiming for Putin's plane. *nymag.com.* Retrieved from http://www.nymag.com

Zubrzycki, G. (2007). The cross, the Madonna and the Jew: Persistent symbolic representations of the nation in Poland. In M. Young & E. Zuelow (Eds.), *Nationalism in a global era: The persistence of nations.* Oxford: Routledge.

4

CONSPIRACY THEORY AS COLLECTIVE MOTIVATED COGNITION

Péter Krekó

The HIV virus was deliberately developed in American state laboratories in order to be spread among the Black community. Behind the 9/11 terrorist attacks that destroyed the World Trade Center, there were no Muslim extremists or Osama bin Laden, but the American government, which aimed to reaffirm its power and to wage a profitable war in the Middle East. The existence of the H1N1 virus is just a fairy tale, and with the antiserum, "they" inject a microchip developed with nanotechnology into our bodies, which does not only gather information about us, but makes us "remote controlled."

All of these are only a few examples of the widespread conspiracy theories that have dominated the last decade. For the skeptical layperson and researchers of the topic, the main questions have remained the same for a long time: Why do we believe in such theories? Do they have any psychological benefits? Why do people sometimes imagine a world inhabited by evil emperors that have total control over us and deceive us with the help of the media? What causes the persistence of conspiracy theories on the one hand and their popularity on the other? In this chapter, relying on the existing literature and my own research, I aim to introduce a theoretical framework that can help people better understand the functions and motivations behind conspiracy theories and their psychological "benefits." This theoretical framework interprets conspiracy theories as a form of *collective motivated cognition*.

Even if these theories are frequently regarded as bizarre delusions, with minor relevance, the negative implications of such belief systems in modern societies would be difficult to overestimate. For example, conspiracy theories that the HIV virus is a governmental creation targeting the Black community could contribute to African Americans' negative attitudes towards condom use and contraception in general, resulting in their disproportionately high affliction with HIV/AIDS, other sexually transmitted infections (STIs), and unintended pregnancy (Bird &

Bogart, 2003; 2005; Bogart & Thorburn, 2006). Antivaccine conspiracy beliefs go hand in hand with weak vaccination intentions (Jolley & Douglas, 2014). The Jewish World Conspiracy (e.g., as it was elaborated in the infamous Protocols of the Elders of Zion) played a key role in legitimizing the Holocaust and the oppression of the Third Reich (Cohn, 1967/1993; see also Winiewski, Soral, & Bilewicz, this volume).

Researchers of conspiracy theories are trying to shoot at a moving and misty target. Highly embedded in social processes, conspiracy theories can evolve over time. Also, they can vary to a great extent in their popularity, malevolence, and degrees of probability. Knowing that it is difficult to set such criteria as completely objective, in our investigations we aim to focus on the conspiracy theories that are popular (widespread in broad segments of the public), malevolent (e.g., conspiracy theories that target specific ethnic groups and justify violence), and seem to be highly improbable in light of logical investigation (e.g., the idea of a successful Jewish World Conspiracy).

Conspiracy theories as normalcy: Motivated, collective, cognitive

In general, conspiracy theories are bound to a general tendency of individuals to make sense of the world in a psychologically comfortable way. It does not necessarily mean that individuals want to know the pure reality, but to receive "knowledge" that satisfies their needs and fits the preexisting beliefs, goals, and values of their community. "Theories of conspiracy represent a permanent temptation for us all" (Groh, 1987, p. 2), as they can explain a broad range of social events while simultaneously satisfying emotional needs and provide an answer to the question, "Why do bad things happen to good people?" The emotionally, motivationally, and collectively determined nature of the cognitive processes behind conspiracy theorizing is the central point in our concept of collective motivated cognition.

Conspiracy theories as normalcy

Conspiracy theories are mostly depicted as abnormal delusions. The expression "conspiracy theory" is an argumentation tool to label the ideas one disapproves of as irrational, foolish, and groundless. Conspiracy theory refers to a kind of stigmatized knowledge (Barkun, 2003), but, of course, only for the skeptics: Believers in plots do not think they are conspiracy theorizing, but rather speaking about the truth. Because of the bad reputation of conspiracy theories, there is a strong temptation to close them into the world of psychopathology, marking them as paranoiac. But the beliefs in conspiracy are not products of individual psychopathology, as some scholars argue, that can be explained with the chronic overproduction of dopamine (e.g., Kapur, 2003). Conspiracy theories, even if they can be harmful, are "normal" in the sense that they are products of normal social psychological processes. In some societies and cultures, especially in epochs of wars and crises, conspiracy theorizing can become a culturally defined norm – a way of normal thinking. Societal conspiracy theories should be distinguished from paranoiac delusions: The perceived plot is directed against a collective as a nation, a group, or a culture, while a paranoid person is afraid of conspiracies personally against him- or herself (Hofstadter, 1965; Barkun, 2003).

While conspiracy mentality can be regarded as isomorphic or similar to paranoid thinking (see Zonis & Joseph, 1994; "political paranoia" by Robins & Post, 1997; the notion of "paranoid style" by Hofstadter, 1965; and "paranoid cognition" by Kramer & Jost, 2002), it is actually a widespread form of thinking. Conspiracy theories are, unlike mental disorders such as schizophrenia and paranoia, abundant in modern societies (Moscovici, 1987; Goertzel, 1994; Abalakina-Paap & Stephan, 1999), and not just in the West (see for example Zonis & Joseph 1994; Pipes, 1998). Using Cas Mudde's (2007) terminology (applied to radical right parties in Europe), conspiracy theories can be understood as a form of pathological normalcy in the sense that sometimes conspiracy theories are based on mainstream views of the society, such as alienation from politics and mistrust in political institutions.

Motivated, collective, cognitive

The idea of collective motivated cognition is partially built upon the concept of "motivated social cognition" (Webster & Kruglanski, 1994; Jost, Glaser, Kruglanski, & Sulloway, 2003) and the concepts of "hot cognition" and "motivated reasoning" (Kunda, 1990). As advocates of the idea of motivated social cognition, we also emphasize the motivational and situational determinants of cognition on other social factors. But we go beyond the concept by emphasizing a) the group and societal context of cognition on others, and b) the importance of cognition on collective others.

Conspiracy theories are *collective* in at least two senses: in terms of the context of their origin and in terms of their targets. Conspiracy theories emerge in groups and are deeply rooted in the social identity of the group. These beliefs help the group and the individual as its member to understand and make sense of the world. They even help draw a line between the in-group and the out-group (see for example "out-group paranoia," Kramer & Jost, 2002). As these theories are anchored to the social identity of the groups, they can reveal the characteristics of the groups where they emerge, spread, and drive collective action. They can mirror the nature and structure of intergroup conflicts. Conspiracy theories are not only explanations about the behavior and intentions of individuals, but about the behavior and intentions of other groups and indeed of the whole social-political system (conspiracy stereotypes, Kofta & Sedek, 2005; see also Bilewicz & Sedek, this volume).

Conspiracy theories are *motivated* as well: These are not just sterile cognitive beliefs, but are deeply rooted in the motivations and emotions of the group. The explanations fit the community's identity, stereotypes, and goals – they are self-assuring, self-serving, and self-justifying in a collective sense. They can justify our prejudices and stereotypes, can serve as an "outlet for hostility" (Abalakina-Paap &

Stephan 1999), and can put the blame on external groups for the problems surrounding us, just defending the own group. In this sense, they sometimes can even serve as a form of wishful thinking: The conspiracy theory widespread in the Muslim world, suggesting that Israeli and/or American governments are responsible for 9/11, can help rid Muslims of the moral burden caused by extreme in-group members by shifting the responsibility back to the out-group. The conspiracy theory can even justify the violence against the out-group (Kofta & Sedek, 2005).

Finally, conspiracy theories are *cognitive*, as they aim to provide the group and its members with an often satisfactory and comfortable explanation of the social and political world, its events and mechanisms. People believe in conspiracy theories because they help to interpret the sociopolitical world around them. Conspiracy theories expose the forces that guide political and economic processes, and thereby history. They help to dissolve contradictions, inconsistencies, and dissonances, and they give simple deductive explanations to a broad range of complex phenomena. This nature of conspiracy theories (drawing conclusions on a wide range of things based on a few premises) makes them the "pornographies of deduction" (Barkun, 2003). Giving similar (or the same) explanation to a wide range of different events and helping to keep and maintain our worldview, they are the best tools for "cognitive conservatism" (Greenwald, 1980): resistance to cognitive change.

Furthermore, conspiracy beliefs, in some cases, can be useful and adaptive as well. From an evolutionary perspective, deception and adverse cooperation against another individual or groups are natural aspects of the fight for survival. "Thus suspiciousness of the adversary's deceptive signals and reading the adversary's mind are adaptive. . . . Natural selection will favor animals that become sensitive to subtle clues of danger" (Robins & Post, 1997, p. 71). "Our behavioral tendencies carry the imprint of our ancestral social past, with a sensitivity to the threatening or safe nature of interpersonal situations" (Ybarra, 2007, p. 275). This principle can be applied to interpersonal, as well as intergroup, situations. Higher suspicion and sensitivity to the clues of danger for the group can be a perfect safety strategy that, while raising the frequency of false alarms, can decrease the probability of the most dangerous scenario: missing the threat (see signal detection model, Green & Swets, 1966).

The functions of conspiracy theories

The notion of collective motivated cognition is basically a functional approach to conspiracy theories. Conspiracy theories fulfill several psychological functions (see Figure 4.1). First, they protect the in-group, both psychologically and physically – a function that is bound to the collective nature of conspiracy theories. Conspiracy theories can help draw and strengthen group boundaries, provide an outlet to hostility, keep and increase collective self-esteem, detect the threats against the in-group, and help interpret the past in a way that fits the group's interest. Second, they explain unusual, atypical, and important events, which is connected to the cognitive nature

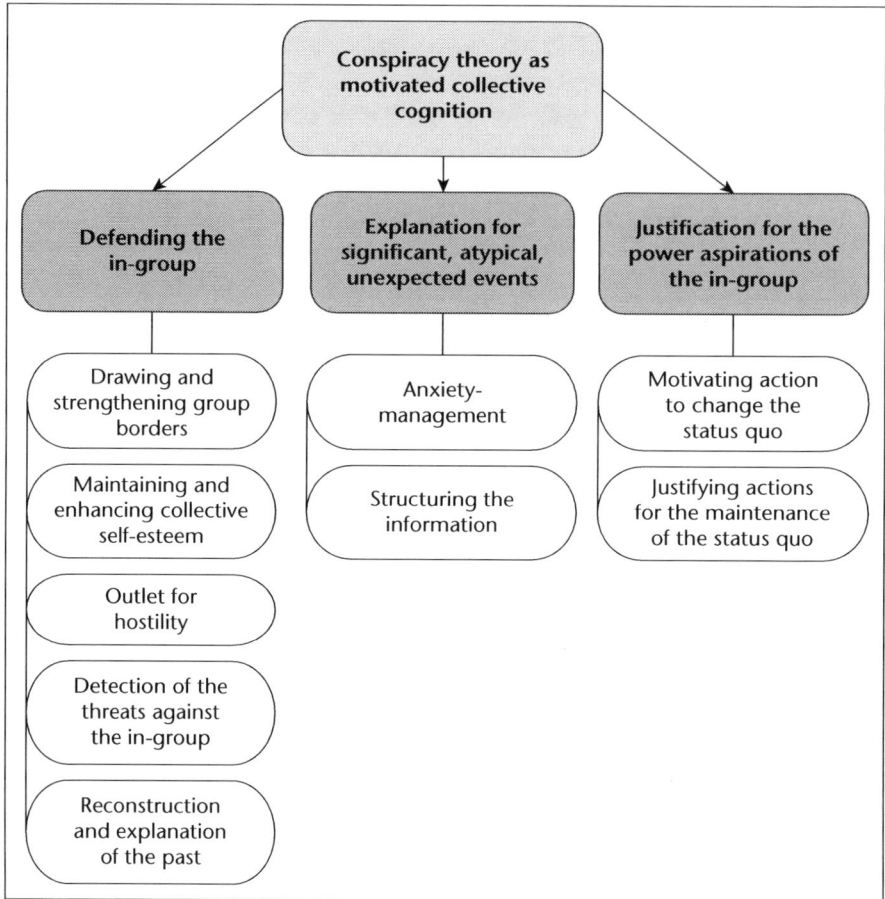

FIGURE 4.1 Functions of conspiracy theories.

of conspiracy theories. Conspiracy theories can help manage the level of in-group anxiety when some unexpected events (tragedies, crises) occur. Third, they justify and support the strivings for in-group power and status, which is bound to the motivated nature of conspiracy theories. Conspiracy theories, emerging above or below in the social-political hierarchy, can motivate actions for changing the status quo, exercise control over the powerful, or, on the contrary, justify oppression and aggression against the lower status groups and cement social hierarchies.

Conspiracy theories as motivated social cognition: Research results

The concept of conspiracy theories as collective motivated cognition is supported by data collected in a series of studies, which aimed to give responses to the following questions: How widespread are conspiracy theories? Do attitudes related to social hierarchy and group identity explain conspiracy theories better than individual psychological variables? When do conspiracy theories aim to strengthen and when do they weaken the group hierarchy (see Imhoff & Bruder, 2014; Sidanius & Pratto, 1999)? Do psychological variables explain a higher ratio of the variance of conspiracy theories than do sociological variables? Will conspiracy theories give explanations of atypical phenomena? And, finally, are conspiracy theories strongly related to the feelings of anxiety in other areas of life?

Conspiracy theories in the context of the crisis

Our first study, conducted in October 2009, was aimed at measuring the level of belief in conspiracy theories, using our own conspiracy worldview scale (CWS, one factor structure, $\alpha = .81$) on a representative sample of Hungarians in the specific context of the economic crisis.[1] The research was conducted in a turbulent and heated political and economic environment, when the effects of the economic crisis were already strong. The research took place during the third quarter of 2009, when the gross national product was 8 percent lower than it was one year earlier. The rate of employment jumped to 10 percent, as opposed to the previous year's 8 percent.[2] In terms of politics, a government change took place: Gordon Bajnai replaced Ferenc Gyurcsány as prime minister (although both had a social-liberal coalition backing in the parliament), and in the summer of 2009 Fidesz and Jobbik made huge gains in the European parliamentary election. The upcoming parliamentary elections in April 2010 obviously foreshadowed a change in government. The public morale at the time is well illustrated by other surveys suggesting that only 13 percent of the respondents believed that the country was heading in the right direction, while 83 percent held the opposite opinion.[3]

In this special social-political context, we found massive support for conspiracy theories. Eighty-eight percent of the respondents tended to agree with at least one item on the list of conspiracies, while 23 percent agreed with all of the items. Seventy-two percent of the sample was above the middle of the scale; that is, the overwhelming majority tended to agree with ideas reflecting a conspiratorial worldview. One particular explanation of this phenomenon can refer to the fact that conspiracy theories breed on the ground of anxieties about the future. In line with this explanation, we observed a significantly stronger correlation between the acceptance of conspiracy theories and the assessment of the future than between conspiracy theories and assessment of the past. Moreover, lower levels of *prospective optimism* (the difference of the assessment of the past and the future) were accompanied by a stronger belief in conspiracy theories.[4] While it seems that people see the future in a brighter light than the past, this optimism in the future all but disappears among people with a strong conspiratorial worldview. Finally, conspiracy beliefs were stronger among respondents who spontaneously mentioned the economic crisis as among the most important social and political issues.

This crisis consciousness seems to be a more important factor in conspiracy beliefs than the objective, sociodemographic factors of economic crisis. Generally, sociological variables appeared to play a marginal role in predicting the conspiracy worldview. For example, employment status did not have any impact on the conspiracy attitudes. Some slight regional differences were observed: Conspiratorial worldview is clearly weaker in the more developed region of central Hungary, while it is stronger in the poorest northeastern part of the country (the real stronghold of the far-right Jobbik party, whose ideology is abundant in conspiracy theories).

The perception of the international environment of the crisis seemed to be important as well. The dissatisfaction with EU membership went hand in hand with a stronger conspiratorial worldview – not surprising, given the strong Eurosceptic rhetoric in Hungary in the last few years, which evoked a strong conspiracy narrative of the EU as a colonizer.

Of course, the scapegoating and conspiracy theorizing in the crisis period is driven by politics (see for example Glick, 2002). Political positions are important in conspiracy theorizing. Rejection of liberal and Roma ethnic parties seemed to be negatively, while identification with the Jobbik party was positively, correlated with conspiracy beliefs.

Conspiracy theories explaining an unexpected and tragic event

On October 15, 2010, after the red mud catastrophe of October 4, a dam containing toxic liquid broke and its content flooded two Hungarian villages, Devecser and Kolontár. Many theories (e.g., Groh, 1987; Glick, 2002) suggest that in the case of such unexpected and tragic events, new conspiracy theories are especially likely to arise. Following the event, conspiracy theories emerged on the left side (e.g., the government deliberately caused the red sludge disaster in order to be able to protect its citizens and provoke a rally around the flag), the right side (e.g., left-wing parties caused the event in order to divert attention from their tragic municipality election results a few days earlier), and the radical right side (the Jews or NATO bombed the reservoir in order to defeat the Hungarian nation to realize their plans for colonization).

We then asked, what role does the preexisting general conspiracy worldview play in forming and acquiring new conspiracy beliefs? In addition, which personality features and attitudinal and situational variables constitute the psychological background of the process? According to our model of collective motivated cognition, variables connected to group identity represent a core of conspiracy theorizing.

To verify our predictions, in our next study we measured the general conspiracy worldview (with an extended version of our conspiracy worldview scale – CWS II[5]), as well as beliefs in specific conspiracies concerning the red sludge catastrophe (with the red sludge catastrophe conspiracy scale – RSCCS[6]). The aim of the latter was to measure specific conspiracy theorizing related to this event. In line with Goertzel's (1994) findings regarding the systemic nature of conspiracy theorizing, general conspiracy worldview was the strongest predictor of specific conspiracy beliefs (regarding the red sludge catastrophe). Moreover, variables related to the group identity (system justification, institutional trust, belief in a just world, Jobbik party preference, perceived collective control) played a more important role in predicting conspiracy theorizing than individual variables (paranoia, animosity, self-esteem). It should be noted that system justification, belief in a just world, and institutional trust were found to be negatively correlated with both conspiracy worldview and beliefs in conspiracies regarding the red sludge catastrophe. Among situational factors, perceived informational ambivalence related to the catastrophe, as well as feelings of anger and fear in reaction it, were positively related with both measures of conspiracy theorizing. Overall, this result indicates the emotional background of conspiracy theorizing, but also refers to the fact that conspiracy theories can function as an outlet for hostility, and moreover as a scheme for providing an explanation for a tragic event.

Conspiracy theories as system justification

In our next study, conducted in April 2011,[7] we pursued further the negative relation between conspiracy beliefs and system justification, belief in a just world, and trust. Thus, we aimed to construe a more sophisticated picture of the relations between social hierarchy, related anxieties, and conspiracy theories.

Our results suggest that conspiracy theories can serve as both hierarchy-weakening (Sidanius & Pratto, 1999) and hierarchy-enhancing social myths. Imhoff and Bruder's (2014) results revealed the importance of conspiracy theories in challenging the existing status quo. However, we have found social Darwinism, the social hierarchy-enhancing attitude, to be positively and strongly related to the conspiracy worldview. Thus, it seems that conspiracy theories can also preserve and conserve the social hierarchy and the status quo. Putting aside the cause of a sometimes different direction of this relationship, one should emphasize the important political function of conspiracy theories.

In addition, we have examined the anxiety-related background of a conspiracy worldview and found that it is collective in its nature; that is, a conspiracy worldview was predicted more by anxiety rooted in the group identity (e.g., a perceived threat to the Hungarian nation) and less by individual anxieties (e.g., poor living standard, crime, liberties). This result provides additional support to our model of conspiracy theories as collective motivated cognition.

Anti-Semitic conspiracy theories and their background

Anti-Semitic conspiracy theories illustrate perfectly the idea of collective motivated cognition. First of all, they provide an ultimate, axiomatic explanation for the world's ills. Furthermore, they name the enemy, therefore helping to legitimize radical measures taken against them, as well as to maintain the collective self-esteem of the group and satisfy its narcissistic needs: If all the political forces are conspiring against the in-group (Hungary and the real Hungarians), they really must be the chosen people! And, of course, these theories are comforting

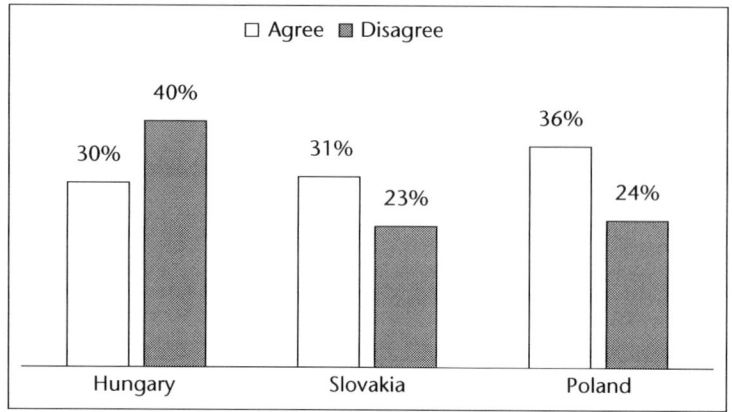

FIGURE 4.2 Agreement with the statement "Jews seek to rule the world"

because they help to distinguish between good and evil and project responsibility onto a named enemy, as well as provide an outlet for hostile feelings.

Researchers in Hungary, Slovakia, and Poland found widespread support for anti-Semitic conspiracy theories. For example, 30, 31, and 36 percent, respectively, agreed with the statement that "Jews seek to rule the world" (see Figure 4.2).

In our recent study, we aimed to explore the connections between a general conspiracy worldview and conspiracy stereotypes of Jews (Kofta & Sedek, 2005; see also Bilewicz & Krzeminski, 2010; Bilewicz & Sedek, this volume). Similar to our previous studies, we found a general conspiracy worldview to be the strongest predictor of specific conspiracy theories (in this case, anti-Semitic conspiracy theorizing), thus supporting the notion of conspiracy theories as monological belief systems (see Goertzel, 1994; Swami, Chamorro-Premuzic, & Furnham, 2010).

In line with the general idea of collective motivated cognition, which emphasizes the psychological instead of the sociological determinants of conspiracy theories, sociodemographic variables seemed to be weak predictors of both the conspiracy worldview and anti-Semitic conspiracy theories. No significant difference has been found among the relevant groups in Hungarian society regarding gender or education. Highly educated groups could also see a Jewish world conspiracy behind everything, which proves again that conspiracy theories are normal and not the "opiate of the fool."

Antipathy towards Jews – at least according to the 2013 Internet sample in Hungary – decreases with age; thus we can find more anti-Semites in the young age groups. Although one-third of the age group between 18 and 39 find Jews repulsive, less than one-sixth of those over 60 share this opinion. The impact on age remains significant, even after controlling for party preference. The fact that youngsters are overrepresented among the voters of Jobbik (see for example Bernát, Juhász, Krekó, & Molnár, 2013) gains a special relevance in this context, given that one of the most characteristic features of the Jobbik camp is anti-Semitism.

Right-wing radicalism building on anti–Semitism seems to have serious strategic reserves in Hungary. And a more general, speculative note that goes beyond the specific results: Anti–Semitism may be starting to be a "fashion trend," perhaps because of its ability to provoke.

Summary

Are conspiracy beliefs widespread? In 2009, more than two-thirds of the Hungarian respondents were at least partly accepting some components of the conspiracy worldview. Comparative research suggests that this is not only a Hungarian phenomenon, as conspiracy theorizing is also widespread in other European countries, such as France and Slovakia (Gyárfásová, Krekó, Mesežnikov, Molnár, & Morris, 2014). It seems that conspiracy theories are general tools for explaining the social–political world. They should be explained as normalcy and not pathology, moreover in social-psychological terms and not in those applied to individual psychology. Among other factors, believing in conspiracies is due to the fact that such theories gain in popularity as an aftermath of political events and trends. Similarly to stereotypes, conspiracy theories are sensitive to political-historical contexts and also tend to change fast. This perspective (see, e.g., Hunyady, 1996; Haslam, Turner, Oakes, McGarty, & Hayes, 1992) is opposite to the one that emphasizes historical anchoring of social beliefs, their rigidness and unchangeableness.

Of particular importance is the observation that attitudes related to social hierarchy and group identity (e.g., collective but not individual anxiety) can explain conspiracy theories in a better way than can individual psychological variables. This is in line with the notion that conspiracy theories are social-psychological, rather than individual psychological, constructs and, as such, also have sociopsychological consequences. They can enhance or undermine social hierarchy and are related to trust. On the one hand, in accordance with previous studies (Imhoff & Bruder, 2014), conspiracy theories are related to attitudes that weaken status hierarchies – as Sidanius and Pratto's (1999) hierarchy-weakening legitimizing myths. Our studies showed that they are positively related to institutional distrust, delegitimization of the system, and lack of belief in a just world, as well as distrust towards "colonizers" (foreign and financial institutions). Moreover, we observed negative correlation between the assessment of EU membership and the conspiratorial worldview, which can be seen as a reflection of the hierarchy-weakening function of the latter. Conspiracy-theory narratives are increasingly dominating the Hungarian political discourse, in which the EU is represented as a superior enemy and colonizing power posing a lethal threat to national sovereignty. The perception of the EU in Hungary is similar to that of the UN in the United States: It is seen as an organization undermining national sovereignty with a secret agenda, a part of an international conspiracy involved in a cover-up (of the latter see Goldberg, 2001). In general, this perspective resembles the proposition of Kramer and Jost (2002), in which a paranoid stance against the establishment may be interpreted as a counterpoint to system justification. On the other hand, as related to social

Darwinism, conspiracy worldview can enhance social hierarchy. The solution to this paradox may rely on the hypothesis positing that hierarchy-enhancing and hierarchy-weakening functions of the conspiracy worldview depend on the actual status and power aspirations of the group. Conspiracy theories against internal and external enemies can be extremely helpful in cementing the power of the ruling elite with ideological tools. This principle is well elaborated in the work of Robins and Post (1997) and frequently encountered in totalitarian regimes such as Nazi Germany, the Soviet Union, or Pol Pot's Cambodia. Populist politicians in power can use a similar conspiracy ideology.

Our studies seem to question the relevance of sociological reductionism when explaining conspiracy theorizing. Our studies – in line with the results of earlier examinations (e.g., Goertzel, 1994) – clearly showed that conspiracy theories are found in every group of society and cannot be localized, for example, to low-status groups. The effects of sociodemographic variables does not seem to be completely insignificant, but at the same time the impact of the attitudinal variables is much stronger. Our studies have proven the hypothesis, however, that belief in conspiracies is widespread and fundamentally not the product of an intellectual "wasteland": We found practically no correlation between the level of education and a conspiratorial worldview.

Conspiracy theories seem to satisfy individuals' motivation to acquire an explanation of atypical phenomena – economic crises or disasters. They seem to direct emotions of anger and fear, and moreover resolve ambivalences, as predicted by the works of Allport and Postman (1947), Festinger (1957), and Rosnow and Fine (1976). Further studies should elucidate the role that environmental factors play in strengthening the attractiveness of a conspiracy theory as an explanation for unexpected, serious events (e.g., Glick, 2005; Groh, 1987; Inglehart, 1987).

Finally, conspiracy theorizing applies not only to past events, but also to beliefs about the future. While it is generally observed that, as a rule, people have a brighter view of the future than the past, forward-looking optimism all but disappears among respondents susceptible to conspiratorial thinking. It seems that conspiracy beliefs act in the service of easing anxieties over an uncertain future (see also Groh, 1987), which may be crucial in explaining unknown, ominous developments and a future of dreadful prospects, all within the context of a symbolic struggle (Wagner, Kronberger, & Seifert, 2002).

Author note

Péter Krekó, ELTE University. Correspondence regarding this chapter should be addressed to Péter Krekó. E-mail: kreko@politicalcapital.hu

Notes

1 The examination took place within the monthly standard omnibus sampling of Median Polling and Market Research Institute. It was carried out between October 2 and 6, 2009, in more than 100 settlements of the country by asking 1,200 randomly chosen adults. The

average age of the sample is 46.8 years; the proportion of women is 53.2%, the proportion of men is 46.8%. The highest schooling is as follows: primary school, 25.1%; vocational school, 31.4%; high school, 29.9%; university, 13.5%.

2 The source of data: KSH website, www.ksh.hu

3 See data in more detail and by timeline at Medián Institute's website: http://www.median. hu/galeria-popup.ivy?artid=b25312f3–25ac-4d74–97c2–192db27276b7&pos=6

4 If the correlation had been zero, it would have meant that in the context of the two variables and CWS there is no substantial difference (because the difference between the two variables is constant).

5 $\alpha = 0.88$, $M = 2.93$, $SD = 0.87$.

6 13-item scale, $\alpha = 0.9$; $M = 2.1$, $SD = 0.9$.

7 The research was part of the research carried out by the Communication Theory Research Group of MTA-ELTE, led by György Hunyady and Katalin Pörzse at ELTE PPK. The survey was conducted with a representative sample regarding sex, age, and type of settlement. The survey polled 1,000 people, identified from an address list provided by the Census Office in April 2011. The average age of the sample was 48.3 years; the male to female ratio of the sample was 52.3% to 47.7%. The percentages of highest educational level obtained are the following: 23% primary school, 27% secondary technical school, 33.1% high school diploma, and 16.8% finished university.

References

Abalakina-Paap, M., & Stephan, W. G. (1999). Beliefs in conspiracies. *Journal of Political Psychology, 20*, 637–647.

Allport, G. W., & Postman L. J. (1947). *The psychology of rumor.* New York: Henry Holt.

Barkun, M. (2003). *A culture of conspiracy.* Berkeley, CA: University of California Press.

Bernát, A., Juhász, A., Krekó, P., & Molnár, C. (2013). The roots of radicalism and anti-Roma attitude among the supporters of the extreme right. In T. Kolosi & I. Gyoörgy Tóth (Eds.), *Social Report 2012* (pp. 355–376). Budapest: TÁRKI.

Bilewicz, M., & Krzeminski, I. (2010). Anti-Semitism in Poland and Ukraine: The belief in Jewish control as a mechanism of scapegoating. *International Journal of Conflict and Violence, 4*(2), 234–243.

Bird, S. T., & Bogart, L. M. (2003). Birth control conspiracy beliefs, perceived discrimination, and contraception among African Americans. *Journal of Health Psychology, 8*, 263–276.

Bird, S. T., & Bogart, L. M. (2005). Conspiracy beliefs about birth control: Barriers to pregnancy prevention among African Americans of reproductive age. *Health Education & Behaviour, 32*, 474–487.

Bogart, L. M., & Thorburn, S. T. (2006). Relationship of African Americans' sociodemographic characteristics to belief in conspiracies about HIV/AIDS and birth control. *Journal of the National Medical Association, 98*, 1144–1150.

Cohn, N. (1967/1993). *Warrant for genocide: The myth of the Jewish world conspiracy and the protocols of the elders of Zion.* New York: Harper & Row.

Festinger, L. (1957). *A theory of cognitive dissonance.* Stanford, CA: Stanford University Press.

Glick, P. (2002). Sacrificial lambs dressed in wolves' clothing: Envious prejudice, ideology, and the scapegoating of Jews. In L. S. Newman & R. Erber (Eds.), *Understanding genocide: The social psychology of the Holocaust* (pp. 113–142). London: Oxford University Press.

Glick, P. (2005). Choice of scapegoats. In J. F. Dovidio, P. E. Glick, & L. A. Rudman (Eds.), *On the nature of prejudice: Fifty years after Allport* (pp. 244–261). Malden, MA: Blackwell.

Goertzel, T. (1994). Belief in conspiracy theories. *Political Psychology, 15*, 733–744.

Goldberg, R. A. (2001). *Enemies within: The culture of conspiracy in modern America.* New Haven, CT: Yale University Press.

Green, D. M., & Swets, J. A. (1966). *Signal detection theory and psychophysics.* New York: Wiley.

Greenwald, A. G. (1980). The totalitarian ego: Fabrication and revision of personal history. *American Psychologist, 35,* 603–618.

Groh, D. (1987). The temptation of conspiracy theory, or: Why do bad things happen to good people? In C. F. Graumann & S. Moscovici (Eds.), *Changing conceptions of conspiracy* (pp. 1–37). New York: Springer.

Gyárfášová, O., Krekó, P., Mesežnikov, G., Molnár, C., & Morris, M. (2014). Conspirational mindset in an age of transition. Retrieved from http://deconspirator.com/wp-content/uploads/2013/12/The_Conspiratorial_Mindset_in_an_Age_of_Transition.pdf

Haslam, S. A., Turner, J. C., Oakes, P. J., McGarty, C., & Hayes, B. K. (1992). Context dependent variation in social stereotyping 1: The effects of intergroup relations as mediated by social change and frame of reference. *European Journal of Social Psychology, 22,* 3–20.

Hofstadter, R. (1965). The paranoid style in American politics. In R. Hofstadter (Ed.), *The paranoid style in American politics and other essays* (pp. 3–40). Cambridge, MA: Harvard University Press.

Hunyady, G. (1996). *Sztereotípiák a változó közgondolkodásban.* Budapest: Akadémiai Kiadó.

Imhoff, R., & Bruder, M. (2014). Speaking (un-)truth to power: Conspiracy mentality as a generalised political attitude. *European Journal of Personality, 28,* 25–43.

Inglehart, R. (1987). Extremist political positions and perceptions of conspiracy: Even paranoids have real enemies. In C. F. Graumann & S. Moscovici (Eds.), *Changing conceptions of conspiracy* (pp. 231–244). New York: Springer.

Jolley, D., & Douglas, K. M. (2014). The effects of anti-vaccine conspiracy theories on vaccination intentions. *PLOS ONE, 9*(2): e89177. doi:10.1371/journal.pone.0089177

Jost, J. T., Glaser, J., Kruglanski, A. W., & Sulloway, F. J. (2003). Exceptions that prove the rule – using a theory of motivated social cognition to account for ideological incongruities and political anomalies: Reply to Greenberg and Jonas. *Psychological Bulletin, 129,* 376–382.

Kapur, S. (2003). Psychosis as a state of aberrant salience: A framework linking biology, phenomenology and pharmacology in schizophrenia. *American Journal of Psychiatry, 160,* 13–23.

Kofta, M., & Sedek, G. (2005). Conspiracy stereotypes of Jews during systemic transformation in Poland. *International Journal of Sociology, 35*(1), 40–64.

Kramer, R. M., & Jost, J. T. (2002). Close encounters of the suspicious kind: Out-group paranoia in hierarchical trust dilemmas. In D. M. Mackie & E. R. Smith (Eds.), *From prejudices to intergroup emotions: Differentiated reactions to social groups* (pp. 173–189). New York: Psychology Press.

Kunda, Z. (1990). The case for motivated reasoning. *Psychological Bulletin, 108*(3), 480–498.

Moscovici, S. (1987). The conspiracy mentality. In C. F. Graumann & S. Moscovici (Eds.), *Changing conceptions of conspiracy* (pp. 151–170). New York: Springer.

Mudde, C. (2007). *Populist radical right parties in Europe.* Cambridge, MA: Cambridge University Press.

Pipes, D. (1998). *The hidden hand: Middle East fears of conspiracy.* New York: St. Martin's Press.

Robins, R. S., & Post, J. M. (1997). *Political paranoia.* New Haven, CT: Yale University Press.

Rosnow, R., & Fine, G. A. (1976). *Rumor and gossip: The social psychology of hearsay.* New York: Elsevier.

Sidanius, J., & Pratto, F. (1999). *Social dominance.* Cambridge: Cambridge University Press.

Swami, V., Chamorro-Premuzic, T., & Furnham, A. (2010). Unanswered questions: A preliminary investigation of personality and individual difference predictors of 9/11 conspiracist beliefs. *Applied Cognitive Psychology, 24*(6), 749–761.

Wagner, W., Kronberger, N., & Seifert, F. (2002). Collective symbolic coping with new technology: Knowledge, images and public discourse. *British Journal of Social Psychology, 41*, 323–343.

Webster, D. M., & Kruglanski, A. W. (1994). Individual differences in need for cognitive closure. *Journal of Personality and Social Psychology, 67*, 1047–1052.

Ybarra, O. (2007). The social prediction dynamic. In J. P. Forgas, M. G. Haselton, & W. von Hippel (Eds.), *Evolution and the social mind*. New York: Psychology Press.

Zonis, M., & Joseph, C. M. (1994). Conspiracy thinking in the Middle East. *Political Psychology, 15*, 443–459.

PART II

Conspiracy theories and ideology

5

MUTUAL SUSPICION AT THE POLITICAL EXTREMES

How ideology predicts belief in conspiracy theories

Jan-Willem van Prooijen and André P. M. Krouwel

People frequently are suspicious of other groups. Societal groups that are particularly the target of substantial distrust are power holders, notably politicians, bankers, or CEOs. Across the EU trust in politicians is low, and people endorse a variety of suspicious perceptions and beliefs pertaining to such powerful leaders (e.g., Andeweg, 2014; Fiske & Durante, 2014). Other societal groups may also be the target of suspicious perceptions among large groups of citizens, such as ethnic minority groups. Frequently, such suspicious perceptions take the form of conspiracy beliefs: the belief that other groups are conspiring in secret agreement to plan and execute an evil goal (e.g., Zonis & Joseph, 1994). Whereas conspiracy beliefs are sometimes sufficiently bizarre to remain obscure (e.g., the belief that the world is ruled by lizards disguised as humans), other conspiracy beliefs are adhered to by rather large portions of citizens, such as the belief in a 9/11 conspiracy (Sunstein & Vermeule, 2009) and conspiracy beliefs pertaining to the assassination of John F. Kennedy (Pipes, 1997).

Many of these well-known conspiracy beliefs have a political element in them, as they assume an active role of elected officials in a scheme designed to deceive the public. As such, it stands to reason that political ideology should be related to conspiracy beliefs. At a very basic level, it has indeed been noted that the political left is inherently suspicious of the political right, and that the political right is inherently suspicious of the political left (Inglehart, 1987). An interesting study in this regard was conducted by Wright and Arbutnoth (1974), which investigated Democrats' and Republicans' perceptions of the Watergate affair. These scholars collected their data while Watergate was still unfolding: The Senate hearing had not taken place yet, and Richard Nixon's personal involvement was not yet known to the public. Their findings revealed that Democrats were more likely than Republicans to believe that Richard Nixon was personally involved in the Watergate affair. This example is ironic in the sense that the conspiracy theory that was under investigation eventually turned out to be true. But for Wright and Arbutnoth's final conclusion, that fact was beside the point: It was ideology that predicted who endorsed or debunked conspiracy beliefs about evil activities committed by others – of a different ideological conviction – in a relevant political context.

While this mutual left versus right distrust certainly is plausible, one may wonder whether the correlation between ideology and conspiracy beliefs is best described by such a simple linear relationship. As a first observation, many conspiracy beliefs are politically neutral and could potentially be adhered to by both the left and the right (e.g., the widely held conspiracy belief that many politicians are connected to organized crime). Second, and perhaps more importantly, a common research finding is that many people have a "conspiratorial mindset" that generalizes to various conspiracy theories on a range of societal and political issues. The best predictor of belief in one conspiracy theory is belief in a different conspiracy theory (Goertzel, 1994), and indeed, one conspiracy theory can reinforce a general worldview of how conspiracies dominate political decision making.

It has been noted that conspiracy beliefs frequently are part of a "monological belief system": an organized set of cognitions about the world that assume the existence of many conspiratorial networks (Goertzel, 1994). Consistent with this assertion, belief in conspiracy theories can be predicted by various stable personality traits or by relatively stable individual differences (e.g., Imhoff & Bruder, 2014; Lewandowsky, Oberauer, & Gignac, 2013; Swami, Chamorro-Premuzic, & Furnham, 2010; Swami et al., 2013). Moreover, research reveals that there is a positive correlation between conspiracy beliefs that are in fact mutually incompatible (e.g., the belief that Princess Diana staged her own death and is still alive vs. the belief that Princess Diana was murdered by the Secret Service) – and belief in these incompatible conspiracy theories is mediated by an overall belief in the deceptiveness of authorities (Wood, Douglas, & Sutton, 2012).

How can we reconcile the insight that specific ideologies predict specific conspiracy beliefs with the insight that there seems to be a general predisposition that makes one susceptible to such beliefs? An interesting suggestion was given by Inglehart (1987), who argued that general susceptibility to conspiracy beliefs is not necessarily predicted by the content or direction of one's ideology, but rather by the strength of one's ideology. In other words, an important predictor of a conspiratorial mindset may be political extremism. The extreme left might believe in different specific conspiracy theories than the extreme right, but for both extremes such beliefs are deeply embedded in an underlying predisposition to be suspicious of the root causes of impactful societal events and to assume an active and intentional role of out-groups in plotting actions that threaten one's own community. To illuminate, the extreme left might believe more strongly in conspiracy theories about, for instance, capitalism (e.g., the belief that various wars were actually started by oil companies, and that bankers and large companies conspire together to start economic crises in order to suppress wages), and the extreme right might believe more strongly in conspiracy theories about, for instance, science or immigration (e.g., the belief that climate change is a hoax used only to extract research funding, or that there is a Muslim conspiracy trying to implement traditional Sharia-laws in the EU), but both extremes share a general tendency of suspiciousness towards power holders and tend to develop conspiracy theories when confronted with societal crises.

In the present chapter, we examine the possibility that political extremism predicts belief in conspiracy theories, and that extremists on all ends of the political spectrum more strongly believe in conspiracy theories than political moderates. To this end, we first provide a few macro-political, historical observations about paranoid responses in different politically extremist regimes. After that, we describe contemporary psychological insight into politically extreme beliefs and develop a theory of why those at the political extremes are most prone to believe in conspiracy theories. We then review a few of our own recent findings on this topic and discuss implications and conclusions.

Historical observations on the extremism-conspiracy link

One basic feature of paranoid responses that are at the core of conspiracy theories is the belief that a different group poses a direct threat to one's own group (e.g., Crocker, Luhtanen, Broadnax, & Blaine, 1999; Kramer & Schaffer, 2014; van Prooijen & van Lange, 2014; see also van Prooijen & van Dijk, 2014). Can we identify such paranoid intergroup perceptions in some of the most extremist regimes that the world has seen in recent history? In this section, we illuminate conspiracy thinking in a few of the most infamous extremist regimes of the 20th century. All the historical observations that follow are well known and well documented by many sources.

One pertinent observation that emerges from the actions of politically extremist regimes is that the extreme left and the extreme right both are highly susceptible to conspiracy beliefs. As Pipes (1997) puts it, "Right and Left engage in similar forms of conspiracism because they share much with each other – a temperament of hatred, a tendency towards violence, a suspiciousness that encourages conspiracism – and little with the political center" (p. 155). Let us examine this statement separately for extremely left-wing and extremely right-wing regimes. A typical feature of extreme-left (e.g., communist, socialist) states is a paranoid stance towards the actions of citizens. Secret services in, for instance, the former Soviet Union and the former East Germany (KGB, Stasi) closely monitored civilians and frequently spied upon them to determine whether they were a threat to the community. Ceausescu's regime in Romania had informants everywhere, frequently even within one's own family. Authorities in these regimes were particularly wary of the possibility that citizens might criticize political leaders and/or have affiliations with the capitalist West – and such affiliations would easily be interpreted as evidence that one was an enemy of the state or a spy. Any sign of sympathy for the capitalist West could get citizens into serious trouble. The authorities were therefore very alert of the possibility that citizens were conspiring against the government to pursue goals that would compromise the goals of the communist state (e.g., Robins & Post, 1997; Pipes, 1997).

Another (potentially even more pernicious) illustration of such extreme-left paranoia is the radically communist Khmer Rouge regime that enforced a bloody rule over Cambodia during the late 1970s. They endorsed the ideology to return to a rural, communitarian way of life that was uncontaminated by outside influences of the capitalist West. Any remote association with the Western way of life – even if only speaking English or wearing reading glasses – was seen as a potential threat to the utopian community that the Khmer Rouge was trying to build, and could get citizens killed. Clearly, the Khmer Rouge was highly suspicious of what they saw as a possible infiltration of a hostile group (the Western world) in their ideal-istic community (Robins & Post, 1997). One might object that the former Soviet Union, East Germany, and Cambodia under the rule of the Khmer Rouge are hard to compare, as each of these cases had different histories, different political and sociocultural backgrounds, and many other different cultural, sociological, and psychological dynamics. But what is striking for the current discussion is that these left extremist regimes, despite their differences, also shared a common denominator: A deep suspiciousness of anyone that was considered "not-us," and that seemed somehow connected with the "evil" capitalist enemy.

Among the most infamous extreme-right regimes was Nazi Germany, as well as Fascist Italy under Mussolini. As a case in point, conspiracy theories were often part of Hitler's speeches and an influential mechanism to fuel hatred against Jews among the German public that ultimately escalated into the Holocaust. Hitler, for instance, warned that communism was a Jewish conspiracy for world domination (at the time also referred to as "Judeo-Bolshevism" – a conspiracy theory that also constituted a substantial part of the justification to wage war against Stalin's Soviet Union; see Pipes, 1997). Likewise, Hitler frequently blamed the Jews for deliberately causing the German defeat in World War I. As such, he singled out a sizeable minority group in German society (i.e., the Jews) and gradually exacer-bated a feeling of intergroup threat among the German population by spreading conspiracy beliefs about this group. Jewish people have been a frequent victim of conspiracy theorizing throughout history, but the conspiracy theories spread by Hitler are an especially dramatic example, with devastating consequences (see also Midlarsky, 2011; Robins & Post, 1997).

Another example of an extreme-right regime was the dictatorial military "Junta" under Jorge Videla that reigned over Argentina during the late 1970s and early 1980s. The Videla regime was keen on protecting Argentina against the threat of communism and was therefore particularly suspicious of those associated with politically left-wing groups, such as labor union leaders, left-wing intellec-tuals, or other people suspected of having left-wing ideologies. This intergroup paranoia led to the disappearance (and killing) of thousands of people (e.g., Rob-ben, 2007). One might again argue that the Argentinian Junta was in many ways incomparable to Nazi Germany, yet despite all their differences both extreme-right regimes uniformly shared the characteristic of being highly suspicious of the potential threat embodied by different societal groups that were considered "them" or "not us." In sum, although the content of left- and right-wing ideologies differ enormously, both the extreme left and the extreme right contributed substantially to the major atrocities that the world witnessed in the 20th century – and a lot of these atrocities were inspired by paranoid, conspiratorial beliefs about competing out-groups, which seemed to flow directly from the extremist ideologies that were endorsed.

We pause here briefly to note that these historical observations should be interpreted with two interrelated and important caveats in mind. First, it is hard to collect research data from people actually living in such extremist regimes (although there are exceptions; see for instance McFarland, Ageyev, & Abalakina-Paap, 1992). One should therefore be careful not to overinterpret research findings on political extremism – of which the data often were collected in the United States or in modern EU countries – as evidence suitable to fully understand the beliefs of citizens that are actually living in such extremist regimes. In addition, the examples above show primarily how elites portrayed a threat by an out-group, and there is no way to say how broadly these conspiracy theories were believed by ordinary citizens. Second, and related, we wish to emphasize that the relatively radical currents in modern EU countries (at least the ones that have actual political significance in democratic elections) are far more moderate than 20th-century communists or fascists. As such, we do not at any point argue that citizens who are currently voting for populist parties in the EU resemble Nazis – such a characterization would be unfair, irresponsible, and inaccurate.

Instead, the historical events described here raise the empirical question of whether there are structural psychological features inherent to relatively extreme political viewpoints, predisposing people to paranoid beliefs about other political groups. We thus seek to examine whether people that lean relatively more towards the political extremes within a specific country are more likely to believe in conspiracy theories than people who oscillate relatively more towards the political center. Put differently, what does contemporary knowledge within psychology teach us about the roots of extreme ideologies, and can we use these insights to make predictions about increased conspiracy beliefs among the relatively more extreme currents that are currently prevalent in the European Union (e.g., anti-immigrant populism) and the United States (e.g., the tea party)?

The psychology of ideological extremism

One common proposition is that ideological extremism is rooted in underlying feelings of uncertainty and fear (e.g., Castano et al., 2011; Greenberg & Jonas, 2003; Hogg, Kruglanski, & Van den Bos, 2013; McGregor, Prentice, & Nash, 2013; Midlarsky, 2011). This proposition fits into a more general research agenda on the psychological origins of political ideology. It has frequently been proposed that particularly right-wing conservatism is associated with uncertainty and fear (Jost, Glaser, Kruglanski, & Sulloway, 2003). This "rigidity of the right" hypothesis is not necessarily alternative to an association between extremism and uncertainty, however, as the radicalization of one's ideological beliefs and the specific content of right-wing ideologies can both independently contribute to managing uncertainty and fear. There is much evidence suggesting that the link between ideology and uncertainty or fear is nonlinear, even when it may be skewed relatively more towards the right. For instance, whereas the political right tends to score higher on indicators of uncertainty and fear in Western societies with a dominant capitalist ideology (Jost et al., 2003), this pattern has been found to reverse in samples collected in the former Soviet Union, a society with a dominant communist ideology (McFarland et al., 1992). Moreover, in a recent large-scale sample ($N > 7500$) that we conducted in the Netherlands, we found that the curvilinear relation between political ideology and socioeconomic fear (i.e., fear that one's well-being is compromised by current societal and economic developments) – revealing more fear at the extremes – was strongly significant, explaining variance above and beyond a simple linear model asserting more fear at the right side of the spectrum (van Prooijen, Krouwel, Boiten, & Eendebak, in press). Given our interest in extremism, as well as our empirical findings on conspiracy beliefs, in the following we will specifically focus on the relationship between extremism and uncertainty.

There is a paradox in the notion that there is an association between uncertainty and extremism, as the political extremes are particularly confident (i.e., certain) of their own ideological viewpoints (Toner, Leary, Asher, & Jongman-Sereno, 2013). This paradox is addressed and resolved in theorizing about "compensatory conviction," which stipulates that underlying feelings of uncertainty and fear instigate meaning-making processes that lead to increased conviction in one's own ideological viewpoints (McGregor, 2006). People thus mentally compensate for underlying uncertainties by an increased conviction in their ideological beliefs. This assertion is consistent with theoretical perspectives positing that uncertainty and fear are associated with sense-making processes designed to regulate such aversive feelings by promoting a sense of understanding the world (Park, 2010; Van den Bos, 2009). The idea that uncertainty and fear drive ideological extremism is also consistent with macro-political insights. For instance, Midlarsky (2011) analyzed what factors predict the rise of extremist regimes and found evidence for a crucial role of "ephemeral gains": Extremist regimes are particularly likely to rise to power in countries that first experienced a brief period of sizable collective gains (e.g., in terms of economic prosperity or territorial expansion), then one followed by a period of critical losses – thereby causing substantial uncertainty among large parts of the population.

Various complementary lines of research examining the micro-level, psychological process of radicalization indeed support the idea that uncertainty and fear increase extremist beliefs. For instance, a study by McGregor and Marigold (2003) reveals that the experience of uncertainty increases peoples' ideological conviction about unrelated societal issues. Moreover, research within the tradition of terror management theory examined how thinking about one's own death (i.e., mortality salience) – thereby activating existential fear – influences political ideology. This theory would predict that existential fear makes people cling more strongly to their ideological worldview, thus increasing extremism in either direction (Pyszczynski, Greenberg, & Solomon, 1999). Indeed, Castano and colleagues (2011) found that mortality salience increased belief in liberal viewpoints among liberals and increased belief in conservative viewpoints among conservatives. Likewise, Weise and colleagues (2008) found that mortality salience has the potential to increase support for both Democratic and Republican presidential candidates, depending on participants' attachment style. Finally, a different line of evidence comes from a study by Hogg, Meehan, and Farqueharson (2010), who investigated the effects of uncertainty on group preference. They found that uncertainty increases people's preference for radical groups (operationalized as groups with a rigid internal structure, a strong norm for consensus, and strong leadership), but not for moderate groups.

The process of radicalization has two interrelated implications. A first implication is that, once radicalized, people have a mental rigidity that promotes intolerance towards other-minded groups (Skitka, Bauman, & Sargis, 2005). Ideologies pertain to moral judgments of right and wrong and hence, almost by definition, extreme faith in the correctness of one's own ideological viewpoints, implying that groups endorsing different ideologies are considered morally inferior, factually incorrect, or otherwise a threat to one's community. As such, both extremes tend to be more prejudiced about, and less tolerant of, other-minded groups in comparison to political moderates.

Consistent with the previous discussion of the rigidity-of-the-right hypothesis, prejudice traditionally has been associated with right-wing ideologies (e.g., Jost et al., 2003; Sears & Henry, 2003). Recent studies, however, have called this truism into question. Specifically, studies reveal that the political left can also be substantially prejudiced, albeit about different societal categories (Chambers, Schlenker, & Collisson, 2013; Whetherell, Brandt, & Reyna, 2013). Examples of social groups that typically are the target of right-wing prejudice are immigrants, Muslims, and homosexuals; examples of social groups that typically are the target of left-wing prejudice are business people, Christians, and bankers. In fact, a survey conducted among highly educated and predominantly liberal social psychologists indicates that the more extremely these academics endorsed liberal values, the more strongly they indicated a willingness to discriminate against openly conservative colleagues, in terms of hiring decisions, symposium invitations, and reviews of grant proposals or papers (Inbar & Lammers, 2012).

The study by Chambers and colleagues (2013) reveals that prejudice among both sides of the political spectrum is mediated by the perception that the other group is dissimilar from one's own ideological group (e.g., the political right's prejudice about immigrants is predicted by their belief that immigrants would mostly vote left wing, and the political left's prejudice about Christians is predicted by their belief that Christians would vote mostly right wing). These effects were linear, such that more extreme ideology towards either the left or the right was associated with more prejudice about the relevant social categories. Given that prejudice is an important aspect of feelings of intergroup threat (Riek, Mania, & Gaertner, 2006), it is likely that such prejudice is closely coupled with suspicious beliefs and conspiracy theories about these social groups (Crocker et al., 1999; Imhoff & Bruder, 2014; van Prooijen & van Lange, 2014).

A second (and related) implication of the process of radicalization is that political extremists embrace a relatively simplified mental processing style characterized by black-and-white thinking, in which social stimuli are rigidly and dichotomously classified as positive or negative, good or bad, and the like (Greenberg & Jonas, 2003). Of particular importance here is the notion that extremists tend to believe in relatively simple solutions for social problems, hence ignoring the complexities that are inherent to many issues subject to intense political debate (Fernbach, Rogers, Fox, & Sloman, 2013; Hardin, 2002; Tetlock, Armor, & Peterson, 1994). To illuminate, the extreme left might be more prone to believe that an economic crisis can be solved simply by increasing taxes for rich people; likewise, the extreme right might be more prone to believe that simply limiting immigration can solve high crime rates. Such a belief in simple political structure is functional to regulate uncertainty: After all, a world where societal problems are easy to understand and solve is comprehensible and predictable; moreover, it is relatively easy to optimize opportunities for success and minimize chances of harm in such a simple and dichotomous world (see also Kruglanski, Pierro, Mannetti, & De Grada, 2006).

One illustration of belief in simple political structure among extremists can be found in a study by Fernbach and colleagues (2013). These authors measured extremism by assessing the extent to which participants had polarized attitudes on a number of policy issues (e.g., the healthcare system). Furthermore, they asked half of their participants to explain how the policy issue in question worked exactly. This intervention confronts people with gaps in their knowledge and increases awareness of the potential complexities that are associated with such policy. In other words, by having to elaborate and explain how the policy works, peoples' ideological certainty about the policy issue decreases; as a consequence, the participants in the study showed a decreased polarization compared to the control condition. The point here is that extremism is associated with a relatively simplistic, snap judgment about social policy – a judgment that is open to more nuance when forced to carefully explain the issue in question.

In sum, due to feelings of uncertainty and fear, people radicalize into extreme ideological viewpoints, which lay the foundation for prejudice about different-minded groups, as well as for a mental simplification of the political world. Hardin (2002) noted that these processes are further perpetuated by a "crippled epistemology" that characterizes politically extremist groups. Such an epistemology entails that once radicalized, people only trust information from their own extremist in-group and naturally distrust any outside information that challenges, or puts some perspective to, their beliefs. This crippled epistemology makes politically extremist beliefs self-sustaining. If extremists are willing to listen only to other extremists with similar beliefs, and are not exposed to different views, there is little basis for deradicalization and moderation.

Implications for conspiracy beliefs

We propose that, taken together, the processes described above provide a strong psychological foundation for belief in conspiracy theories. As a first and general notion, the uncertainty-regulating function of political radicalization has also been identified as a core predictor of belief in conspiracy theories. The classic work by Hofstadter (1966) already noted that conspiracy beliefs constitute a mental attempt to develop causal explanations for events that are hard to understand otherwise. It is no coincidence that conspiracy beliefs surge particularly following distressing events, such as 9/11 or the assassination of JFK, as people are strongly motivated to find coherent explanations of such impactful uncertainty-eliciting events (van Prooijen & van Dijk, 2014; see also Bale, 2007). The assertion that conspiracy theories emerge in response to threatening, uncertainty-eliciting events is consistent with generic insights on sense-making motivation, stipulating that uncertainty and threat are potent factors for people to start mental sense-making processes aimed at understanding the social world (Park, 2010; Van den Bos, 2009; see also Kossowska & Bukowski, this volume). These sense-making processes are closely tied to political paranoia. For instance, Kramer (1998) noted that sense-making processes are at the heart of what he termed "paranoid social cognition," that is, a suspicious state of mind that is particularly attentive to the possible evil intentions of others. These arguments suggest that political radicalization and belief in conspiracy theories serve a similar underlying psychological function, which is to make sense of the world as a means for regulating the uncertainties that people encounter in their life.

Various research studies indeed support the idea that conspiracy beliefs particularly flourish in uncertain situations (see also Kossowska & Bukowski, this volume). For instance, Whitson and Galinsky (2008) found that the experience of lacking control increases people's tendency to perceive illusory patterns, including seeing patterns in random noise, seeing patterns in random stock market information, and perceiving conspiracies. Sullivan, Landau, and Rothschild (2010) found that lacking control leads people to perceive their enemies as more influential. Such exaggerated influence is also part of many conspiracy theories, which frequently attribute superhuman power to the alleged conspirators (Bale, 2007). Finally, various studies found effects of inducing subjective uncertainty on belief in conspiracy theories (Newheiser, Farias, & Tausch, 2011), a finding that is moderated by the extent to which the implicated authorities are considered to be moral or immoral (van Prooijen & Jostmann, 2013).

Additionally, the two mentioned psychological features of extremists – prejudice and belief in simple political structure – are likely to be strongly related to conspiracy beliefs. It has been noted that conspiracy beliefs essentially are a form of intergroup threat – that is, the perception of an evil out-group (e.g., politicians, CEOs) posing a direct threat to one's in-group (e.g., fellow citizens, fellow employees) (Kramer & Schaffer, 2014; van Prooijen & van Dijk, 2014; van Prooijen & van Lange, 2014). Consistent with this perspective, empirical evidence reveals that particularly cohesive groups that face realistic threats in society – such as ethnic minority groups that are frequent victims of stigmatization – are particularly susceptible to conspiracy beliefs (Crocker et al., 1999). As argued by Riek and colleagues (2006), an important feature of perceived intergroup threat is a prejudiced perspective of the out-group, and such an intergroup threat is particularly exacerbated when a perceiver considers the out-group to be powerful. Prejudice allows one to characterize other-minded people as an "evil out-group" – a group that cannot be trusted, that might be potentially dangerous, which could secretly be plotting to cause serious harm on the in-group, and hence should be closely monitored. It is therefore likely that prejudice is associated with conspiracy beliefs that imply an accusation of the target out-group (see also Cichocka, Golec de Zavala, Marchlewska, & Olechowski, this volume; Golec de Zavala & Cichocka, 2012).

Related to prejudice are the implications of belief in simple political structure for the suspicious assumptions that people make about a threatening out-group. In a dichotomous, simple, and rigid world, the problems that one's in-group faces (e.g., an economic crisis) can be attributed solely to the suspected evil actions of a despised out-group, instead of to a plethora of interdependent situational factors (e.g., complex political and economic developments that jointly influence international trade and markets). In other words, belief in simple political structure facilitates scapegoating of different groups to explain social problems. Consistent with this assertion, there is evidence that people are more likely to blame other groups for social problems if they experience uncertainty. A study by Rothschild, Landau, Sullivan, and Keefer (2012) reveals that people scapegoated different social groups more strongly in conditions where they experienced a lack of control. The black-and-white thinking that is inherent to political extremism is also part of belief in conspiracy theories, in which "they" are simply identified as a homogeneous group and uniformly bad.

The above review illuminates the theoretical basis for a strong association between ideological extremism (in either political direction) and belief in conspiracy theories. Both phenomena are a natural response to the uncertainty and fear that can be elicited by distressing socioeconomic developments. Ideological extremism prompts prejudice and belief in simple political structure, and these interrelated processes are both highly likely to fuel belief in conspiracy theories. And, in fact, it has been noted that the crippled epistemology that characterizes extremist groups is also inherent to conspiracy believers, who often only trust information provided by other conspiracy believers (Sunstein & Vermeule, 2009; Swami et al., 2013). All these cues point towards the theory that belief in conspiracy theories is rooted in similar psychological processes as political extremism, and that a conspiratorial mindset closely matches the rigid thinking style that characterizes political extremism. Building on these theoretical insights, it is now time to evaluate empirical data. In the following, we review the findings of recent empirical studies on the association between political ideology and belief in conspiracy theories that we conducted.

Empirical findings

Based on the above review, we propose that there are three possible hypothesized relations that may emerge between political ideology and belief in conspiracy theories. All three hypothesized effects are quadratic relations, and they are displayed graphically in Figures 5.1a, 5.1b, and 5.1c. The pattern depicted in Figure 5.1a represents left-wing conspiracy beliefs. This is the pattern that might be expected for conspiracy beliefs about societal topics that match a right-wing ideology, but violates a left-wing ideology. A possible example would be conspiracy beliefs pertaining to powerful multinationals (e.g., beliefs about malevolent practices of the pharmaceutical industry in third-world countries). Importantly, the pattern is nonlinear, as the slope becomes steeper to the extent that ideology moves more to the left end of the political spectrum. In other words, left-wing conspiracy theories are expected to be particularly prominent among the *extreme* left.

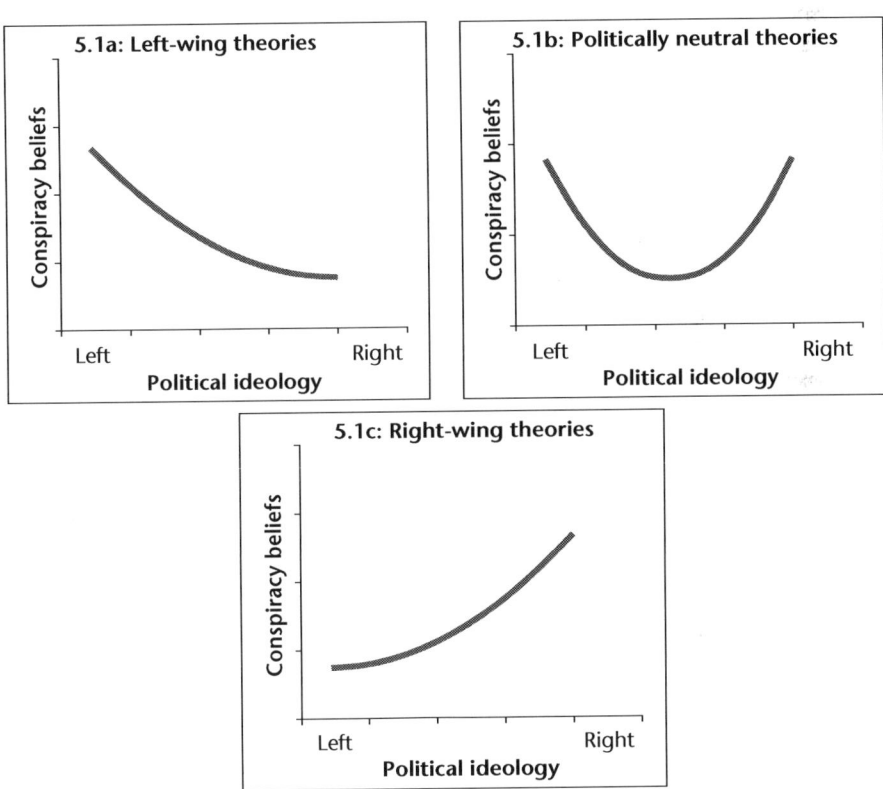

FIGURE 5.1 Hypothesized quadratic relations between political ideology and belief in conspiracy theories. Figure 5.1a indicates the hypothesized relation for left–wing conspiracy theories; Figure 5.1b indicates the hypothesized relation for politically neutral conspiracy theories; and Figure 5.1c indicates the hypothesized relation for right-wing conspiracy theories.

The pattern depicted in Figure 5.1b represents conspiracy beliefs about societal issues that are not clearly left wing or right wing. Such politically neutral conspiracy beliefs may pertain to a wide range of issues, including relatively abstract, global beliefs (e.g., the general belief that there are many secret meetings between powerful societal actors behind closed doors to pursue some evil goal), or issues such as natural disasters, plane crashes, or political issues that both extremes are suspicious of (e.g., the transition of power from national governments to the EU).

Finally, the pattern depicted in Figure 5.1c represents right-wing conspiracy beliefs. This is the nonlinear pattern that might be expected for conspiracy beliefs about issues that match a left-wing ideology, but that violate a right-wing ideology. A possible example would be conspiratorial climate-skepticism (e.g., the belief that scientists deliberately create panic about climate change to further their own careers). Of course, this nonlinear pattern reflects the reverse pattern as for left-wing conspiracy theories.

In a study conducted on U.S. participants, van Prooijen, Krouwel, and Pollet (in press) tested the linear and quadratic relations between political ideology (scored on a scale ranging from extreme left wing to extreme right wing) and two conspiracy beliefs: conspiracy beliefs about the financial crisis (an example item is "the financial crisis was caused by some banks to win the competition from other banks") and conspiracy beliefs about climate change (an example item is "Do you believe that scientists are pressured to portray climate change differently than is actually the case?"). Results on the endorsement of conspiracy theories about the financial crisis did not reveal a linear effect of ideology. The results did show a quadratic effect, however, matching the hypothesized pattern depicted in Figure 5.1b. At first glance this finding might seem surprising, given that banks are mostly associated with capitalism; unlike the extreme right, the extreme left particularly has negative stereotypes about bankers (Chambers et al., 2013). This would suggest a pattern corresponding with Figure 5.1a. However, these data were collected shortly after the crisis, and people at both the political left and the political right were financially hit – and hence threatened – by this development. Put differently, people from the political right also lost a lot of money due to the financial crisis, possibly explaining why the extreme right endorsed this conspiracy theory as well.

On conspiracy beliefs pertaining to climate change, results indicated both a linear and a quadratic effect. The linear effect is not surprising: The political right endorsed climate conspiracy theories more strongly than the political left. The quadratic effect closely matched the pattern depicted in Figure 5.1c, although it must be added that in the specific case of climate conspiracies, the quadratic effect was driven specifically by right-wing extremist men – a finding that future research may elaborate on. One might be tempted to say that belief in a climate conspiracy theory is a right-wing phenomenon. But these findings suggest that it would be more accurate to say that belief in a climate conspiracy theory is an *extremely* right-wing phenomenon. To give an example, there is a lot of climate-skepticism within the tea party – the relatively extreme branch of the Republican Party in the United States. This does not mean that the entire Republican Party is climate-skeptic. In fact, John McCain – a relatively moderate Republican senator and 2008 Republican presidential candidate – wrote an opinion piece in the *Boston Globe* with political independent Joe Lieberman in which they stated, for instance, that "there is now broad consensus in this country, and indeed in the world, that global warming is happening, that it is a serious problem, and that humans are causing it" (February 13, 2007).

Van Prooijen, Krouwel, and Pollet (in press) also conducted two independent studies with samples nationally representative for the Dutch voting population. In both samples, belief in conspiracy theories was measured by a series of statements about various conspiracy beliefs (cf. Douglas & Sutton, 2011), some referring to politically neutral beliefs (e.g., the belief that many politicians have connections with organized crime), some referring to politically left-wing beliefs (e.g., the belief that the political arena was infiltrated by oil companies when waging war on Iraq), and some referring to politically right-wing beliefs (e.g., belief in a climate conspiracy). Together these very different beliefs formed a highly reliable scale, which is consistent with the proposition that conspiracy beliefs are part of a monological belief system (e.g., Goertzel, 1994; Lewandowsky et al., 2013; Swami et al., 2010; 2013). The results did not reveal a consistent linear effect of ideology: In the first representative sample, the linear association between political ideology and belief in conspiracy theories was not significant, and in the second representative sample the linear effect was significant, pointing towards slightly stronger conspiracy beliefs at the right end of the political spectrum. But more important was that the results consistently indicated a quadratic effect, matching the hypothesized relation displayed in Figure 5.1b. On such a composite scale assessing participants' belief in various conspiracy theories, the extreme left and the extreme right displayed more political paranoia than political moderates.

In both of these nationally representative samples, we included a measure of participants' belief in simple political structure (i.e., participants' agreement with the statement: "With the correct policies, most societal problems can be solved very easily"). Results also revealed a quadratic effect on participants' belief in simple political structure, matching the hypothesized relation of Figure 5.1b. This finding is consistent with the assertion that both political extremes have a relatively simplistic political worldview (Fernbach et al., 2013; Hardin, 2002; Tetlock et al., 1994). More important for the current purposes, however, were the results of a curvilinear mediation analysis. Unlike linear mediation analysis that only yields one confidence interval – or Sobel test – for the entire mediation model, a curvilinear analysis tests for mediation at various (usually three) points of the regression line[1] (Hayes & Preacher, 2010). Results in both samples revealed that belief in simple political structure mediated the association between political ideology and conspiracy beliefs among participants at the left extreme (−1 *SD*) and among participants at the right extreme (+1 *SD*), but not among participants in the political center. These results are consistent with the assertion that the rigid thinking style that characterizes the political extremes is closely coupled with the psychological processes that produce belief in conspiracy theories.

Implications and Conclusions

In the present chapter, we sought to illuminate the relationship between political ideology and conspiracy beliefs. The main conclusion that we draw – based on a combination of historical observations, theoretical arguments, and empirical data – is that the political extremes are more likely to believe in conspiracy theories than are political moderates. There are, of course, typical "left-wing" conspiracy theories and typical "right-wing" conspiracy theories – but even for such theories, extremism is a potent factor to take into account, as the relationship also seems to be nonlinear for topics of which opinions, sentiments, and suspicious beliefs are likely influenced by the content of one's ideology (cf. Figures 5.1a and 5.1c). Thus, whereas specific ideologies may predict what specific conspiracy theories a perceiver endorses, it is strength of political ideology – not direction – that predicts whether or not people have a general conspiratorial mindset that is reflected in a tendency to perceive the world as being filled with evil conspiracies.

The present chapter was inspired significantly by the seminal chapter of Inglehart (1987), which first raised the idea that political extremism predicts conspiracy beliefs. As such, it is interesting to note that Inglehart proposes a different explanation for this extremity-conspiracy link than we do. Inglehart specifically reasons that extremist groups often operate at the fringes of society, which explains their suspiciousness towards societal events, as well as their suspiciousness towards more mainstream ideologies. People at the political fringes will also have a general suspicion of the major power-holders in society. Certainly we concur that this assertion has merit, at least when explaining the ideologies, beliefs, and behaviors of relatively obscure extremist groups (e.g., contemporary groups of neo-Nazis). Empirical research suggests that being in a minority group is an important predictor of belief in conspiracy theories (Crocker et al., 1999). At the same time, we argue that the minority status of extremist groups is unsatisfactory to fully explain the conspiratorial mindset among the political extremes. Various populist parties in the EU are quite remote from the fringes of society, as they receive substantial and broad support in democratic elections (see Krouwel, 2012), yet we find increased conspiracy beliefs in our data among participants that voted for such parties compared to participants that did not vote for such parties. Moreover, we also described how some of the most infamous extremist regimes of the 20th century had a suspicious, conspiratorial attitude towards specific societal groups. These regimes were not at the fringes of society, but were the main power holders with broad national support.

There is another group-related aspect of politically extremist groups that we have not explicitly addressed yet, and that is nationalism. Many extremist political parties – particularly on the right – are highly nationalistic, as for instance reflected in EU skepticism that rejects the transfer of sovereignty to European institutions, and hold a negative attitude to factors that threaten one's national identity (e.g., immigrants; see Startin & Krouwel, 2013). This observation matches well with the arguments presented earlier. Specifically, we noted that conspiracy beliefs essentially are a form of intergroup threat (Kramer & Schaffer, 2014; van Prooijen & van Dijk, 2014). We propose that there are two aspects of intergroup threat relevant here. One is a more negative (e.g., prejudiced) perception of the relevant competing out-group. But the other aspect is a stronger psychological tie to the in-group that one cares about. The assertion that intergroup threat increases in-group identification follows directly from classic social-psychological theories such as realistic intergroup conflict theory (Sherif & Sherif, 1969) and social identity theory (Tajfel & Turner, 1979). It has been noted that, paradoxically, conspiracy beliefs might be pro-socially motivated, in the sense that such beliefs reflect a parochial desire to protect an in-group that one cares about against factors – including out-groups – that one considers threatening (van Prooijen & van Lange, 2014; see also Cichocka et al., this volume). The notion that the extremes have relatively stronger nationalistic values are in line with this reasoning.

The intergroup nature of conspiracy beliefs is also reflected in the type of paranoia that can be observed among the extremes. In the previously discussed study that we conducted on a U.S. sample, we also included the 20-item paranoia scale by Fenigstein and Vanable (1992). This paranoia scale differs from conspiracy beliefs in that it assesses people's feelings that they *personally* are being persecuted (example items are "I sometimes feel as if I'm being followed" and "I have often felt that strangers were looking at me critically"). Such a conceptualization of paranoia is relatively more in line with how paranoid beliefs are conceptualized in the clinical sciences that study a range of mental and psychiatric disorders (i.e., persecutory delusions; see for instance Bentall, Corcoran, Howard, Blackwood, & Kinderman, 2001). These personally paranoid beliefs are different from conspiracy beliefs, as they lack an intergroup element stipulating, for instance, that fellow citizens also are being deceived by the authorities. Of interest here is that political ideology did not show a linear or a quadratic relation with such personal paranoia. The extremes did not feel personally persecuted any more or less than political moderates did. Apparently, the political extremes only experience increased intergroup paranoia that is focused specifically on the root causes of social and political events.

Admittedly, the present chapter highlighted mostly the harmful side of extremism and the rigid thinking style that is associated with it. In that respect, we urge one to note that not all extremist rigidity is "bad" and can sometimes even be essential for moral progress. An excellent case in point is offered by Tetlock and colleagues (1994), who content analyzed speeches about slavery by political leaders shortly before the U.S. Civil War. They found that not only the speeches by extreme advocates of slavery, but also those by extreme abolitionists, were characterized by low integrative complexity, at least according to scientific definitions ("slavery is wrong and can never be allowed, period"). The more 'nuanced' political center displayed more integrative complex reasoning, but with it an increased willingness to compromise on this issue. Sometimes, it can be necessary to stand up for basic human rights by taking an extreme, uncompromising ideological position about pressing societal issues.

One challenge for further research is establishing causality. The data collected thus far are correlational, and it is hence impossible to draw conclusions about cause and effect. Theoretically, either causal direction for the extremism–conspiracy relationship is conceivable: Belief in conspiracy theories can be a potent source of uncertainty and fear, which may prompt radicalization into extremist political beliefs. At the same time, radicalization promotes a rigid thinking style that has many commonalities with the conspiratorial mindset, as argued in this chapter. As such, we suspect that the relationship is bidirectional and self-reinforcing. But we lack the data to support this bidirectional hypothesis. A fruitful avenue for future research would therefore be to examine both the possible causal relations between politically extreme ideologies and belief in conspiracy theories. One way to achieve this would be to design longitudinal research, in which participants' political radicalization and deradicalization are tracked over time, along with their belief in conspiracy theories.

In closing, much research on political ideology has focused on the question of how the left versus the right differ from one another psychologically (e.g., Jost et al., 2003). Identifying such differences between specific ideologies is important, as it may further scientists' understanding of the origins of the various belief systems that people endorse. In the present chapter, however, we took a somewhat different perspective on these issues by paying attention not only to the differences, but also to the similarities, between the left and the right. One such similarity may be found in the politically paranoid mindset that produces belief in conspiracy theories. Our review consistently suggests that there is a remarkable convergence between the psychological processes that drive radicalization into extreme left- and right-wing ideologies and the psychological processes underlying conspiracy beliefs. It is concluded that suspicion is strongest at the political extremes.

Author note

Jan-Willem van Prooijen, VU University Amsterdam, Department of Social and Organizational Psychology and the Netherlands Institute for the Study of Crime and Law Enforcement (NSCR). André P. M. Krouwel, VU University Amsterdam, Department of Communication Science and Kieskompas (Election Compass) Amsterdam. Address correspondence to Jan-Willem van Prooijen, Department of Social and Organizational Psychology, VU University Amsterdam, Van der Boechorststraat 1, 1081BT, Amsterdam, the Netherlands. Telephone: (+31) 205988851. Email: j.w.van.prooijen@vu.nl

Note

1 The statistical logic behind this is that, in a linear regression model, it does not matter for the mediation statistic where on the regression line the test is performed, given that the regression line is equally steep at all points of the model – which is different if the regression line is nonlinear (Hayes & Preacher, 2010).

References

Andeweg, R. B. (2014). A growing confidence gap in politics? Data versus discourse. In J.-W. van Prooijen & P. A. M. van Lange (Eds.), *Power, politics, and paranoia: Why people are suspicious of their leaders* (pp. 176–196). Cambridge: Cambridge University Press.

Bale, J. M. (2007). Political paranoia vs. political realism: On distinguishing between bogus conspiracy theories and genuine conspirational politics. *Patterns of Prejudice, 41,* 45–60.

Bentall, R. P., Corcoran, R., Howard, R., Blackwood, N., & Kinderman, P. (2001). Persecutory delusions: A review and theoretical integration. *Clinical Psychology Review, 21,* 1143–1192.

Castano, E., Leidner, B., Bonacossa, A., Nikkah, J., Perrulli, R., Spencer, B., & Humphrey, N. (2011). Ideology, fear of death, and death anxiety. *Political Psychology, 32,* 601–621.

Chambers, J. R., Schlenker, B. R., & Collisson, B. (2013). Ideology and prejudice: The role of value conflicts. *Psychological Science, 24,* 140–149.

Crocker, J., Luhtanen, R., Broadnax, S., & Blaine, B. E. (1999). Belief in U.S. government conspiracies against Blacks among Black and White college students: Powerlessness or system blame? *Personality and Social Psychology Bulletin, 25*(8), 941–953.

Douglas, K. M., & Sutton, R. M. (2011). Does it take one to know one? Endorsement of conspiracy theories is influenced by personal willingness to conspire. *British Journal of Social Psychology, 50*(3), 193–364.

Fenigstein, A., & Vanable, P. A. (1992). Paranoia and self-consciousness. *Journal of Personality and Social Psychology, 62,* 129–138.

Fernbach, P. M., Rogers, T., Fox, C. R., & Sloman, S. A. (2013). Political extremism is supported by an illusion of understanding. *Psychological Science, 24,* 939–946.

Fiske, S. T., & Durante, F. (2014). Never trust a politician? Collective distrust, relational accountability, and voter response. In J.-W. van Prooijen & P. A. M. van Lange (Eds.), *Power, politics, and paranoia: Why people are suspicious of their leaders* (pp. 91–105). Cambridge: Cambridge University Press.

Goertzel, T. (1994). Belief in conspiracy theories. *Political Psychology, 15,* 733–744.

Golec de Zavala, A., & Cichocka, A. (2012). Collective narcissism and anti-Semitism in Poland. *Group Processes & Intergroup Relations, 15,* 213–229.

Greenberg, J., & Jonas, E. (2003). Psychological motives and political orientation – The left, the right, and the rigid: Comment on Jost et al. (2003). *Psychological Bulletin, 129,* 376–382.

Hardin, R. (2002). The crippled epistemology of extremism. In A. Breton, G. Galeotti, P. Salmon, & R. Wintrobe (Eds.), *Political extremism and rationality* (pp. 3–22). Cambridge: Cambridge University Press.

Hayes, A. F., & Preacher, K. J. (2010). Quantifying and testing indirect effects in simple mediation models when the constituent paths are nonlinear. *Multivariate Behavioral Research, 45,* 627–660.

Hofstadter, R. (1966). The paranoid style in American politics. In R. Hofstadter (Ed.), *The paranoid style in American politics and other essays* (pp. 3–40). New York: Knopf.

Hogg, M. A., Kruglanski, A., & Van den Bos, K. (2013). Uncertainty and the roots of extremism. *Journal of Social Issues, 69,* 407–418.

Hogg, M. A., Meehan, C., & Farqueharson, J. (2010). The solace of radicalism: Self-uncertainty and group identification in the face of threat. *Journal of Experimental Social Psychology, 46,* 1061–1066.

Imhoff, R., & Bruder, M. (2014). Speaking (un-)truth to power: Conspiracy mentality as a generalized political attitude. *European Journal of Personality, 28,* 25–43.

Inbar, Y., & Lammers, J. (2012). Political diversity in social and personality psychology. *Perspectives on Psychological Science, 7,* 496–503.

Inglehart, R. (1987). Extremist political positions and perceptions of conspiracy: Even paranoids have real enemies. In C. F. Graumann & S. Moscovici (Eds.), *Changing conceptions of conspiracy* (pp. 231–244). New York: Springer.

Jost, J. T., Glaser, J., Kruglanski, A. W., & Sulloway, F. J. (2003). Political conservatism as motivated social cognition. *Psychological Bulletin, 129,* 339–375.

Kramer, R. M. (1998). Paranoid cognition in social systems: Thinking and acting in the shadow of doubt. *Personality and Social Psychology Review, 2,* 251–275.

Kramer, R. M., & Schaffer, J. (2014). Misconnecting the dots: Origins and dynamics of out-group paranoia. In J.-W. van Prooijen & P. A. M. van Lange (Eds.), *Power, politics, and paranoia: Why people are suspicious of their leaders* (pp. 199–217). Cambridge: Cambridge University Press.

Krouwel, A. P. M. (2012). *Party transformations in European democracies.* Albany: State University of New York Press.

Kruglanski, A. W., Pierro, A., Mannetti, L., & De Grada, E. (2006). Groups as epistemic providers: Need for closure and the unfolding of group-centrism. *Psychological Review, 113,* 84–100.

Lewandowsky, S., Oberauer, K., & Gignac, G. E. (2013). NASA faked the moon landing – Therefore (climate) science is a hoax: An anatomy of the motivated rejection of science. *Psychological Science, 24,* 622–633.

McFarland, S. G., Ageyev, V. S., & Abalakina-Paap, M. A. (1992). Authoritarianism in the former Soviet Union. *Journal of Personality and Social Psychology, 63,* 1004–1010.

McGregor, I. (2006). Offensive defensiveness: Toward an integrative neuroscience of compensatory zeal after mortality salience, personal uncertainty, and other poignant self-threats. *Psychological Inquiry, 17,* 299–308.

McGregor, I., & Marigold, D. C. (2003). Defensive zeal and the uncertain self: What makes you so sure? *Journal of Personality and Social Psychology, 85,* 838–852.

McGregor, I., Prentice, M., & Nash, K. (2013). Anxious uncertainty and reactive approach motivation (RAM) for religious, idealistic, and lifestyle extremes. *Journal of Social Issues, 69,* 537–563.

Midlarsky, M. L. (2011). *Origins of political extremism.* Cambridge: Cambridge University Press.

Newheiser, A.-K., Farias, M., & Tausch, N. (2011). The functional nature of conspiracy beliefs: Examining the underpinnings of belief in the *Da Vinci Code* conspiracy. *Personality and Individual Differences, 51,* 1007–1011.

Park, C. L. (2010). Making sense of the meaning literature: An integrative review of meaning making and its effects on adjustment to stressful life events. *Psychological Bulletin, 136,* 257–301.

Pipes, D. (1997). *Conspiracy: How the paranoid style flourishes and where it comes from.* New York: Simon & Schuster.

Pyszczynski, T., Greenberg, J., & Solomon, S. (1999). A dual-process model of defense against conscious and unconscious death-related thoughts: An extension of terror management theory. *Psychological Review, 106,* 835–845.

Riek, B. M., Mania, E. W., & Gaertner, S. L. (2006). Intergroup threat and outgroup attitudes: A meta-analytic review. *Personality and Social Psychology Review, 10,* 336–353.

Robben, A. C. G. M. (2007). *Political violence and trauma in Argentina.* Philadelphia: University of Pennsylvania Press.

Robins, R. S., & Post, J. M. (1997). *Political paranoia: The psychopolitics of hatred.* New Haven, CT: Yale University Press.

Rothschild, Z. K., Landau, M. J., Sullivan, D., & Keefer, L. A. (2012). A dual-motive model of the motives underlying scapegoating: Displacing blame to reduce guilt or increase control. *Journal of Personality and Social Psychology, 102,* 1148–1163.

Sears, D. O., & Henry, P. J. (2003). The origins of symbolic racism. *Journal of Personality and Social Psychology, 85*, 259–275.

Sherif, M., & Sherif, C. W. (1969). Ingroup and intergroup relations: Experimental analysis. In M. Sherif & C. W. Sherif (Eds.), *Social psychology* (pp. 221–266). New York: Harper & Row.

Skitka, L. J., Bauman, C. W., & Sargis, E. G. (2005). Moral conviction: Another contributor to attitude strength or something more? *Journal of Personality and Social Psychology, 88*, 895–917.

Startin, N., & Krouwel, A. P. M. (2013). Euroscepticism re-galvanized: The consequences of the 2005 French and Dutch rejections of the EU constitution. *Journal of Common Market Studies, 51*(1), 65–84.

Sullivan, D., Landau, M. J., & Rothschild, Z. K. (2010). An existential function of enemyship: Evidence that people attribute influence to personal and political enemies to compensate for threats to control. *Journal of Personality and Social Psychology, 98*, 434–449.

Sunstein, C. R., & Vermeule, A. (2009). Conspiracy theories: Causes and cures. *Journal of Political Philosophy, 17*, 202–227.

Swami, V., Chamorro-Premuzic, T., & Furnham, A. (2010). Unanswered questions: A preliminary investigation of personality and individual difference predictors of 9/11 conspiracist beliefs. *Applied Cognitive Psychology, 24*(6), 749–761.

Swami, V., Pietschnig, J., Tran, U. S., Nader, I. W., Stieger, S., & Voracek, M. (2013). Lunar lies: The impact of informational framing and individual differences in shaping conspiracist beliefs about the moon landings. *Applied Cognitive Psychology, 27*, 71–80.

Tajfel, H., & Turner, J. C. (1979). An Integrative Theory of Intergroup Conflict. In W. G. Austin & S. Worchel (Eds.), *The Social Psychology of Intergroup Relations*. Monterey, CA: Brooks-Cole.

Tetlock, P. E., Armor, D., & Peterson, R. S. (1994). The slavery debate in antebellum America: Cognitive style, value conflict, and the limits of compromise. *Journal of Personality and Social Psychology, 66*, 115–126.

Toner, K., Leary, M., Asher, M. W., & Jongman-Sereno, K. P. (2013). Feeling superior is a bipartisan issue: Extremity (not direction) of political views predicts perceived belief superiority. *Psychological Science, 24*, 2454–2462.

Van den Bos, K. (2009). Making sense of life: The existential self trying to deal with personal uncertainty. *Psychological Inquiry, 20*, 197–217.

van Prooijen, J.-W., & Jostmann, N. B. (2013). Belief in conspiracy theories: The influence of uncertainty and perceived morality. *European Journal of Social Psychology, 43*, 109–115.

van Prooijen, J.-W., Krouwel, A. P. M., Boiten, M., & Eendebak, L. (in press). Fear among the extremes: How political ideology predicts negative emotions and outgroup derogation. *Personality and Social Psychology Bulletin*.

van Prooijen, J.-W., Krouwel, A. P. M., & Pollet, T. (in press). Political extremism predicts belief in conspiracy theories. *Social Psychological and Personality Science*.

van Prooijen, J.-W., & van Dijk, E. (2014). When consequence size predicts belief in conspiracy theories: The moderating role of perspective taking. *Journal of Experimental Social Psychology, 55*, 63–73.

van Prooijen, J.-W., & van Lange, P. A. M. (2014). The social dimension of belief in conspiracy theories. In J.-W. van Prooijen & P. A. M. van Lange (Eds.), *Power, politics, and paranoia: Why people are suspicious of their leaders* (pp. 237–253). Cambridge: Cambridge University Press.

Weise, D. R., Pyszczynski, T., Cox, C. R., Arndt, J., Greenberg, J., Solomon, S., & Kosloff, S. (2008). Interpersonal politics: The role of terror management and attachment processes in shaping political preference. *Psychological Science, 19*, 448–455.

Whetherell, G. A., Brandt, M. J., & Reyna, C. (2013). Discrimination across the ideological divide: The role of value violations and abstract values in discrimination by liberals and conservatives. *Social Psychological and Personality Science, 4,* 658–667.

Whitson, J. A., & Galinsky, A. D. (2008). Lacking control increases illusory pattern perception. *Science, 322,* 115–117.

Wood, M. J., Douglas, K. M., & Sutton, R. M. (2012). Dead and alive: Beliefs in contradictory conspiracy theories. *Social Psychological and Personality Science, 3,* 767–773.

Wright, T. L., & Arbuthnot, J. (1974). Interpersonal trust, political preference, and perceptions of the Watergate affair. *Personality and Social Psychology Bulletin, 1,* 168–170.

Zonis, M., & Joseph, C. M. (1994). Conspiracy thinking in the Middle East. *Political Psychology, 15,* 443–459.

6

ARE THE HIGH AUTHORITARIANS MORE PRONE TO ADOPT CONSPIRACY THEORIES?

The role of right-wing authoritarianism in conspiratorial thinking

Monika Grzesiak-Feldman

Although there have always been conspiracy theories, it seems that nowadays – in the time of the continuous development of the Internet (Coady, 2006) – there are more conspiracy theories than ever, and they are on the rise (Leman, 2007; Parish, 2001). On the other hand, despite playing an important role in society (Leman, 2007) and despite being ubiquitous, conspiracy theories "had been left, almost completely, to the mercy of disciplines such as history and the other social sciences" (Byford, 2014, p. 84). Although significant advances in understanding the psychological roots of conspiracy theorizing have been made in the last few years, the body of work is still underrepresented compared to other disciplines of psychology, such as that of stereotypes and prejudices. That is probably the reason why psychologists studying conspiracy theories often begin their papers expressing surprise that so little research has been attempted to understand the psychological processes that underlie conspiracy thinking (e.g., Douglas & Sutton, 2011; Jolley & Douglas, 2014; Leman & Cinnirella, 2013), and to explore the psychological variables that lead to conspiratorial thoughts (Leman & Cinnirella, 2013; Swami & Coles, 2010; Swami, Chamorro-Premuzic, & Furnham, 2010). In this chapter, we will focus on the latter case, particularly on associations between right-wing authoritarianism and two distinct categories of conspiracy beliefs: about events and about groups (conspiracy stereotypes).

Multiplicity of conspiracy beliefs

Scholars (Abalakina-Paap, Stephan, Craig, & Gregory, 1999) distinguish between beliefs in specific conspiracies and a general propensity to believe in the existence of conspiracies. The latter is consistent with the idea of a generalized conspiracy mentality – a tendency to prefer explanations based on conspiracy theories – which was first introduced by Michael Billig (1978), continued by Serge Moscovici

(1987), and freshly developed and empirically proofed by other researchers (Bruder, Haffke, Neave, Nouripanah, & Imhoff, 2013; Imhoff & Bruder, 2014). Conspiracy theories may vary in their narratives and are attached to almost every big event, such as John F. Kennedy's assassination (Butler, Koopman, & Zimbardo, 1995; McHoskey, 1995) and the Polish presidential plane crash near Smolensk in 2010 (Grzesiak-Feldman & Haska, 2012), as well as being built around a particular group of people, for example witches, freemasons, or Jews (Dillinger, 2004; Groh, 1987; Kofta & Sedek, 2005). Conspiracy theories may concern religion, politics, health, or business, as well as past versus present versus future events, inside versus outside forces, natural versus supernatural phenomena, etc. (Furnham, 2013). Conspiracy theories can also be divided into system conspiracy theories versus minority conspiracy theories (Wagner-Egger & Bangerter, 2007). The last classification corresponds to the sociological distinction between evil elites versus evil others (Campion-Vincent, 2005). Using a social cognition approach, conspiracy theories about groups (minority conspiracy theories) can be considered as cognitive schemata (Kofta, 1995). As has been already mentioned in Chapter 6, Kofta and Sedek developed a new and important approach to conspiracy theorizing, which allows for the conceptualization of conspiracy beliefs in terms of social cognition. They described a holistic representation of the entire out-group as a collective enemy, which consists of three main elements: an obsessive striving for power or domination, acting in conspiracy, and a high degree of group egoism. They used to label it a *group-soul stereotype*, and this term was constantly used in their early writings (Kofta & Sedek, 1992; 1995; Kofta 1995). Later, the term was replaced with the term *conspiracy stereotype* (Kofta, 2001; Kofta & Narkiewicz-Jodko, 2001; Kofta & Sedek, 2005; see also Bilewicz & Sedek, this volume). The latter term is nowadays used widely, not only by Kofta and Sedek but also by other researchers (e.g., Golec de Zavala & Cichocka, 2012; Grzesiak-Feldman, 2013; Grzesiak-Feldman & Irzycka, 2009).

The conspiracy stereotype is based on the causal, conspiracy theory of an entire out-group as a highly integrated being, having intentions, values, programs, and actions. The idea of perceiving a group as an entity corresponds with the common modern social psychology concept of group entitativity (e.g., Castano, Yzerbyt, Paladino, & Sacchi, 2002; Lickel et al., 2000; Pickett, 2001). It has been demonstrated that conspiracy stereotypes of various nationalities can be predicted both by group entitativity and by essentialism (Więckowska, 2004). Essentialism is usually defined as a belief in the essential nature of a group, or more precisely in the existence of an essence that links together all the members of a group or a category (e.g., Lickel, Hamilton, & Sherman, 2001; Yzerbyt, Judd, & Corneille, 2004).

The content of conspiracy stereotype is universal, based on the diabolic causation schema, according to which the out-group is perceived as working out secretly evil plans with the help of dark powers (Groh, 1987; Kofta, 1995). Conspiracy stereotypes of various nationalities are usually strongly correlated with each other (Kofta & Sedek, 1992; 1999; 2005) and with conspiracy beliefs about events (Grzesiak-Feldman, 2012), which is consistent with the idea of a generalized conspiracy mentality (Bruder et al., 2013).

Why authoritarianism should be associated with conspiracy thinking

Right-wing authoritarianism (RWA) is defined as the covariation of three attitudinal clusters: authoritarian submission, authoritarian aggression, and conventionalism (Altemeyer, 1996). Authoritarian submission is a general acceptance of established and legitimate authorities – in a society in which one lives – plus a high degree of willingness to submit to those authorities. Authoritarian aggression is a hostility and general aggressiveness towards others, particularly "social deviants" (Altemeyer, 1996, p. 10), out-groupers, and members of minority groups. Authoritarian aggression is usually accompanied by the feeling of certainty that authority approves it or that it will help keep the authority in the right position by maintaining the status quo. Conventionalism is connected with adherence to social conventions, which are perceived as sanctioned and endorsed by both authorities and society. It is also connected with a belief that others should also be required to adhere to these norms.

According to Altemeyer (1996; 2004), right-wing authoritarians belong to the most prejudiced group of people. Particularly, they are prejudiced against a variety of out-groupers, such as members of racial, ethnic, and nationalistic minorities, homosexuals, and feminists. They also have conservative political attitudes (Altemeyer, 1996; 1998; 2004; Altemeyer & Hunsberger, 1992; Duriez, Van Hiel, & Kossowska, 2005; McFarland, Ageyev, & Abalakina-Paap, 1992; Van Hiel, Duriez, & Kossowska, 2006). RWA is a significant predictor of political paranoia, as well as conspiratorial thinking about various political phenomena (Korzeniowski, 2009; 2010).

Why, at least on a theoretical level, should authoritarianism be associated with conspiracy thinking? The first hint can be taken straight from the famous Authoritarian Personality Theory by Adorno, Frenkel-Brunswik, Levinson, and Sanford (1950). The original researchers on authoritarianism (Adorno et al., 1950) speculated – using their psychodynamic approach – that belief in conspiracies is a characteristic of individuals high in authoritarianism. They regarded this as an aspect of projectivity, particularly of projecting one's own dangerous impulses onto the world at large. Recently, Bruder and his collaborators (2013; see also Imhoff, this volume) have emphasized that projectivity is closely related to their conception of generalized conspiracy mentality.

In the present chapter, the focus is on connections between right-wing authoritarianism – which is a modern reconstruction of the original idea of an authoritarian personality – and various forms of conspiracy thinking, in the expectation that RWA makes belief in conspiracy theories more likely. People high in right-wing authoritarianism "make many incorrect inferences from evidence"

(Altemeyer, 1996, p. 301), which theoretically may lead, *inter alia*, to constructing and endorsing conspiratorial plots.

Is there an empirically proven link between authoritarianism and conspiracy thinking?

The first serious attempt to specify the role of individual differences and personality dimensions – including authoritarianism – in the endorsement of conspiracies has been proposed by Marina Abalakina-Paap and her collaborators (1999). Measuring authoritarianism with 12-item scale derived from the Altemeyer (1988) original RWA scale, they found that RWA was a good predictor of beliefs in specific conspiracies, such as assassination of President John F. Kennedy, the taking control of the banking system by Jews, or government cover-ups of alien landings. However, they found no significant association between authoritarianism and general attitudes towards the existence of conspiracies. In more recent research (Bruder et al., 2013), it has been demonstrated that RWA, measured with Funke's 12-item scale, turned out to be positively related with both the general tendency to endorse conspiracies (measured with 5 items assessing a conspiratorial view of the world and with 12 items measuring generic conspiracy beliefs) and the endorsement of 33 specific conspiracies, including the death of Princess Diana, alien landings, and business relations between the Mafia and the Vatican Bank. However, in further studies by the same researchers (Imhoff & Bruder, 2014), RWA, which was again measured with Funke's scale, showed only small (e.g., $r = .15$ in Study 3, $r = .29$ in Study 4, and $r = .22$ in Study 5) or statistically insignificant correlations with conspiracy mentality (Studies 1 and 2). Imhoff and Bruder (2014) have also observed that conspiracy mentality was a stronger predictor of prejudices against powerful groups (e.g., Jews) than RWA and social dominance orientation (SDO – a variable reflecting the degree to which people prefer hierarchy within any social system and domination over lower-status groups; Sidanius & Pratto, 1999). This is in line with the former findings of Kofta and Sedek (2005), who found that conspiracy stereotypes (particularly conspiracy stereotypes of Jews) are excellent predictors of ethnic prejudices.

Two recent survey studies (Bilewicz, Winiewski, Kofta, & Wójcik, 2013), both conducted in Poland on nationwide representative samples, yield a similar discrepancy in results as do the German studies described by Imhoff and Bruder (2014). Particularly, the two surveys found mixed evidence regarding the relationship between RWA and a belief in Jewish conspiracy. In the first study, which had the form of an in-house survey, RWA – measured with 11 items derived from Altemeyer's (1981) RWA scale – correlated significantly ($r = .23$, $p < .001$) with belief in Jewish conspiracy. In the second study, which had the form of an Internet survey on a quota nationwide representative sample, RWA – measured with a short four-item scale – did not correlate with a belief in Jewish conspiracy. Swami (2012), who examined conspiracy theories among Malays in Malaysia, has also reported some mixed evidence, in particular, a positive relationship between

RWA, which was measured with 15 items taken from Altemeyer's RWA scale, and a belief in Jewish conspiracy ($r = .33$, $p < .001$) and a negative relationship between RWA and the general conspiracist ideation ($r = -.22$, $p < .001$). In another study by Swami (2012), also conducted in Malaysia, the scores on the Attitudes to Authority Scale (Reicher & Emler, 1985) correlated positively with general conspiracy ideation, ($r = .17$, $p < .05$) and did not correlate with a belief in Jewish conspiracy ($r = .07$, ns).

In another line of studies that were conducted in Poland and described below (e.g., Grzesiak-Feldman & Irzycka, 2009; Grzesiak-Feldman, 2012), RWA, which was assessed with Funke's scale, was not only a significant correlate but also proved to be the strongest predictor of conspiracy beliefs about events and about groups (conspiracy stereotypes). To begin with, a correlational study on 354 volunteer high school students (Grzesiak-Feldman & Irzycka, 2009; Irzycka, 2008) indicated that there is a relationship between RWA and conspiracy stereotypes of Jews ($r = .32$, $p < .001$), Arabs ($r = .31$, $p < .001$), Germans ($r = .39$, $p < .001$), and Russians ($r = .38$, $p < .001$). Regression analyses, with stepwise procedure, yielded the same pattern of results for conspiracy stereotypes of all nationalities. Paranoia, assessed with the self-reported Paranoia Scale (Fenigstein & Vanable, 1992) and entered in the first step, turned out to be a positive predictor of conspiracy stereotypes of Germans $\Delta R^2 = .07$, $\beta = .24$, $p < .001$; Russians $\Delta R^2 = .03$, $\beta = .17$, $p < .01$; Jews $\Delta R^2 = .07$, $\beta = .26$, $p < .001$; and Arabs $\Delta R^2 = .04$, $\beta = .21$, $p < .001$. RWA entered into the regression equation in the second step was a significant predictor of conspiracy stereotypes of Germans $\Delta R^2 = .16$, $\beta = .40$, $p < .001$; Russians $\Delta R^2 = .15$, $\beta = .39$, $p < .001$; Jews $\Delta R^2 = .10$, $\beta = .32$, $p < .001$; and Arabs $\Delta R^2 = .10$, $\beta = .31$, $p < .001$. It is worth noticing that entering RWA into the regression equations increased significantly the amount or variance of conspiracy stereotypes that were explained. It seems that RWA, compared to paranoia, is a more powerful predictor of conspiracy stereotypes.

In our next study (Grzesiak-Feldman, 2012), the focus was on the relationship between RWA, SDO, and conspiracy thinking. Specifically, we investigated whether both RWA and SDO, which is defined as "a very general individual difference orientation expressing the value that people place on nonegalitarian and hierarchically structured relationships among social groups" (Sidanius & Pratto, 1999, p. 61), allow for the prediction of conspiracy stereotypes, as well as conspiracy beliefs about events. SDO is usually related to beliefs that support social hierarchy. Despite being both theoretically and conceptually distinct, RWA and SDO usually correlate with each other, but those correlations are average or low. Both RWA and SDO are strong predictors of prejudices and therefore cannot be redundant. They are additive rather than interactive in their nature (Duckitt & Sibley, 2007; 2010). According to Altemeyer (2004), people who score highly on both the RWA and SDO scales are the most prejudiced persons on the world. Altemeyer (2004) called them the "double high" or "dominating authoritarians." According to a dual process approach, RWA and SDO differentially predict attitudes towards specific groups (Duckitt, Wagner, du Plessi, & Birum, 2002). Particularly, RWA, which is an expression of the motivational need for social control and security, predicts attitudes towards dangerous or threatening groups, whereas SDO predicts attitudes towards derogated groups (Duckitt, 2001; Duckitt et al., 2002). RWA is connected with perceiving the social world as dangerous and threatening and as such influences both group defense motivation and threat-control motivation, whereas SDO is connected with seeing the social world as a competitive jungle (Duckitt, 2001). In the majority of modern studies on social and political psychology, RWA and SDO are included simultaneously in the studies' designs.

Participating in the study (see Grzesiak-Feldman, 2012) were 368 students from various universities in Warsaw (252 women and 116 men, mean age 21.83, $SD = 3.11$). RWA was assessed with Funke's scale, whereas SDO was assessed with the 16-item Social Dominance Orientation Scale (Pratto, Sidanius, Stallworth, & Malle, 1994). Conspiracy stereotypes were assessed on six items, three of which referred to power strivings and the other three to acting in conspiracy. The items were similar to those used in previous studies on conspiracy beliefs (Kofta & Narkiewicz-Jodko, 2001; Kofta & Sedek, 2005; see also Grzesiak-Feldman, 2013). Conspiracy beliefs about events were assessed on nine items, which referred to the death of Princess Diana, the economic crisis, and the A/H1N1 influenza outbreak.

RWA correlated significantly with conspiracy beliefs about the death of Princess Diana ($r = .15$, $p < .01$), the economic crisis ($r = .13$. $p < .05$) and the A/H1N1 influenza outbreak ($r = .13$, $p < .05$). RWA also correlated with conspiracy stereotypes towards Jews ($r = .34$, $p < .01$), Germans ($r = .22$, $p < .01$), and Russians ($r = .13$, $p < .05$), whereas SDO correlated with conspiracy stereotypes towards Jews ($r = .21$, $p < .01$) and Germans ($r = .15$, $p < .01$). There was no significant association between SDO and conspiracy stereotype of Russians. Regression analysis, with all predictors mean centered prior to conducting the analyses (see Aiken & West, 1991), revealed that RWA explained almost all kinds of conspiracy beliefs, whereas SDO explained only conspiracy stereotypes, which are strictly connected to the domain of intergroup relations (see Table 6.1). Moreover, the association between RWA and conspiracy stereotypes of Germans and Russians was dependent on SDO. There was a significant interaction of those two predictors (RWA and SDO). Simple slope analyses, conducted to interpret these interactions (see Aiken & West, 1991; Preacher, Curran, & Bauer, 2006), revealed that when SDO was low (one standard deviation below the mean), RWA positively predicted conspiracy stereotypes of Germans and Russians. In contrast, when SDO was high (one standard deviation above the mean), RWA did not predict conspiracy stereotypes of Germans and Russians. Together, these findings show that RWA is more predictive for conspiracy stereotyping when SDO is low (Grzesiak-Feldman, 2012).

According to a dual process approach (Duckitt, 2001), RWA should be predictive for the attitudes towards dangerous and threatening groups. On the other hand, those groups that are objects of conspiracy theories are usually perceived as politically, culturally, or militarily threatening (Bergmann, 2008; Bilewicz, 2007; Kofta & Sedek, 2005), and this in turn may lead to the ascription of conspiracy motives to those groups (Byford, 2003; Bergmann, 2008; Groh, 1987; Kofta & Sedek, 2005; Krzemiński, 1993; Pipes, 1997).

TABLE 6.1 Summary of the multiple regression analysis predicting conspiracy stereotypes and belief in conspiracy theories from RWA and SDO in a Polish sample ($n = 252$).

| | Conspiracy stereotypes | | | | | | Jews $R^2 = .13$; $F_{(3,314)} = 16.61^{**}$ | | | Belief in conspiracy theories about events $R^2 = .04$; $F_{(3,318)} = 4.88^{**}$ | | |
| | Russians $R^2 = .04$; $F_{(3,314)} = 4.81^{**}$ | | | Germans $R^2 = .07$; $F_{(3,313)} = 8.91^{**}$ | | | | | | | | |
Predictors	B	SE B	β	B	SE B	β	B	SE B	β	B	SE B	β
RWA	.38	.20	.11*	.59	.17	.19**	1.10	.19	.30**	.75	.27	.16**
SDO	.27	.20	.07	.38	.18	.11*	.59	.21	.15**	.54	.29	.10
RWA × SDO	−.04	.16	−.14*	−.33	.14	−.12*	−.10	.17	.03	−.15	.23	−.04

Source: Grzesiak-Feldman (2012).

* $p < .05$,
** $p < .01$

Swami, Chamorro-Premuzic, and Furnham (2010) showed that the Big Five personality factors of agreeableness and openness were associated with 9/11 conspiracy beliefs. In another study by Swami and Furnham (2012), there was a correlation ($r = -.12$, $p < .001$) between the Big Five factor of agreeableness and a belief in conspiracy explanations of the disappearance of Amelia Earhart, an American aviation pioneer and the first woman to fly solo across the Atlantic Ocean. In other recent research (Brotherton, French, & Pickering, 2013), the Big Five factor of conscientiousness correlated with generic conspiracy beliefs ($r = .16$, $p < .05$). Our next study examined the relation between Big Five personality dimensions, RWA, and both conspiracy stereotypes and conspiracy beliefs about events. The Big Five personality traits were assessed using the Polish adaptation (Zawadzki, Strelau, Szczepaniak, & Śliwińska, 1998) of the NEO Five-Factor Inventory (NEO-FFI). RWA was assessed with Funke's scale, and paranoia was assessed with the 20-item Paranoia Scale (Fenigstein & Vanable, 1992). Subjects consisted of 168 first-year volunteer students from the University of Warsaw, Poland (124 women and 44 men, mean age 20.76, $SD = 3.76$). They completed the NEO–FFI, Paranoia Scale (Fenigstein & Vanable, 1992), and Funke's RWA scale. Conspiracy beliefs were assessed on (1) 6 items measuring conspiracy stereotypes towards Jews, Germans, and Russians; (2) 21 items measuring beliefs in various conspiracy theories about events, e.g., the A/H1N1 influenza outbreak, the death of Princess Diana, the JFK assassination, and UFO landings; and (3) 14 items measuring conspiracy beliefs about the presidential plane crash in Smolensk (Piłat, 2012). No significant correlations were found between conspiracy beliefs about events and Big Five personality dimensions. Small significant correlations were found between neuroticism and conspiracy stereotypes of Russians ($r = .21$, $p < .01$) and Germans ($r = .23$, $p < .01$), as well as between extraversion and conspiracy stereotypes of Jews ($r = -.16$, $p < .05$). RWA correlated significantly with conspiracy beliefs about events ($r = .33$, $p < .01$), conspiracy stereotypes towards Jews ($r = .34$, $p < .01$), conspiracy stereotypes towards Germans ($r = .44$, $p < .01$), and conspiracy stereotypes towards Russians ($r = .31$, $p < .01$). Paranoia was positively associated with conspiracy beliefs about events ($r = .30$, $p < .01$) and conspiracy stereotypes towards Jews ($r = .25$, $p < .01$), Russians ($r = .29$, $p < .01$), and Germans ($r = .28$, $p < .01$).

Additionally, in order to test the predictive validity of the Big Five personality traits, paranoia, and RWA, a series of multiple regression analyses were inspected on conspiracy beliefs about events, conspiracy beliefs about the Polish presidential plane crash in Smolensk, and conspiracy stereotypes towards Jews, Russians, and Germans. The Big Five personality traits were entered on the first step of the regression equations, whereas paranoia and RWA were entered on the second step of the regression equations. Table 6.2 shows the results of hierarchical regressions for those three measures of conspiracy beliefs. As it can be seen, the Big Five personality factors explained no or little variability in conspiracy thinking, whereas RWA proved to be the most important predictor of the belief in various conspiracies.

Consistent with other evidence reviewed above, the data from our next study (Grzesiak–Feldman & Haska, 2012) indicated that RWA, which was assessed with

TABLE 6.2 Summary of the regression analyses predicting various forms of conspiracy beliefs from the Big Five personality factors, RWA, and paranoia in a Polish sample ($n = 168$).

| Predictor | Conspiracy stereotypes | | | | | | Belief in conspiracy theories about events | | Conspiracy beliefs about the residential plane crash in Smolensk | |
| | Russians | | Germans | | Jews | | | | | |
	ΔR^2	β	ΔR^2	β	ΔR^2	β	ΔR^2	β	ΔR^2	β
Step 1	.07*		.12***		.03		.03		.02	
Openness		-.14		-.18*		.02		-.09		-.12
Conscientiousness		-.01		-.12		-.02		.03		.09
Extraversion		.06		.14		-.13		.10		.01
Agreeableness		-.07		.08		.04		.01		-.03
Neuroticism		.22*		.24**		.07		.14		-.01
Step 2	.11**		.17***		.18***		.18**		.16***	
Paranoia		.24*		.18**		.29**		.41***		.27**
RWA		.29***		.41***		.38***		.30***		.36***

* $p < .05$,
** $p < .01$,
*** $p < .001$

Funke's scale, was an important predictor of conspiracy beliefs surrounding the Polish presidential plane crash in Smolensk (Russia). Subjects were 432 adult volunteers from Warsaw, Poland (286 women and 146 men, mean age 38.75, $SD =$ 15.51), who participated in the study for no reward. They responded to 14 questions concerning conspiracy beliefs about the Smolensk plane crash (Piłat, 2012), 6 items measuring conspiracy stereotypes towards Jews and Russians, and 4 items concerning prejudice towards Russians and Jews. RWA correlated significantly with conspiracy beliefs surrounding the plane crash ($r = .22$, $p < .01$) and conspiracy stereotypes towards Jews ($r = .11$, $p < .05$) and towards Russians ($r = .10$, $p < .05$). In addition, the data also showed that RWA was related to prejudice towards Russians and Jews ($r = .13$, $p < .01$ and $r = .19$, $p < .01$ respectively). To get a better idea of exactly what the results are telling us, we computed a multiple linear regression with conspiracy beliefs surrounding the Polish presidential plane crash in Smolensk entered as the dependent variable, and RWA, prejudice towards Russians and Jews, and conspiracy stereotypes towards Jews and Russians entered as predictors. Results showed that the regression was significant $F(5, 420) = 14.91$, $p < .001$, $Adj. R^2 = .14$. There were three significant predictors of conspiracy beliefs surrounding the Smolensk plane crash: (1) RWA, $\beta = .21$, $t = 4.56$, $p < .001$; (2) prejudice towards Russians, $\beta = .31$, $t = 4.93$, $p < .001$; and (3) conspiracy stereotypes towards Jews, $\beta = -.18$, $t = -3.16$, $p < .01$. Both conspiracy stereotypes towards Russians and prejudices towards Jews did not appear to be significant predictors of conspiracy beliefs connected with the plane crash.

Although a majority of recent studies, described in the previous paragraphs, showed that endorsement of conspiracy theories is associated with authoritarianism, one exception should be also mentioned. In an often-cited study by McHoskey (1995), RWA was associated with an increased endorsement of evidence consistent with the official stance of the U.S. government, rather than of evidence supporting a conspiracy theory about John F. Kennedy's assassination. However, this study (McHoskey, 1995) has some self-evident limitations. First, some of the subjects did not complete the RWA scale. Second, the negative relationship between authoritarianism and believing in a conspiracy theory about John F. Kennedy's assassination was found in a relatively small subsample ($N = 33$). According to McHoskey (1995, p. 407), "due to the small number of Oswald theory advocates, the nonsignificance of this correlation may be the result of range restriction. This issue must await future investigation." Finally, the trouble with the study by McHoskey (1995) is related to the choice of JFK assassination as a conspiracy example. JFK was a liberal, which means that he would have been a member of the out-group for right-wing authoritarians, so it could also be hypothesized that the responses were a projection of aggression towards an out-group (see Grzesiak-Feldman & Irzycka, 2009). To sum up, this study (McHoskey, 1995), contrary to other research described in this chapter, has not answered the question about whether there is a significant and direct relationship between authoritarianism and believing in conspiracy theories (see Grzesiak-Feldman & Irzycka, 2009). A summary of all the studies described in this chapter appears in Table 6.3.

TABLE 6.3 Overview of results (in chronological order) on relationships between authoritarianism and various forms of conspiracy thinking, including both specific and general measures of conspiracist ideation.

Participants	RWA Scale	Type of conspiracy beliefs	Measurement of conspiracy beliefs	Relations with RWA	Source
253 psychology students (116 women and 137 men) in mean age of 19.3, $SD = 3.1$. The relationship between RWA and attitudes towards conspiracy explanations of JFK assassination was assessed only in small ($N = 33$) subsample [sic]	30-item RWA Scale (Altemeyer, 1988)	Attitudes towards JFK assassination	One item: "Do you believe that President John F. Kennedy was killed by a lone assassin named Lee Harvey Oswald, or that there were multiple assassins, and therefore a conspiracy to kill President Kennedy?" (McHoskey, 1995)	Significant negative correlation between RWA and the evidence evaluation index $r = -.30$, $N = 33$, $p < .05$	McHoskey (1995)
156 students (50% males and 50% females) at New Mexico State University, U.S. Average age 20 years (range: 18–34 years)	12-item scale, derived from the RWA Scale (Altemeyer, 1988)	Belief in specific conspiracies	22 items, each addressing beliefs in a different conspiracy, e.g., JFK assassination conspiracy theory	Significant, positive relationship between beliefs in specific conspiracies and RWA, $p < .02$	Abalakina-Paap et al. (1999)
		Attitudes towards the existence of conspiracies	19 items addressing attitudes concerning the existence of conspiracies in general	Lack of any significant relationship	
354 volunteer high school students from Warsaw (180 women, 174 men) in mean age of 17.5 years, $SD = .06$	12-item RWA Scale (Funke, 2005)	Conspiracy stereotypes towards Jews, Germans, Russians, and Arabs	18-item Conspiracy Beliefs Scale (Kofta & Narkiewicz-Jodko, 2001)	Significant, positive correlations between RWA and conspiracy stereotypes from $r = .39$, $p < .001$ for Germans to $r = .31$, $p < .001$ for Arabs	Grzesiak-Feldman and Irzycka (2009)

(Continued)

TABLE 6.3 (Continued)

Participants	RWA Scale	Type of conspiracy beliefs	Measurement of conspiracy beliefs	Relations with RWA	Source
368 students from Warsaw (252 women and 116 men) in mean age of 21.83, $SD = 3.11$	12-item RWA Scale (Funke, 2005)	Conspiracy stereotypes towards Jews, Germans, and Russians	6 items delivered from 18-item Conspiracy Beliefs Scale (Kofta & Narkiewicz-Jodko, 2001)	Significant, positive correlations between RWA and conspiracy stereotypes from $r = .34$, $p < .01$ for Jews to $r = .13$, $p < .05$ for Russians	Grzesiak-Feldman (2012)
		Conspiracy beliefs about events	9-item scale of conspiracy beliefs about events (Grzesiak-Feldman, 2012)	Significant, positive correlation between RWA and conspiracy beliefs about A/H1N1 influenza ($r = .13$, $p < .05$), financial crisis ($r = .13$, $p < .05$), and the death of Princess Diana ($r = .15$, $p < .05$)	
432 adult volunteers from Warsaw (286 women and 146 men) in mean age of 38.75, $SD = 15.51$	12-item RWA Scale (Funke, 2005)	Conspiracy beliefs concerning Smolensk plane crash	14 items concerning conspiracy beliefs about the Smolensk plane crash (Piłat, 2012)	Significant, positive correlations between RWA and conspiracy beliefs concerning Smolensk plane crash, $r = .22$, $p < .01$	Grzesiak-Feldman and Haska (2012)
		Conspiracy stereotypes towards Russians and Jews	6 items delivered from 18-item Conspiracy Beliefs Scale (Kofta & Narkiewicz-Jodko, 2001)	Significant, positive correlations between RWA and conspiracy stereotypes of Jews, $r = .11$, $p < .05$ and Russians, $r = .10$, $p < .05$	

Study	Sample	Scale	Construct	Measure	Result
Swami (2012)	368 Malays (180 women and 188 men) in mean age 44.15, SD = 12.90	Attitudes to Authority Scale (Reicher & Emler, 1985)	Belief in the Jewish conspiracy theory	A novel, 12-item scale to measure belief in the Jewish conspiracy theory (Swami, 2012)	Lack of significant correlation between attitudes to authority and belief in Jewish conspiracy, $r = 0.07$, ns.
			General conspiracy ideation (belief in general conspiracy theories)	The Belief in Conspiracy Theories Inventory – a 15-item measure (Swami et al., 2010; 2011)	Significant, positive correlation between attitudes to authority and general conspiracy ideation, $r = .17$, $p < .05$
	314 Malays (162 women and 152 men) in age from 18 to 68 years ($M = 40.89$, SD = 13.04)	The Right-Wing Authoritarianism Scale (Zakrisson, 2005)	Belief in the Jewish conspiracy theory	A novel, 12-item scale to measure belief in the Jewish conspiracy theory (Swami, 2012)	Significant, positive correlation between RWA and belief in the Jewish conspiracy, $r = .33$, $p < .001$
			General conspiracy ideation (belief in general conspiracy theories)	The Belief in Conspiracy Theories Inventory – a 15-item measure (Swami et al., 2010; 2011)	Significant, negative correlation between RWA and general conspiracy ideation, $r = -.20$, $p < .001$
Bilewicz et al. (2013)	A nationwide representative sample of 979 Polish participants (534 women and 445 men) in mean age of 48.22, SD = 18.03	11 items derived from Altemeyer's (1981) RWA scale	Jewish conspiracy	6 items delivered from Conspiracy Beliefs Scale (Kofta & Sedek, 2005)	Significant, positive correlation between RWA and Jewish conspiracy, $r = .23$, $p < .001$
	A nationwide representative sample of 600 young Poles (310 women and 290 men) in mean age 24.89, SD = 6.311	4 items			Lack of significant correlation between RWA and Jewish conspiracy, $r = -.02$, p ns.

(Continued)

TABLE 6.3 (Continued)

Participants	RWA Scale	Type of conspiracy beliefs	Measurement of conspiracy beliefs	Relations with RWA	Source
274 students from German universities (96 men and 178 women) in mean age of 25.6, $SD = 8.1$	12-item RWA Scale (Funke, 2005)	Conspiracy mentality	5-item Conspiracy Mentality Questionnaire (Bruder et al., 2013) – assessing generic conspiracy beliefs	Significant, positive correlation between RWA and conspiracy mentality, $r = .28$, $p < .001$	Study 4 Bruder et al. (2013)
			Conspiracy Mentality Scale – 12-item measure of generic conspiracy beliefs	Significant, positive correlation between RWA and conspiracy mentality, $r = .29$, $p < .001$	
		Beliefs in specific conspiracies	33 items on specific conspiracy beliefs	RWA predicted 18 items (from 33) on beliefs in specific conspiracies with average $\beta = .17$	
497 participants (245 women and 240 men, 1 other, 11 missing) in mean age of 33.49, $SD = 12.25$	12-item RWA Scale (Funke, 2005)	Conspiracy mentality	Conspiracy Mentality Scale – 12-item measure of generic conspiracy beliefs	a) $r = .05$, p ns.– for correlation with RWA b) moderately related ($r = .15$) with RWA facet of authoritarian aggression	Study 1 Imhoff and Bruder (2014)
294 (133 men and 161 women) in mean age of 28.09, $SD = 10.41$				Lack of significant correlation between RWA and conspiracy mentality, $r = .16$, p ns.	Study 2 Imhoff and Bruder (2014)

208 participants from a German university (110 men and 165 women, 5 unidentified) in mean age of 23.71, $SD = 4.93$	Significant, positive correlation between RWA and conspiracy mentality, $r = .15, p < .01$	Study 3 Imhoff and Bruder (2014)
280 students of a German university (97 men and 181 women) in mean age of 25.63, $SD = 8.13$	Significant, positive correlation between RWA and conspiracy mentality, $r = .29, p < .001$	Study 4 Imhoff and Bruder (2014)
1,852 participants recruited online (1,086 women and 735 men) in mean age of 30.68, $SD = 11.97$	Significant, positive correlation between RWA and conspiracy mentality, $r = .22, p < .01$	Study 5 Imhoff and Bruder (2014)

General conclusions and discussion

The starting point for the present chapter was the observation that nowadays there are more conspiracy theories than ever and they are on the rise (Leman, 2007; Parish, 2001). An adequate theoretical understanding of this phenomenon should not ignore the role of dispositional variables, *inter alia* the right-wing authoritarianism (RWA), that are associated with conspiratorial thinking. The present chapter takes a first step towards summarizing the role of RWA in conspiracy theorizing. I have described several studies (the brief summary appears in Table 6.3) showing, with only few exceptions, significant connections between RWA and conspiracy beliefs. Moreover, RWA turned out to be a much better predictor of conspiracy thinking than SDO or Big Five personality traits.

In sum, in the present chapter I have referred to 9 papers on the relationship between authoritarianism and conspiracy thinking, 15 empirical studies conducted on 15 samples, and at least 28 statistical analyses (see Table 6.3). The majority of them, as one can easily see, yield a significant relationship between RWA and conspiracy thinking. In particular, RWA was significantly related to conspiracy thinking in the case of 23 statistical analyses. What about the remaining five cases? Does a pattern emerge from those analyses suggesting different effects of authoritarianism on different kinds of conspiracy beliefs? In the case of Study 2 by Bilewicz et al. (2013), the problem (i.e., lack of significant relationship) may have been connected to the fact that RWA was assessed with only four single items. Putting that study aside, more interesting is that in the other survey study by the same researchers (Bilewicz et al., 2013, Study 1), RWA, measured with 11 items, correlated significantly with Jewish conspiracy beliefs. The study by McHoskey (1995), showing links between RWA and the increased endorsement of evidence consistent with the official stance of the U.S. government rather than with evidence supporting conspiracy, had some serious limitations, which have already been discussed. In the cases of the three other studies (Abalakina–Paap et al., 1999 – one study; Imhoff & Bruder, 2014 – two studies), the lack of any significant relationship between authoritarianism and conspiracy thinking was observed when conspiracy ideation was conceptualized and measured as a general predisposition (respectively, a general conspiracy mentality in Imhoff and Bruder's studies or attitudes concerning the existence of conspiracies in general in Abalakina–Paap's study). Does it mean that generic measures of conspiracy ideation are unrelated with authoritarianism? The answer is "no." In the other three studies by Imhoff and Bruder (2014), generic measures of conspiracy mentality were linked significantly with authoritarianism. The studies by Swami (2012), which were conducted among Malaysian Malays, have also yielded unexpected, mixed results showing a negative relationship between RWA and belief in general conspiracy theories in Study 2 and no significant relationship between RWA and Jewish conspiracy beliefs in Study 1. At the same time, RWA correlated positively with general conspiracy ideation in Study 1 and with the belief in Jewish conspiracy in Study 2. These results were interpreted by Swami (2012), with regard to cultural specificity of the Malaysian sample. In my opinion, they can be considered to be a very special case or an aberration.

What is interesting is that conspiracy stereotypes, as a general rule, depend on both RWA and SDO, whereas conspiracy beliefs about events depend only on RWA. Presumably, it is because conspiracy stereotypes are related to both threat and the perception of hierarchical intergroup relation. Using Duckitt's dual process model (2001; Duckitt et al., 2002), we can expect conspiracy stereotyping to be connected to both a perception of the world as a dangerous and threatening place and a perception of the world as a competitive jungle. Groups that are objects of conspiracy stereotypes, as well as of other conspiracy theories, are usually perceived as dangerous, as well as powerful and dominating (e.g., Kofta & Sedek, 2005; Bergmann, 2008; Byford & Billig, 2001). It is important to note that perceiving an out-group as conspiring against an in-group will be more likely when the out-group is in power and less likely when the out-group is not in power (Uscinski, 2014). According to Uscinski (2014), being in power is strictly connected with a potential threat posed by the out-group. On the other hand, conspiracy beliefs about events seem to be associated most of all with perceptions of the world as dangerous and threatening, not with a hierarchical view of social relations (i.e., the world as a competitive jungle).

Much of the concentration in the current chapter was on conspiracy stereotyping, an important approach to conspiracy beliefs in terms of social cognition (Kofta & Sedek, 2005). In his interesting essay published on an Internet blog (March 14, 2013) and dedicated to the psychology of conspiracy theories, Michael Wood noted that the association between RWA and conspiracy theories "seems to depend on the specifics of the theory in question." Conspiracy stereotypes, for certain, belong to the category of conspiracy theories that are constantly related with authoritarianism. RWA consistently turns out to be a good predictor and a significant correlate of conspiracy stereotypes.

The research suggests that the higher the scores on RWA, the higher the scores on various conspiracy beliefs scales. "And anyone who thinks two measures will correlate just because they appear in the same booklet has not tried it very often," wrote Bob Altemeyer (1996, p. 39) in his famous book *The Authoritarian Specter.* Thus, the relationship between right-wing authoritarianism and conspiracy thinking cannot be an artifact. RWA should be considered as one of the psychological antecedents of conspiracy theorizing, which may draw people towards a wide range of conspiracy theories. Nevertheless, it should be also remembered that in all the studies described in the current chapter, the amount of variability of conspiracy beliefs that may be explained by RWA has been relatively low or average. This leaves much of the variability of conspiracy thinking still to be accounted for by other variables, which should be the starting point for further studies on psychological correlates of conspiracy beliefs. The degree to which people believe in conspiracy theories may depend, for instance, on high reality testing deficits (Drinkwater, Dagnall, & Parker, 2012), which may lead to less critical reasoning; paranoia and paranoid ideation (Grzesiak-Feldman & Ejsmont, 2008; Darwin,

Neave, & Holmes, 2011; Holm, 2009); and various kinds of situational threat or anxiety (Bergmann, 2008; Byford & Billig, 2001; Kofta & Sedek, 2005; Grzesiak-Feldman, 2007; 2013; Parish, 2001; Uscinski, 2014).

Altemeyer (1996) links authoritarianism with religiosity, claiming that religious training can sometimes make people authoritarian. At the same time, conspiracy theories can be considered as kind of modern myths (Raab, Ortlieb, Auer, Guthmann, & Carbon, 2013), analogues to religious beliefs (Franks, Bangerter, & Bauer, 2013) in the sense that they allow an explanation for threatening events (Franks et al., 2013). Hence, religiosity is one of the variables that may be included in further research on conspiracy theories and authoritarianism. Findings from a study using functional magnetic resonance imaging (fMRI) also show that religiosity and beliefs in supernatural phenomena are connected with decreased cognitive inhibition (Lindeman, Svedholm, Riekki, Raij, & Hari, 2013). This fMRI study (Lindeman et al., 2013) demonstrated the importance of searching for a possible brain basis for conspiratorial thinking. It would be a fascinating possibility that believing in conspiracy theories may be associated, analogically as are religiosity and beliefs in the supernatural, with weaker cognitive inhibition. Parenthetically, it is also worth mentioning that both religion and conspiracy theories can be considered as memes (see Goertzel, 2010; 2012), units of human cultural evolution, transmitted from one mind to another, that are self-replicating, mutating, and surviving or dying out through natural selection (Dawkins, 1976).

As previously mentioned, it is extremely difficult to find any sensible, universal explanation for all the studies that yielded no significant effects of authoritarianism on conspiracy thinking. It demonstrates the importance of searching for possible mediators of the relationship between RWA and conspiracy thinking. Researchers should not forget about the studies showing no relationship between RWA and conspiracy beliefs and should try to discover under which circumstances RWA does not lead towards conspiracy ideation. This question should be answered in future research and would provide an excellent agenda for further studies on both conspiracy beliefs (especially on the psychological ascendants of conspiracy beliefs) and on the nature of authoritarianism per se. In searching for this answer, one should remember what Swami (2012, p. 7) has written: "Conspiracist ideation may play different roles in different cultural contexts." Therefore, not only individual differences but also intercultural differences should be regarded in future research. Gaining a better understanding of conspiracy theorizing is the first step towards correcting those beliefs, which are often false or lead towards serious social consequences (see Jolley & Douglas, 2014).

Author note

Monika Grzesiak-Feldman, Faculty of Psychology, University of Warsaw. Work on this chapter was supported by a grant from the National Science Centre (Decision No 2013/09/B/HS6/02626) to Monika Grzesiak-Feldman. Correspondence regarding this chapter should be directed to Monika Grzesiak-Feldman, University of Warsaw, Faculty of Psychology, Stawki 5/7, Warsaw (Poland). E-mail: ika@psych.uw.edu.pl

References

Abalakina-Paap, M., Stephan, W.G., Craig, T., & Gregory, W.L. (1999). Beliefs in conspiracies. *Political Psychology, 20*(3), 637–647.

Adorno, T. W., Frenkel-Brunswik, E., Levinson, D. J., & Sanford, R. N. (1950). *The authoritarian personality.* New York: Harper & Row.

Aiken, L.S., & West, S.G. (1991). *Multiple regression: Testing and interpreting interactions.* Newbury Park, CA: Sage.

Altemeyer, B. (1981). *Right-wing authoritarianism.* Winnipeg: University of Manitoba Press.

Altemeyer, B. (1988). *Enemies of freedom: Understanding right-wing authoritarianism.* San Francisco: Jossey-Bass.

Altemeyer, B. (1996). *The authoritarian specter.* Cambridge, MA: Harvard University Press.

Altemeyer, B. (1998). The other "authoritarian personality." *Advances in Experimental Social Psychology, 30,* 47–92.

Altemeyer, B. (2004). Highly dominating, highly authoritarian personalities. *Journal of Social Psychology, 144,* 421–447.

Altemeyer, B., & Hunsberger, B.E. (1992). Authoritarianism, religious fundamentalism, quest, and prejudice. *International Journal for the Psychology of Religion, 2,* 113–133.

Bergmann, W. (2008). Anti-Semitic attitudes in Europe: A comparative perspective. *Journal of Social Issues, 64,* 343–362.

Bilewicz, M. (2007). History as an obstacle: Impact of temporal-based social categorizations on Polish-Jewish intergroup contact. *Group Processes and Intergroup Relations, 10,* 551–563.

Bilewicz, M., Winiewski, M., Kofta, M., & Wójcik, A. (2013). Harmful ideas, the structure and consequences of anti-Semitic beliefs in Poland. *Political Psychology, 34*(6), 821–839.

Billig, M. (1978). *Fascists: A social psychology of the National Front.* London: Academic Press.

Brotherton, R., French, C.C., & Pickering, A.D. (2013). Measuring belief in conspiracy theories: The generic conspiracist beliefs scale. *Frontiers in Psychology, 4,* 279.

Bruder, M., Haffke, P., Neave, N., Nouripanah, N., & Imhoff, R. (2013). Measuring individual differences in generic beliefs in conspiracy theories across cultures: Conspiracy mentality questionnaire (CMQ). *Frontiers in Psychology, 4,* 225.

Butler, L.D., Koopman, C., & Zimbardo, P.G. (1995). The psychological impact of viewing the film "JFK": Emotions, beliefs, and political behavioural intentions. *Political Psychology, 16,* 237–257.

Byford, J. (2003). Anti-Semitism and the Christian Right in post-Milošević Serbia: From conspiracy theory to hate crime. *Internet Journal of Criminology, 1,* 1–27.

Byford, J. (2014). Beyond belief: The social psychology of conspiracy theories and the study of ideology. In C. Antaki and S. Condor (Eds.), *Rhetoric, ideology and social psychology: Essays in honour of Michael Billig* (pp. 83–94). London: Routledge.

Byford, J., & Billig, M. (2001). The emergence of antisemitic conspiracy theories in Yugoslavia during the war with NATO. *Patterns of Prejudice, 35,* 50–63.

Campion-Vincent, V. (2005). From evil others to evil elites: A dominant pattern in conspiracy theories today. In G.A. Fine, V. Campion-Vincent, & C. Heath (Eds.), *Rumor mills: The social impact of rumor and legend* (pp. 103–122). New Brunswick, NJ: Aldine Transaction.

Castano, E., Yzerbyt, V., Paladino, M., & Sacchi, S. (2002). I belong, therefore, I exist: Ingroup identification, ingroup entitativity, and ingroup bias. *Personality and Social Psychology Bulletin, 28*, 135–143.

Coady, D. (2006). *Conspiracy theories: The philosophical debate.* Hampshire, England: Ashgate.

Darwin, H., Neave, N., & Holmes, J. (2011). Belief in conspiracy theories. The role of paranormal belief, paranoid ideation and schizotypy. *Personality and Individual Differences, 50*, 1289–1293.

Dawkins, R. (1976). *The selfish gene.* New York: Oxford University Press.

Dillinger, J. (2004). Terrorists and witches: Popular ideas of evil in the early modern period. *History of European Ideas, 30*, 167–182.

Douglas, K. M., & Sutton, R. M. (2011). Does it take one to know one? Endorsement of conspiracy theories is influenced by personal willingness to conspire. *British Journal of Social Psychology, 50*(3), 544–552.

Drinkwater, K., Dagnall, N., & Parker, A. (2012). Reality testing, conspiracy theories, and paranormal beliefs. *Journal of Parapsychology, 76*, 57–78.

Duckitt, J. (2001). A dual-process cognitive-motivational theory of ideology and prejudice. *Advances in Experimental Social Psychology, 33*, 41–114.

Duckitt, J., & Sibley, C. G. (2007). Right-wing authoritarianism, social dominance orientation and the dimensions of generalized prejudice. *European Journal of Personality, 21*, 113–130.

Duckitt, J., & Sibley, C. G. (2010). Right-wing authoritarianism and social dominance orientation differentially moderate intergroup effects on prejudice. *European Journal of Personality, 24*, 583–601.

Duckitt, J., Wagner, C., du Plessis, I., & Birum, I. (2002). The psychological bases of ideology and prejudice: Testing a dual process model. *Journal of Personality and Social Psychology, 83*, 75–93.

Duriez, B., Van Hiel, A., & Kossowska, M. (2005). Authoritarianism and social dominance in Western and Eastern Europe: The importance of the socio-political context and of political interest and involvement. *Political Psychology, 62*, 299–321.

Fenigstein, A., & Vanable, P. A. (1992). Paranoia and self-consciousness. *Journal of Personality and Social Psychology, 62*, 129–138.

Franks, B., Bangerter, A., & Bauer, M. W. (2013). Conspiracy theories as quasi-religious mentality: An integrated account from cognitive science, social representations theory and frame theory. *Frontiers in Psychology, 4*, 424.

Funke, F. (2005). The dimensionality of right-wing authoritarianism: Lessons from the dilemma between theory and measurement. *Political Psychology, 26*, 195–218.

Furnham, A. (2013). Commercial conspiracy theories: A pilot study. *Frontiers in Psychology, 4*, 379.

Goertzel, T. (2010). Conspiracy theories in science. *EMBO Reports, 11*, 493–499.

Goertzel, T. (2012). The conspiracy meme. *Skeptical Inquirer, 35*, 28–37.

Golec de Zavala, A., & Cichocka, A. (2012). Collective narcissism and anti-Semitism in Poland. *Group Processes & Intergroup Relations, 15*, 213–229.

Groh, D. (1987). The temptation of conspiracy theory, or: Why do bad things happen to good people? Part I: Preliminary draft of a theory of conspiracy theories. In. C. F. Graumann and S. Moscovici (Eds.), *Changing conceptions of conspiracy* (pp. 1–13). New York: Springer.

Grzesiak-Feldman, M. (2007). Conspiracy thinking and state-trait anxiety in young Polish adults. *Psychological Reports, 100*, 199–202.

Grzesiak-Feldman, M. (2012). *Prawicowy autorytaryzm oraz orientacja na dominację społeczną jako predyktory różnych form myślenia spiskowego* [Predicting conspiracy beliefs: The role of right-wing authoritarianism and social dominance orientation]. *Psychologia Społeczna [Social Psychology]*, 7, 48–63.

Grzesiak-Feldman, M. (2013). The effect of high-anxiety situations on conspiracy thinking. *Current Psychology, 32*(1), 100–118.

Grzesiak-Feldman, M., & Ejsmont, A. (2008). Paranoia and conspiracy thinking of Jews, Arabs, Germans, and Russians in a Polish sample. *Psychological Reports, 102*, 884–886.

Grzesiak-Feldman, M., & Haska, A. (2012). Conspiracy theories surrounding the Polish presidential plane crash near Smolensk, Russia. Retrieved from the Deconspirator Project website: http://deconspirator.com/2012/11/22/conspiracy-theories-surrounding-the-polish-presidential-plane-crash-near-smolensk-russia/

Grzesiak-Feldman, M., & Irzycka, M. (2009). Right-wing authoritarianism and conspiracy thinking in a Polish sample. *Psychological Reports, 105*(2), 389–393.

Holm, N. (2009). Conspiracy theorizing surveillance: Considering modalities of paranoia and conspiracy in surveillance studies. *Surveillance and Society, 7*, 36–48.

Imhoff, R., & Bruder, M. (2014). Speaking (un-)truth to power: Conspiracy mentality as a generalised political attitude. *European Journal of Personality, 28*, 25–43.

Irzycka, M. (2008). *Stereotypy spiskowe i uprzedzenia gorące w zależności od środowiska szkolnego, wybranych zmiennych osobowościowych oraz eksperymentalnego wzbudzenia poczucia powszechności vs. rzadkości występowania stereotypów w społeczeństwie* [Conspiracy stereotypes and hot prejudices depending on school background, selected personality variables and the experimental arousal of the sense of commonness vs. rarity of the occurrence of the stereotypes in society]. (Unpublished master's thesis). University of Warsaw, Warsaw.

Jolley, D., & Douglas, K. M. (2014). The social consequences of conspiracism: Exposure to conspiracy theories decreases the intention to engage in politics and to reduce one's carbon footprint. *British Journal of Psychology, 105*(1), 35–56.

Kofta, M. (1995). The stereotype of a group-as-a-whole: The role of diabolic causation schema. *Polish Psychological Bulletin, 26*, 83–96.

Kofta, M. (2001). *Stereotyp spiskowy jako centralny składnik antysemityzmu* [Conspiracy stereotype as a central component of anti-Semitism]. In M. Kofta & A. Jasińska-Kania (Eds.), *Stereotypy i uprzedzenia: Uwarunkowania społeczno kulturowe* [Stereotypes and prejudice: Psychological and cultural determinants] (pp. 274–297). Warsaw: Wydawnictwo Naukowe Scholar.

Kofta, M., & Narkiewicz-Jodko, W. (2001). *Wartości a bytowość grupy, stereotypy spiskowe, i uprzedzenia* [Values, group entitativity, and conspiracy stereotypes as determinants of prejudice]. In D. Doliński & B. Weilg (Eds.), *Od myśli i uczuć do decyzji i działań* [From thoughts and feelings to decisions and action] (pp. 59–74). Warsaw: Wydawnictwo Instytutu Psychologii PAN.

Kofta, M., & Sedek, G. (1992). *Struktura poznawcza stereotypu etnicznego, bliskość wyborów parlamentarnych, a przejawy uprzedzeń antysemickich* [Cognitive structure of ethnic stereotype, election campaign, and anti-Semitism]. In Z. Chlewiński & I. Kurcz (Eds.), *Stereotypy i uprzedzenia* [Stereotypes and prejudices] (pp. 67–86). Warsaw: Wydawnictwo Instytutu Psychologii PAN.

Kofta, M., & Sedek, G. (1999). *Stereotyp duszy grupowej a postawy wobec obcych: wyniki badań sondażowych* [Group-soul stereotypes and attitudes toward "strangers": Results of survey research]. In B. Wojciszke & M. Jarymowicz (Eds.), *Psychologia rozumienia zjawisk społecznych* [Understanding societal phenomena: A psychological approach] (pp. 173–208). Warsaw: PWN.

Kofta, M., & Sedek, G. (2005). Conspiracy stereotypes of Jews during systemic transformation in Poland. *International Journal of Sociology, 35*(1), 40–64.

Korzeniowski, K. (2009). *O dwóch psychologicznych przesłankach myślenia spiskowego: Alienacja i autorytaryzm* [On two psychological determinants of conspiratorial thinking: Alienation and authoritarianism]. *Psychologia Społeczna [Social Psychology]*, *3*, 144–154.

Korzeniowski, K. (2010). *Polska paranoja polityczna. Źródła, mechanizmy i konsekwencje spiskowego myślenia o polityce* [Polish political paranoia. Sources, mechanisms and consequences of conspiratorial thinking about politics]. Warszawa: Wydawnictwo Instytutu Psychologii PAN.

Krzemiński, I. (1993). Anti-Semitism in today's Poland. *Patterns of Prejudice*, *27*, 127–135.

Leman, P. J. (2007). The born conspiracy. *New Scientist*, *195*, 35–37.

Leman, P. J., & Cinnirella, M. (2013). Beliefs in conspiracy theories and the need for cognitive closure. *Frontiers in Psychology*, *4*, 378.

Lickel, B., Hamilton, D. L., & Sherman, S. J. (2001). Elements of a lay theory of groups: Types of groups, relational styles, and the perception of group entitativity. *Personality and Social Psychology Review*, *5*, 129–140.

Lickel, B., Hamilton, D. L., Wieczorkowska, G., Lewis, A., Sherman, S. J., & Uhles, A. N. (2000). Varieties of groups and the perception of group entitativity. *Journal for Personality and Social Psychology*, *78*, 223–246.

Lindeman, M., Svedholm, A. M., Riekki, T., Raij, T., & Hari, R. (2013). Is it just a brick wall or a sign from the universe? An fMRI study of supernatural believers and skeptics. *Social Cognitive and Affective Neuroscience*, *8*, 943–949.

McFarland, S. G., Ageyev, V. S., & Abalakina-Paap, M. A. (1992). Authoritarianism in the former Soviet Union. *Journal of Personality and Social Psychology*, *63*, 1004–1010.

McHoskey, J. W. (1995). Case closed? On the John F. Kennedy assassination: Biased assimilation of evidence and attitude polarization. *Basic and Applied Social Psychology*, *17*(3), 395–409.

Moscovici, S. (1987). The conspiracy mentality. In C. F. Graumann & S. Moscovici (Eds.), *Changing conceptions of conspiracy* (pp. 151–169). New York: Springer.

Parish, J. (2001). The age of anxiety. In J. Parish & M. Parker (Eds.), *The age of anxiety: Conspiracy theory and the human sciences* (pp. 1–16). Oxford: Blackwell.

Pickett, C. L. (2001). The effects on entitativity beliefs on implicit comparisons between group members. *Personality and Social Psychology Bulletin*, *27*, 515–525.

Piłat, A. (2012). *Wiara w teorie spiskowe dotyczące katastrofy smoleńskiej a prawicowy autorytaryzm, orientacja na dominację społeczną, stereotypy spiskowe i uprzedzenia* [Conspiracy beliefs about Smolensk crash, right-wing authoritarianism, social dominance orientation, conspiracy stereotyping and prejudices] (Unpublished master's thesis). University of Warsaw, Warsaw.

Pipes, D. (1997). *Conspiracy: How the paranoid style flourishes and where it comes from*. New York: Free Press.

Pratto, F., Sidanius, J., Stallworth, L. M., & Malle, B. F. (1994). Social dominance orientation: A personality variable predicting social and political attitudes. *Journal of Personality and Social Psychology*, *67*, 741–763.

Preacher, K. J., Curran, P. J., & Bauer, D. J. (2006). Computational tools for probing interaction effects in multiple linear regression, multilevel modeling, and latent curve analysis. *Journal of Educational & Behavioral Statistics*, *31*, 437–448.

Raab, M. H., Ortlieb, S. A., Auer, N., Guthmann, K., & Carbon C. (2013). Thirty shades of truth: Conspiracy theories as stories of individuation, not of pathological delusion. *Frontiers in Psychology*, *4*, 406.

Reicher, S., & Emler, N. (1985). Delinquent behaviour and attitudes to formal authority. *British Journal of Social Psychology*, *24*, 161–168.

Sidanius, J., & Pratto, F. (1999). *Social dominance: An intergroup theory of social hierarchy and oppression.* Cambridge: Cambridge University Press.

Swami, V. (2012). Social psychological origins of conspiracy theories: The case of the Jewish conspiracy theory in Malaysia. *Frontiers in Psychology, 3,* 280.

Swami, V., Chamorro-Premuzic, T., & Furnham, A. (2010). Unanswered questions: A preliminary investigation of personality and individual difference predictors of 9/11 conspiracist beliefs. *Applied Cognitive Psychology, 24*(6), 749–761.

Swami, V., & Coles, R. (2010). The truth is out there: Belief in conspiracy theories. *Psychologist, 23,* 560–563.

Swami, V., Coles, R., Stieger, S., Pietschnig, J., Furnham, A., Rehim, S., & Voracek, M. (2011). Conspiracist ideation in Britain and Austria: Evidence of a monological belief system and associations between individual psychological differences and real-world and fictitious conspiracy theories. *British Journal of Psychology, 102*(3), 443–463.

Swami, V., & Furnham, A. (2012). Examining conspiracist beliefs about the disappearance of Amelia Earhart. *Journal of General Psychology, 139,* 244–259.

Uscinski, J. (2014). Placing conspiratorial motives in context: The role of predispositions and threat, a comment on Bost and Prunier (2013). *Psychological Reports, 115,* 1–6.

Van Hiel, A., Duriez, B., & Kossowska, M. (2006). The presence of left-wing authoritarianism in Western Europe and its relationship with conservative ideology. *Political Psychology, 27,* 769–793.

Wagner-Egger, P., & Bangerter, A. (2007). *La vérité est ailleurs: Corrélats de l'adhésion aux théories du complot* [The truth lies elsewhere: Correlates of belief in conspiracy theories]. *Revue Internationale de Psychologie Sociale-International [Review of Social Psychology], 20,* 31–61.

Więckowska, J. (2004). *Percepcja bytowości i esencjalizm kategorii społecznych a stereotypy spiskowe i uprzedzenia* [Perception of group entitativity, essentialism of social categories, stereotypes and prejudices]. In M. Kofta (Ed.), *Myślenie stereotypowe i uprzedzenia. Mechanizmy poznawcze i afektywne* [Stereotypical thinking and prejudices. Cognitive and affective mechanisms] (pp. 79–94). Warsaw: Wydawnictwo Instytuty Psychologii PAN.

Wood, M. (2013, March 14). Authoritarianism and conspiracy theories – What's the connection? Is there one? Retrieved from http://conspiracypsychology.com/2013/03/14/authoritarianism-and-conspiracy-theories-whats-the-connection-is-there-one/

Yzerbyt, V., Judd, C. M., & Corneille, O. (2004). The psychology of group perception: Perceived variability, entitativity, and essentialism. In V. Yzerbyt, C. M. Judd, & O. Corneille (Eds.), *The psychology of group perception: Perceived variability, entitativity, and essentialism* (pp. 1–24). London: Psychology Press.

Zakrisson, I. (2005). Construction of a short version of the Right-wing Authoritarianism (RWA) scale. *Personality and Individual Differences, 39,* 863–872.

Zawadzki, B., Strelau, J., Szczepaniak, P., & Śliwińska, M. (1998). *Inwentarz osobowości Inwentarz osobowości NEO-FFI Costy i McCrae* [NEO Five-Factor Inventory of Costa and McCrae]. Warsaw: Pracownia Testów Psychologicznych PTP.

7

BEYOND (RIGHT-WING) AUTHORITARIANISM

Conspiracy mentality as an incremental predictor of prejudice

Roland Imhoff

In the 2014 FIFA World Cup, Croatian defender Josip Simunic was missing in the Croatian team. The reason for that was not an injury, but a FIFA ban on him for having made a fascist salute to the Croatian fans after the final qualification match in November 2013. Simunic, of course, is not an isolated case: Time and again political commentators point to the rise of the far right within Europe – whether it is Jobbik in Hungary, the terrorist neo-Nazi underground organization NSU, or far-right parties NPD in Germany, Chrysi Avgi (Golden Dawn) in Greece, and many others. Although the right has traditionally been understood as conservative and law abiding, what many of these groups have in common is a fierce opposition to the system and those in power. In the present chapter, I will argue that part of this seeming paradox may be resolved by widening our scope on more predisposing personality variables and leaving the dominant view, whereby prejudices and other far-right attitudes are predominantly the result of an authoritarian character and a belief in inequality. Fully understanding the role of individual differences in prejudicial beliefs may require turning our attention to a previously largely neglected personality factor that might add incremental power in explaining such attitudes. Specifically, I will argue for the predictive power of a view of the world as being run by a few powerful groups via secretly made plans – a conspiracy mentality. Such a Manichean worldview may not be an exclusive feature of the far right, but nevertheless it holds the promise to reconcile the paradox of the authoritarian and, at the same time, subversive appearance of the far right.

Who is most likely to harbor prejudicial beliefs, and who is most likely to endorse negative views of minorities? The question of which personality traits and individual experiences constitute extreme right-wing and misanthropic attitudes has been at the core of social psychologists' interest since the 1940s. One of the first ambitious and comprehensive efforts to explore such personality predictors were the studies on the "authoritarian personality" (Adorno, Frenkel-Brunswik,

Levinson, & Sanford, 1950). Looking for a solution to the question of unravelling what exactly makes a fascist personality, Adorno and colleagues suggested that we understand such an authoritarian personality as a syndrome made up of nine interconnected facets. According to this influential concept, authoritarians can be described by their willingness to subordinate under existing authorities (authoritarian submission), their willingness to punish anyone who does not do so (authoritarian aggression), and a strong adherence to conventions (conventionalism), as well as by superstition; stereotypical thinking; exaggerated preoccupation with power, toughness, and sex; general destructiveness and cynicism; a strong opposition to anything tender-minded (anti-intraception); and finally, the belief that dangerous things go on in the world out there (projectivity). In general, the evidence provided by Adorno and colleagues was relatively supportive of their notion: High scores on this F scale correlated quite consistently with anti-Semitism, which was seen as the main validity criterion given to the centrality of anti-Semitic hatred in German Nazi ideology. Later studies found that, as late as 1965, former SS members still scored higher on the F scale than former Wehrmacht officers (Steiner & Fahrenberg, 1970).

Despite these findings, the authoritarian personality soon lost its appeal as an explanatory construct. First, modern social psychology believed in the power of situations much more than in personality as a latent unalterable disposition. Second, the original concept of the authoritarian personality was based on psychodynamic reasoning (originally developed in Fromm's theorizing on the sadomasochistic[1] character; Fromm, 1941), as most evident in the subcomponent of projectivity that implies that authoritarians project their own unconscious emotional impulses outwards (current psychology asserts that "people like to see themselves as similar to others, but the evidence does not show this to be a defense mechanism that helps people avoid recognizing their own bad traits," Baumeister, Dale, & Sommer, 1998, p. 1090). In scientific psychology, there was little room for such psychodynamic speculation (but see Baumeister et al., 1998, for a thorough review on the issue), so the authoritarian personality was laid aside until it was revived by Bob Altemeyer. Altemeyer (1988) suggested a revised conceptualization of authoritarianism, unburdened from psychodynamic concepts as right-wing authoritarianism (RWA), consisting only of the three core components of authoritarian submission, authoritarian aggression, and conventionalism. This reinvention can only be considered a success story, as RWA is widely accepted as one of the two strongest differential predictors of ethnocentric (or racist) attitudes (Asbrock, Sibley, & Duckitt, 2010; Whitley, 1999).

In light of this success, very few have asked whether the reduction down to RWA might have come with a cost, whether certain aspects included in the original conceptualization were desperately missing from the new one. In particular, the projectivity subscale (with items worded like "Most people don't realize how much our lives are controlled by plots hatched in secret places") captured what I call a conspiracy mentality, the idea that the world is a dangerous place, full of sinister-minded powerful groups that hatch plots against one's own welfare in secret. Although there is little empirical evidence supporting the original notion that the reason for this mentality is an outward projection of one's own impulses to act in such a way (but see Douglas & Sutton, 2011, for the role of personal willingness to conspire on an endorsement of conspiracy theories), the projectivity subscale grasped an important aspect of Manichaean thinking that is no longer included in modern RWA conceptions. I argue that such a conspiracy-laden worldview is precisely the dominant feature of some of the current extreme right-wing rhetoric that construes an ultranationalist identity as a subversive and antiestablishment subculture. Such a phenomenon is difficult to reconcile with the view of the extreme right as (orthodox) authoritarians who predominantly follow traditions and subordinate to the state.

Instead of this, right-wing extremists complain about being victimized by a conspiracy against the "White race" that installs multiculturalism to dismantle cohesive and patriotic bonds – plotted by allegedly evil forces sometimes described as Jews (as in the conspiracy about Zionist Occupied Governments) or as a less-specified secret power elite (as in the conspiracy about a New World Order). The deplorable state of the world is blamed on sinister forces that act behind the curtain and exert control over the institutions that ostensibly rule the world, such as the UN, the World Bank, or the G8. This conception brings the defenders of the White nation in opposition to power, acting in resistance to the overwhelming enemy. Such a conspiracy also forms the nucleus of modern anti-Semitic ideology: the protocols of the elders of Zion. From their very first appearance in Russian czardom in 1903, via German National Socialism, to the Hamas Charter in 1988, these fully fictional "protocols" have served as evidence for a Jewish conspiracy and as a legitimation for one's own anti-Semitism (Benz, 2011). In the book, a wide array of real existing phenomena (e.g., economic crises, war, national debt, and abolishment of aristocratic privileges) are portrayed as intentional doings of the "elderly" in order to disintegrate organically grown communities and reach world domination. The projectivity scale by Adorno and colleagues tapped exactly into such a thinking style of attributing visible phenomena to the hidden intentions of sinister forces. This facet of thinking has been lost in the new conception of RWA. I thus want to discuss what I call conspiracy mentality and specifically its relation to extreme right-wing worldviews.

Conspiracy mentality and political attitudes

The term conspiracy mentality (Moscovici, 1987) is best summarized in the words of Karl Popper (1966) as "a view that an explanation of a social phenomenon consists in the discovery of the men or groups who are interested in the occurrence of this phenomenon . . . and who have planned and conspired to bring it about" (p. 295), further characterized as a "mistaken theory that, whatever happens in society – especially happenings such as war, unemployment, poverty, shortages, which people as a rule dislike – is the result of direct design by some powerful individuals and groups" (Popper, 1966, p. 295). Conspiracy mentality thus describes the generalized attitude that some sinister-minded conspirators determine the fate of the world, relatively irrespective of the concrete example. As the notion of a mentality already suggests, it is not so much the specific content of a given conspiracy theory that determines an individual's endorsement of this belief, but rather one's general tendency to either endorse conspiracy beliefs or not.

In support of such a generalized tendency to either agree or disagree with conspiracy theories, we were able to show that a wide range of beliefs in conspiracies – ranging from a conspiracy to cover the truth behind alien landings or the assassination of celebrities like JFK and Princess Diana to secret plots to suppress technological and medical progress – were all highly intercorrelated and loaded on only one factor in three different languages (German, Turkish, English; total $N = 7,673$; Bruder, Haffke, Neave, Nouripanah, & Imhoff, 2013). As an illustration, agreement with the statement "I think the international banking system is controlled by Jews" was positively and significantly correlated with every single other item, mean $r = .42$. Further sharpening the idea that individuals consistently agree with (almost) any conspiracy theory or not, recent research findings suggest that the endorsement of logically mutually exclusive conspiracy theories is positively correlated (Wood, Douglas, & Sutton, 2012). Respondents who saw it as plausible that Princess Diana fell victim to an assassination plot also gave greater credibility to the notion that she faked her own death and was still alive. Likewise, in a second study, participants who were convinced that Osama Bin Laden was already dead before his hideout was raided by U.S. forces also believed that he was still alive years later, when the study was carried out.

Based on this remarkable consistency in conspiracy beliefs, the development of a generic scale tapping into conspiracy mentality without mentioning any concrete groups or events (Imhoff & Bruder, 2014) allows an identification of the connection between the general propensity to endorse conspiracy theories and fragments of right-wing ideology. Anti-Semitism serves as a case in point here, as it can be shown that it is not only part and parcel of the anti-Semitic stereotype that Jews operate on the basis of sinister plots hatched in secret (Kofta & Sedek, 2005), but that there exists an intrinsic affinity between conspirational thinking and anti-Semitic ideology. Even if anti-Semitism is measured without any reference to a Jewish conspiracy and conspiracy mentality is measured without any reference to Jews, the two show a substantial positive correlation (Imhoff & Bruder, 2014, Study 2).

Another benefit of this approach to a generic (not content-contaminated) conspiracy mentality lies in the possibility of testing the role of this generalized attitude as an explanatory nexus between manifestations of beliefs in sinister, albeit powerful, others. Many scholars (e.g., Bergmann & Wetzel, 2003; Horkheimer & Adorno, 1969; Postone, 1986) have pointed to the concurrence of anti-Semitic ideology and personalized anticapitalism, also evident in National Socialist rhetoric of the money grubbing (*raffend*) Jewish capital that was seen as the opposite of the productive (*schaffend*) German capital. In fact, anticapitalist rhetoric that does not target the systemic and structural core of the capitalist economy but tries to blame a few bad apples of sinister and morally corrupt bankers, lobbyists, or brokers has been called structurally anti-Semitic in German political discourse (Brumlik, Kiesel, & Reisch, 1991). One infamous incident was during an interview with then head of the German Social Democratic Party, Franz Münterfering, in 2005, in which he used an animal analogy to describe investment bankers: "Some investors don't waste a thought on the people whose jobs they destroy. They remain anonymous and faceless, raiding companies like a cloud of locusts: grazing them and leaving them deserted." This led to a public debate, and many saw the metaphor of a plague in close relation to Nazi rhetoric and its goals to exterminate such plagues.

An empirical approach to whether such a form of personalized anticapitalism that blames the existing downsides of a capitalist economy on a few mean-intending others does indeed have an affinity to anti-Semitic ideology would be to, as a first step, look at the correlation between the two. A previously unpublished study with 60 students on anti-Semitism (Imhoff, 2010) and personalized anticapitalism (Imhoff & Bruder, 2014; items included the direct quote of Franz Münterfering cited above and statements like, "Everyone in this world would be better off if there were fewer international financial speculators" or "As a result of their greed, CEOs have lost all their morals") showed a positive correlation of $r = .34$, $p < .01$. More central to the current argument, however, is our rationale that this superficial affinity may be due to the fact that both ideologies represent manifestation of a Manichaean worldview of a few evil powerful others (Jews, bankers) controlling the world (i.e., conspiracy mentality). In line with this assumption, conspiracy mentality showed a positive correlation with anti-Semitism, $r = .52$, $p < .01$, and personalized anticapitalism, $r = .56$, $p < .01$, and the correlation between these two was reduced to nonsignificance when controlling for conspiracy mentality, $r_p = .07$, $p > .05$.[2] I thus propose that personalized anticapitalism and anti-Semitism co-occur because they are both grounded in a worldview of a few powerful people hatching plots in secret.

A more systematic approach to the manifestation of conspiracy mentality as a generalized political attitude was provided by Imhoff and Bruder (2014). They specifically argued that conspiracy mentality entails a generalized distrust against groups that are seen as powerful. This is in contrast to the other two well-established generalized political attitudes: RWA and social dominance orientation (SDO; Pratto, Sidanius, Stallworth, & Malle, 1994). Authoritarianism is a generalized negative attitude towards groups or individuals seen as deviant or disruptive to the social order, whereas SDO entails a devaluation of groups or individuals perceived as low in the social hierarchy, presumably as a system-justifying ideology. In line with these different conceptualizations, conspiracy mentality only predicted prejudices against groups perceived as powerful (i.e., Americans, capitalists), whereas RWA and SDO both (incrementally) predicted prejudice against traditional targets of such discriminatory attitudes (i.e., Muslims, "Gypsies"). Note that anti-Semitism served a special role here because Jews are often seen as deviant and low status, but also – due to their scheming – as powerful. Anti-Semitism was thus predicted by all three generalized political attitudes and all three added a unique contribution. As an even clearer indication, two further studies tapped into intraindividual associations between power and threat across 32 social groups. Participants high in conspiracy mentality associated high power with greater threat, whereas participants high in RWA and participants high in SDO associated powerless groups with greater threat.

How is this conspiracy mentality related to extreme right-wing attitudes? Although the forms of prejudice cited above are clearly part and parcel of right-wing ideologies, it could be argued that the reliance on student samples poses a problem. For most prejudice scales, we have a restricted range in these samples in the sense that university students predominantly try to present themselves as unprejudiced, and therefore almost only differ in their degree of disagreement (e.g., less than 20% of respondents scored on the complete upper half of a scale tapping into prejudice against Turks, Banse & Gawronski, 2003; highly similar distributions can be observed for prejudices against Romani people and Jews, Imhoff & Bruder, 2014). Treating a less-pronounced disagreement as fully equivalent to an actual endorsement of an attitude may, however, constitute an unwarranted extrapolation. We therefore included a short version of the conspiracy mentality scale in a nationally representative survey of the German population (for the item wording and psychometric properties of the scale, see Imhoff, 2013a). In such samples, the actual frequency of extreme right-wing participants can be assumed to be large enough to make an informative statement.[3] Also, representative sampling allows for estimating the distribution of conspiracy mentality in the larger population. The scale was thus included in the 2012 version of the "Mitte" studies, a biannual study on extreme right-wing attitudes in the German population published by the Friedrich-Ebert-Foundation (the full questionnaire used in the studies and all results are described in more detail in Decker, Brähler, & Kiess, 2012).

The 5-item scale (2 items reverse-coded) proved to be sufficiently reliable and almost perfectly normally distributed around the scale midpoint in the general population.[4]

To answer the question of whether conspiracy mentality is associated with extreme right-wing ideology and prejudices, there are several possible avenues for empirical investigation. One could be to test the potency of conspiracy mentality in predicting endorsement of prejudice above and beyond established predictors of prejudice. Typically, RWA and SDO are regarded as the best-established predictors of prejudice, with no other psychological variable explaining any incremental variance (Asbrock et al., 2010; but see Imhoff & Bruder, 2014). In the present study, only a measure of RWA was included for reasons of succinctness. It consisted of 4 items tapping into authoritarian submission and aggression (important to show obedience towards authorities, tougher stand against criminality and sexual immorality, gratitude for leaders, and children should be obedient to their parents; $\alpha = .76$).[5] Social identity theory (Tajfel & Turner, 1986; Turner, Hogg, Oakes, Reicher, & Wetherell, 1987) posits that an identification with and glorification of one's own group often comes at the cost of derogating out-groups. As the glorification of the in-group and agitation against (minority) out-groups is one of the core elements of extreme right-wing ideology, national identification was included as an additional predictor. National identification was assessed with a scale of increasingly over-lapping circles, with the instruction to estimate one's closeness with the group of Germans (Schubert & Otten, 2002).

The criteria were different fragments or manifestations of right-wing ideol-ogy. As a specificity of the German context, any extreme form of nationalism has to take the era of National Socialism somehow into account. Although there exists a neo-Nazi subculture that openly celebrates Nazi Germany, it is much more common to trivialize the Nazi crimes by referring to the supposedly exaggerated insistence on commemorating Nazi evil or by referring to the fact that there were also positive aspects about National Socialism (*trivialization of National Socialism*; for a discussion of current Germans' relation to National Socialism, see Frei, 2005). Other aspects that are less specific to the German context are the active *support for an authoritarian dictatorship*, *social Darwinism* (insistence of the difference between valuable and worthless beings and survival of the toughest), and the glorification of and belief in the superiority of one's own nation (*chauvinism*). Finally, three different forms of out-group derogation against Jews (e.g., "Jews use more decep-tion than others," "Jews are peculiar and don't suit us"; *anti-Semitism*), foreign-ers in general (e.g., "Foreigners exploit our welfare system," "Germany is being swamped with foreigners"; *xenophobia*), and Muslims (*Islamoprejudice*; Imhoff & Recker, 2012; Imhoff, 2013b; $\alpha = .88$) were added as criteria. As an analytic strat-egy, these fragments of right-wing ideology were simultaneously regressed on RWA and national identification (Step 1) before it was tested whether the inclu-sion of conspiracy mentality added incremental validity in explaining variance (Step 2).

As can be seen from Table 7.1, RWA was indeed a potent predictor of all chosen fragments of right-wing ideology. This is well in line with the original concept of authoritarianism, a plethora of research on the issue, and of course the apparent semantic overlap in some cases (e.g., between RWA and the support for an authori-tarian dictatorship). National identification produced a more interesting pattern, as it was indeed (relatively weakly) related to in-group glorification (chauvinism) and out-group derogation (xenophobia, Islamoprejudice), but showed a mark-edly differing relation to all ideological fragments even only remotely related to National Socialism. Feeling closely connected to other Germans was related to less agreement with the central aspect of the Nazi ideology (social Darwinism, anti-Semitism,[6] authoritarian dictatorship) and less trivialization of the era of National Socialism. This finding is not only well reconcilable with the theoretically mean-ingful differentiation between in-group glorification and (less defensive) in-group attachment (e.g., Golec de Zavala, Cichocka, & Bilewicz, 2013; Roccas, Klar, & Liviatan, 2006), but also resonated with Theodor W. Adorno's (1955) dictum that a specific attachment to and identification with Germany would entail taking responsibility for the Nazi history and coming to terms with it.

TABLE 7.1 Fragments of right-wing ideology as a function of right-wing authoritarianism, national identification, and conspiracy mentality in a nationally representative sample of Germans.

	Trivialization of National Socialism		Support for Authoritarian Dictatorship		Social Darwinism		Chauvinism		Anti-Semitism		Xenophobia		Islamoprejudice	
	ΔR^2	β	ΔR^2	β	ΔR^2	β	ΔR^2	β	ΔR^2	β	ΔR^2	β	ΔR^2	β
Step 1	.16**		.25**		.23**		.16**		.14**		.15**		.10**	
Right-Wing Authoritarianism		.41**		.50**		.48**		.36**		.38**		.35**		.27**
National Identification		−.07**		−.07**		−.05**		.12**		−.05*		.14**		.13**
Step 2	.02**		.03**		.05**		.09**		.12**		.08**		.05**	
Right-Wing Authoritarianism		.39**		.47**		.45**		.32**		.32**		.30**		.24**
National Identification		−.06**		−.07**		−.04*		.13**		−.04*		.15**		.14**
Conspiracy Mentality		.14**		.16**		.23**		.30**		.35**		.29**		.22**
Total R^2			.27**		.28**		.24**		.26**		.23**		.15**		
n	2493		2494		2493		2492		2489		2493		2485	

Note: Exact numbers may differ slightly from Imhoff and Decker (2013), as their regressions were computed only for participants for whom all scales were present (equal N for all criteria)

** $p < .01$,

* $p < .05$

More central to the current chapter, however, is the question of whether conspiracy mentality adds any incremental predictive power in explaining right-wing ideology fragments. Including conspiracy mentality as a predictor led to a significant increase in explained variance in each and every case (Table 7.1), suggesting that it may indeed form a previously (or intermittently) overlooked factor in extreme right-wing ideology. Painting the world as being ruled by a few evil-minded and powerful groups forms an integral part of – particularly subcultural – right-wing rhetoric. In such a delusional worldview, German superiority has to be actively defended against the sinister plan of the evil-minded, almost almighty, enemy that tried to undermine German purity and dominance by means of infiltrating the country with foreigners and using the memory of National Socialism to suppress legitimate German national pride.

Conspiracy mentality – an exclusive phenomenon of the extreme right?

With the analyses provided above, I aimed to demonstrate that a conspirational belief system constitutes a personal vulnerability to adapt right-wing ideology (although empirical support for any causal direction is missing). Does this, however, suggest that conspiracy mentality is an exclusive phenomenon of the extreme right? Already at the level of the content of most popular conspiracy theories, such an assumption seems implausible. Whereas beliefs in Jewish conspiracies or in an almighty and supposedly overly liberal surveillance state are well compatible with right-wing ideology, other conspiracy theories bear less of a right-wing connotation. For instance, several conspiracy theories focus on the extent to which American government institutions conspired to keep African American people down (e.g., Crocker, Luthanen, Broadnax, & Blaine, 1999). The abovementioned oversimplified approach to the downsides of a capitalist economy by blaming it on evil-minded individuals is not only to be found in neo-Nazi agitation, but also is part and parcel of many left-wing activist groups' rhetoric. As a different approach to the question of the role of conspiracy beliefs in political ideologies, I thus explored the distribution of conspiracy mentality across the political spectrum. Specifically, I explored the average extent of conspiracy mentality and RWA as a function of political party leaning ("Who would you vote for if parliamentary elections were held next Sunday?") (see Figure 7.1).

In line with its characterization as *right-wing* authoritarianism, RWA shows a linear increase from left to right of the political spectrum (lower dotted line; linear contrast: $t(1649) = 4.50, p < .001$).[7] Voters of parties that are generally considered more right-wing also have higher scores on RWA. The pattern looks markedly different, however, for conspiracy mentality. Clearly, there exists no linear relation between political affiliation and conspiracy mentality (upper dotted line, linear contrast: $t(1645) = 1.06, p = .29$). Instead, supporters of the extreme right, as well as voters of rather left-wing parties, show the strongest endorsement of the conspiracy worldview, resulting in a curvilinear relation (continuous line; quadratic

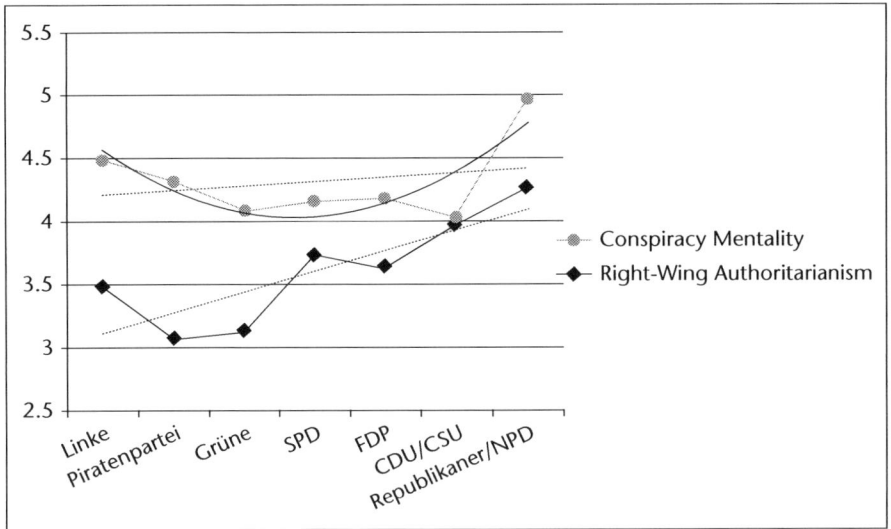

FIGURE 7.1 Conspiracy mentality and right–wing authoritarianism as a function of preference for political party (voting intentions if elections were next Sunday). Due to small absolute numbers, Republikaner and NPD were combined into one category. Dotted lines represent linear trends; the straight line represents a quadratic trend.

contrast: $t(1645) = 3.79$, $p < .001$). As puzzling as this result seems to be at first sight, a highly similar finding has been reported previously (Inglehart, 1987). As an important caveat, this is not meant to abet an oversimplified version of the theory of totalitarianism, whereby left and right essentially are totalitarian twins of the same make. Clearly, the left and the right differ on many crucial aspects (e.g., their general take on equality, civil liberties, acceptance of difference), but they seem to share a tendency to see the world's fate in the hand of a few powerful people. This fact and the intrinsic relation between conspiracy mentality and anti-Semitism might constitute one explanation for the often heralded anti-Semitism on the left (Brumlik et al., 1991; Haury, 2002).

Potentially, it is not so much the exact political standpoint but the distance to power that explains this pattern. Voters of the ruling party might see much less necessity to develop alternative theories about how important decisions are being made than individuals who repeatedly experience that their own political ideas are not realized. Voters on the margins of the political spectrum might therefore perceive their own position as one of low power, making it tempting to blame one's powerless position on the system of conspiracies (rather than oneself), as this is more advantageous for both personal and collective self-esteem (Crocker et al., 1999). An equally plausible explanation as to why the political margin shows greater conspiracy mentality is that there are predisposing factors that make it not only more likely to endorse conspiracy ideas but also to vote for marginal parties. One candidate of such a predisposing factor might be the abovementioned feeling of lacking power and control.

Lack of control and conspiracy mentality

What predisposes individuals to construe explanations of most happenings in the world as the result of the direct design of mean-intending people, and what is functional about adopting conspiracy theories? At first sight, such conspiracy theories seem to provide an easy answer to understand complex world events (Groh, 1987), but more often than not, they build up to immensely complicated theories, by far outperforming the complexity of attributing events to chance or bad luck. In light of this, it does not seem likely that conspiracy theories are merely mental shortcuts to generate maximally simple answers (note also the finding that conspiracy mentality is entirely unrelated to individuals' need for cognitive closure, the desire to reach easy and conclusive answers; Imhoff & Bruder, 2014). So far, the most prominently discussed factor in predisposing conspiracy theory endorsement is a perceived lack of control.

Humans are assumed to have an intrinsic motivation to perceive their fate and environment as controllable, and the more this motivation is deprived, the more eager they are to engage in compensatory acts to regain a sense of control. Based on this basic premise, it has been argued that situations in which an individual feels powerless and at the mercy of uncontrollable happenings feel more controllable to the extent that they are not attributed to pure chance but the secret plotting of other humans. In a way, the individual engages in an act of empowerment because he or she saw through the conspiracy and has identified the enemy. Although very little evidence exists for this presumed palliative function of endorsing conspiracies, the link between control deprivation and conspiracy thinking seems to be robustly established.

In a pioneering study, Whitson and Galinsky (2008) asked participants to either remember a threatening situation in which they had no control or to remember a threatening situation in which they had control. Afterwards they were presented with two fictitious narratives that described how something aversive happened to a main character (e.g., not being promoted at work) and were asked to indicate to what extent they thought this was the result of a secret conspiracy. In line with the hypotheses, attribution to conspiracies was greater for participants who had remembered a situation in which they had no control. In a less hypothetical and more realistic setting, Sullivan, Landau, and Rothschild (2010) asked participants to estimate the likelihood that their preferred candidate for an election to senate would become the victim of a conspiracy of the opposing candidate's party (e.g., manipulation of electronic ballots). Again, the experimentally induced subjective lack of control increased the rated likelihood of such conspiracies to have taken place.

In my own research, I have tested the idea that such experimentally induced lack of control may even (temporarily) increase the generalized tendency to endorse conspiracies (in contrast to the endorsement of one specific conspiracy theory). Participants completed a concept identification task in which they had to identify a concept that the computer selected. In each trial a pair of two symbols was provided, out of which only one concept was realized. Across several trials, participants could determine the concept through the feedback provided by the computer (correct or incorrect) to the options they chose (Whitson & Galinsky, 2008; originally introduced by Pittman & Pittman, 1979). To deprive feelings of control in the experimental condition, the feedback provided was fully random and noncontingent on participants' response, whereas the control condition received no feedback. Although the results showed a descriptive trend in the expected direction with higher scores in conspiracy mentality for the control deprivation condition ($M = 4.08$, $SD = 1.00$) than the condition with no feedback ($M = 3.89$, $SD = 0.87$), this difference was very small, Cohen's $d = 0.20$, and far from statistical significance, $t < 1$, given the relatively small sample size ($N = 44$).

For a second attempt, I relied on the manipulation introduced by Sullivan and colleagues (2010), in which participants either had to report how much control they have over events over which one typically has at least some degree of control (e.g., how much TV one watches, who one chooses as a date; *no control threat*) or events over which one typically has no control (e.g., whether one is exposed to a disease, whether family members suffer; *control threat*). Again, there was a descriptive increase in conspiracy mentality after control threat, $M = 4.55$, $SD = 1.05$, compared to no control threat, $M = 4.32$, $SD = 1.12$. Nevertheless, the much larger sample, $N = 168$, still did not provide enough statistical power to decide that this modest difference, Cohen's $d = 0.21$, was statistically different from zero, $t(166) = 1.35$, $p = .18$. This is even less surprising when one realizes that the manipulation check (the last item of the questions about control read, "In general, how much control do you feel you have over what happens in your life?") produced absolutely no difference between the control threat, $M = 3.38$, $SD = 0.77$, and the no threat, $M = 3.38$, $SD = 0.78$, condition, $t < 1$.

As a last attempt, I resorted to an even stronger, and arguably ecologically more valid, manipulation. Participants played a stock market game (adapted from Bröder, 2000) in which they could invest 1,000 virtual currency units to buy shares of different companies in 25 consecutive rounds. Importantly, a raffle was announced whereby three participants would be randomly determined who could exchange their virtual currency at the end of the experiment for real money with an exchange rate of 500:1 (resulting in a maximum payoff of €20). Before each decision, participants could buy cues on each company (for 2% of the benefit they would receive in that round) that provided information about the companies (e.g., recent developments of sales volume, profit, and dividends). Whereas in the control condition the cues differed in their validity but linearly predicted the economic development (with a minor random factor included in the calculation), in the experimental condition, the development of the share was completely noncontingent on the presented cues. Participants thus had absolutely no control over their (potentially very real) financial outcome. Despite this arguably stronger manipulation, I again did not observe an increase in conspiracy mentality after exposing participants to an uncontrollable and random environment. In fact, there were even descriptively lower scores in the experimental, $M = 3.04$, $SD = 0.59$, than in the control condition, $M = 3.16$, $SD = 0.57$, $t < 1$.

Based on these file drawer studies, it thus seems safe to conclude that experimental manipulations of control deprivation do not reliably increase conspiracy mentality. Conspiracy mentality (in contrast to spontaneous endorsement of specific conspiracy theories; Whitson & Galinsky, 2008; Sullivan et al., 2010) thus can be regarded as a relatively robust interindividual difference, which is also corroborated by its high retest reliability (Imhoff & Bruder, 2014). Given this, it is still conceivable that repeated and outlasting experiences of lacking control over one's own fate may be responsible for chronic differences in the extent of conspiracy thinking. To entertain this possibility, I explored the relation between conspiracy mentality and indicators of lack of control in one's daily life.

One potential source of deprived feelings of control is an unstable working life in the form of precarious working conditions or phases of unemployment. Among all participants who ever were unemployed in their previous professional life, the duration of this unemployment phase was (weakly) positively correlated with conspiracy mentality, $r = .09$, $p = .02$. Thus, individuals who have longer experiences with a phase in life during which they could not find a job again and, therefore, likely experienced a lack of control at least over their work life, were generally more likely to exhibit greater degrees of conspiracy mentality. For those in the workforce, the feeling of being treated unfairly at work (also indicating a lack over control over one's outcomes) was also a positive predictor of conspiracy mentality, $r = .08$, $p < .001$. Directly comparing individuals with a structurally greater level of security and control (permanent work contract) with less secure (i.e., fixed-term contracts) or no work contract revealed a similar pattern: A secure job was associated with the lowest levels of conspiracy mentality, $M = 4.07$, $SD = 1.15$, followed by fixed-term contracts, $M = 4.30$, $SD = 1.31$, and unemployed individuals, $M = 4.34$, $SD = 1.41$, $F(2, 1162) = 3.47$, $p = .03$. Although each single association of conspiracy mentality with insecure working conditions was relatively small, their combination consistently suggests that a precarious and insecure professional life may be a risk factor for developing conspirational worldviews.

Feelings of control deprivation, however, cannot only be inferred indirectly from objective criteria like the professional situation. Potentially more relevant, individuals have subjective feelings of uncertainty and control deprivation they can report. Based on Paulhus's (1983) conception of different spheres of control, participants were asked to indicate the extent to which they perceived to have or lack political control (e.g., "People like me have no influence on what the government does"). Perceiving such a lack of political control was associated with conspiracy mentality, $r = .13$, $p < .001$. This may not seem very surprising and invite speculation about a reverse causal order: If one is convinced that political decisions are the results of plots hatched in secret, it is only logical to conclude that one has no influence over them. Yet, lack of control outside of the political sphere exhibited a correlation of identical magnitude: Lack of interpersonal control (e.g., "In my immediate surroundings, there are not enough people who take me as I am") showed the same correlation with conspiracy mentality, $r = .13$, $p < .001$.

As a last pathway to individuals' feelings of insecurity and lack of control over one's outcomes, I choose subjective financial prospects. To the extent that one has the feeling that one will be worse off financially in the future, one experiences low control over this outcome and only sees few opportunities to create a better one. In line with this idea, conspiracy mentality showed a significant negative correlation with respondents' estimation of their own, $r = -.19$, $p < .001$, or Germany's, $r = -.23$, $p < .001$, financial situation one year from now. Thus, perceiving little control in creating an (economically) brighter future either as an individual or collectively was systematically related to the extent to blame powerful conspirators for world happenings (and likely this economic hardship).

Speaking (un)truth to power – conspiracy mentality and political engagement

One of the downsides of the dominant view of authoritarianism as the central personality dimension predicting extreme right-wing attitudes is that this creates an apparent contradiction. The subcultural image and behavior of neo-Nazis and their rhetoric to fight the "system" do not fit well with the RWA core components. The concept of RWA and its focus on authoritarian submission and conventionalism can explain the adherence to alleged cultural traditions and nostalgic ideas about ethnically homogeneous societies. Regarding the political goals of extreme right-wing movements, however, one would have to expect that they comply with the government (authoritarian submission) in order to preserve the status quo (conventionalism). Quite obviously, this is not the case for most extreme right-wing groups. At least in Germany, neo-Nazi groups openly act against the (supposedly corrupt) state, demanding a "national revolution" and a violent overthrow of the system.[8] This subversive opposition to the status quo stands in marked contrast to authoritarian ideas but is part and parcel of conspiracy mentality. Because conspiracy mentality can be characterized as a generalized distrust against those in power (Imhoff & Bruder, 2014), it predisposes individuals to challenge the status quo and precisely those sinister forces who hold power.

We have no data on right-wing activism specifically but have data that support the general idea that conspiracy mentality brings one in opposition to power and the status quo. In a study conducted in the aftermath of the Fukushima Daiichi nuclear disaster following an earthquake and a tsunami in March 2011, we asked participants about their attitude towards nuclear power and their willingness to engage in individual (change to eco-friendly power supplier), normative collective (sign a petition), or nonnormative collective (engage in civil disobedience by blocking a transport of nuclear waste) antinuclear actions (Imhoff & Bruder, 2014, Study 5). Results consistently showed for all three forms of political engagement a positive relation with conspiracy mentality and a negative prediction by RWA.

The present national representative sample offered an opportunity to bolster this finding with a larger and more diverse sample. Participants indicated what kind of action they would take in order to achieve their political goals. In concordance with the previously reported results, the extent to which participants indicated a willingness to take political action was positively related to conspiracy mentality, $\beta = .05$, $p = .02$, but negatively related to RWA, $\beta = -.10$, $p < .001$. In contrast to the cited earlier findings, this was particularly true for normative actions but not for nonnormative or even illegal actions. As an additional caveat, the relation is significantly different from zero but very small, suggesting that there exist a plethora of unidentified other predictors and moderating factors. Nevertheless, two large-scale studies provided consistent support for the idea that conspiracy mentality and RWA are inversely related to the readiness to alter the status quo by taking political action.

At first sight, this seems to be at odds with recent findings that showed that exposure to conspiracy theories led to feelings of powerlessness and thereby to a reduced willingness to engage politically (Jolley & Douglas, 2014). At closer inspection, however, there is a number of important differences between the two approaches that could be responsible for this difference, and future research could take these as a starting point to further elucidate the role of conspirational thinking in political activism. First, I measured (relatively stable) convictions that the world is ruled by conspiracies, whereas Jolley and Douglas (2014) confronted participants with a text including insinuations to potential conspiracy actions. Although participants showed greater endorsement of conspiracy beliefs in a manipulation check, it seems premature to equate this with a lasting interpretational bias of the world and the happenings therein. As a second difference, at least in Study 1, Jolley and Douglas operationalized political engagement as participants' "intended behaviors over the next 12 months (e.g., 'Will you vote in the next election'; 'Do you intend to contribute money to a candidate, a political party, or any organization that supports candidates?')" (p. 39f). Thus, political engagement was defined as participation in a parliamentary system that was earlier described as being corruptly involved in assassinations and terrorist attacks. In contrast, some of the behaviors we looked at were clearly extraparliamentary. Although Jolley and Douglas use a less institutionally involved dependent variable (personal reduction of carbon footprint) in Study 2, here the definition of political engagement might be too narrow. Reading (and, according to the manipulation check, believing) that climate change is a hoax will clearly lower the willingness to reduce carbon footprints. To tap into the motivating power of conspiracy ideas, it might have been more useful to target forms of political engagement that have the potential to undermine the influence of the conspirators (e.g., protesting against the UN climate summit) rather than to follow their lies. Nevertheless, in light of the existing inconsistency, introducing the target of political engagement as a moderating variable might constitute a fruitful avenue to reconcile the seemingly contradictory findings.

Summary

People differ in the degree to which they believe the world to be controlled by powerful groups that determine our mutual fate far away from public transparency, let alone control. I have argued and showed that such a worldview may constitute a long-overlooked incremental personality variable to account for prejudiced and other far-right attitudes. Despite this strong relation, conspiracy mentality is not a unique feature of the far right but a normally distributed interindividual difference variable that may express itself differently in other subcultures. Although it is relatively robust over time and hardly susceptible to experimental manipulations of control deprivation, it shows consistently stronger in individuals with structurally reduced control in their work life, their financial prospects, or their interpersonal relations. Whether and to what extent conspiracy thinking motivates or demotivates action to alter the status quo is currently open to debate in light of contradictory findings.

Future research may dig deeper into the motivational or cognitive underpinnings of conspiracy thinking. Are conspiracies just the results of an increased willingness to detect agency and intentionality (see Imhoff & Bruder, 2014) or do they follow from the more general tendency to interpret (more or less random) co-occurrences as causally connected? Are conspiracy theories indeed endorsed to gain a sense of control and if so, is that a successful strategy? Are there identifiable subtypes of supporters of conspiracy belief than can be bifurcated in simplifiers (who reduce complexity of real events by blaming one responsible agent) and complicators (who increase complexity by creating intertwined narratives of how things came about by the evil intentions of conspirators instead of simply attributing it to chance or randomness)? These and many other questions guarantee that the study of conspirational thinking (in relation to right-wing extremism and beyond that) will supply a plethora of fascinating questions for the near and not so near future.

Author note

Roland Imhoff, Faculty of Human Sciences, University of Cologne. This chapter is largely based on analyses and arguments previously outlined in the German language chapter by Imhoff and Decker (2013). Correspondence related to this chapter should be addressed to Roland Imhoff, Richard-Strauss-Str. 2, 50931 Köln, Germany. E-mail: rimhoff@uni-koeln.de

Notes

1 Fromm does not understand sadomasochism in any sexual sense but in relation to the admiration of authority and the joy of subordinating (masochism), as well as the will to exert authority (sadism).
2 In the same dataset, conspiracy mentality also significantly correlated with anti-Zionism and anti-Americanism, the latter having been replicated in a larger dataset (Imhoff & Bruder, 2014).
3 Depending on the criterion – votes for extreme parties or specific attitudes – the frequency of right-wing extremists is estimated to lie between 1% and 20%. Internal consistency was Cronbach's $\alpha = .74$ in the sample of respondents who completed at least 4 items ($n = 2,502$ out of a total $N = 2,510$; 1,167 men, 1,335 women; mean age of 49.4 years,

SD = 18.0). A visual inspection of the histogram, normal Q-Q plot, and boxplot suggested normal distribution

4 Around a mean value of M = 4.17, SD = 1.19 (scale midpoint 4), with a skewness of −0.073 (SE = 0.049) and a kurtosis of −0.019 (SE = 0.098). Note that the significant Shapiro-Wilk test, p < .001, is nondiagnostic as it is biased for significance in large samples (Royston, 1982).

5 Unlike the conspiracy mentality scale, the distribution of scores on this measure deviated from normality, mostly due to a relatively large frequency of extremely nonauthoritarian responses and a resulting left skewness.

6 The study also included a short form (Imhoff, 2013c) of an anti-Semitism scale (Imhoff & Banse, 2009; Imhoff, 2010) designed to differentiate between primary (authentic) anti-Semitism and secondary anti-Semitism (blaming Jews for still bringing up the Nazi past). If this scale was used as a criterion, it became apparent that national identification was associated with (descriptively) less primary anti-Semitism but pronouncedly more secondary anti-Semitism.

7 It has been criticized by some scholars that the very conception of RWA is problematic, as the core psychological elements of fiercely defending in-group norms and punishing deviants could be found in any political reference group (e.g., the Green party; Stellmacher & Petzel, 2005). For the current case, however, the politically laden phrasing of the RWA scale (denying equal rights to women and gay men), makes it clear that such an ideological stand is more easily reconcilable without a political right leaning in the context of the current German society.

8 On an ideological level, this of course might be restricted to authorities that are seen as weak and therefore do not justify one's submission under their authority. To the extent that democratic governments are seen as weak, they may face a hard time in providing a cohesive power for right-wing movements. It is unclear, however, whether followers of strong, authoritarian, and racist governments would be of the same psychological make as proponents of such a system in the current democratic system. It is conceivable that followers of the most authoritarian and brutal regimes could indeed be better characterized by the banality of their evil (Arendt, 1963) than their similarity to extreme right-wing groups in current Western societies. Likewise, the most outspoken proponents of such totalitarian systems might take an equally deviant position in such a society as they do today. This of course is as equally speculative as the opposite idea that neo-Nazis would follow authoritarian ideals of conventionalism and authoritarian submission if only the surrounding system was the right one.

References

Adorno, T. W. (1955). Schuld und Abwehr. In F. Pollock (Ed.), *Gruppenexperiment* (pp. 278–428). Frankfurt: Europäische Verlagsanstalt.

Adorno, T. W., Frenkel-Brunswik, E., Levinson, D. J., & Sanford, R. N. (1950). *The authoritarian personality.* New York: Harper & Row.

Altemeyer, B. (1988). *Enemies of freedom: Understanding right-wing authoritarianism.* San Francisco, CA: Jossey-Bass.

Arendt, H. (1963). *Eichmann in Jerusalem: A report on the banality of evil.* New York: Viking Press.

Asbrock, F., Sibley, C. G., & Duckitt, J. (2010). Right-wing authoritarianism and social dominance orientation and the dimensions of generalized prejudice: A longitudinal test. *European Journal of Personality, 24,* 324–340.

Banse, R., & Gawronski, B. (2003). *Die skala motivation zu vorurteilsfreiem verhalten: Psychometrische eigenschaften und validität* [The scale motivation to act without prejudice: Psychometric properties and validity]. *Diagnostica, 49*(1), 4–13.

Baumeister, R. F., Dale, K., & Sommer, K. L. (1998). Freudian defense mechanisms and empirical findings in modern social psychology: Reaction formation, projection, displacement, undoing, isolation, sublimation, and denial. *Journal of Personality, 66*, 1081–1124.

Benz, W. (2011). *Die Protokolle der Weisen von Zion. Die Legende von der jüdischen Weltverschwörung.* Munich: C. H. Beck.

Bergmann, W., & Wetzel, J. (2003). *Manifestations of antisemitism in the European Union. Synthesis Report on behalf of the European Monitoring Centre on Racism and Xenophobia.* Retrieved November 28, 2011, from http://www.hagalil.com/antisemitismus/europa/eu-studie.htm

Bröder, A. (2000). Assessing the empirical validity of the "Take the Best"-heuristic as a model of human probabilistic inference. *Journal of Experimental Psychology: Learning, Memory, and Cognition, 26*, 1332–1346.

Bruder, M., Haffke, P., Neave, N., Nouripanah, N., & Imhoff, R. (2013). Measuring individual differences in generic beliefs in conspiracy theories across cultures: Conspiracy mentality questionnaire. *Frontiers in Psychology, 4*, 225.

Brumlik, M., Kiesel, D., & Reisch, L. (1991). *Der Antisemitismus und die Linke.* Frankfurt: Haag + Herchen.

Crocker, J., Luthanen, R., Broadnax, S., & Blaine, B. E. (1999). Belief in U.S. government conspiracies against Blacks among Black and White college students: Powerlessness or system blame? *Personality and Social Psychology Bulletin, 25*, 941–953.

Decker, O., Brähler, E., & Kiess, J. (2012). *Die Mitte im Umbruch: Rechtsextreme Einstellungen in Deutschland 2012.* Bonn: Dietz.

Douglas, K. M., & Sutton, R. M. (2011). Does it take one to know one? Endorsement of conspiracy theories is influenced by personal willingness to conspire. *British Journal of Social Psychology, 50*(3), 544–552.

Frei, N. (2005). *1945 und wir. Das Dritte Reich im Bewusstsein der Deutschen* [1945 and us. The Third Reich in Germans' collective consciousness]. Munich: Beck.

Fromm, E. (1941). *Escape from freedom.* New York: Farrar and Rinehart.

Golec de Zavala, A., Cichocka, A., & Bilewicz, M. (2013). The paradox of in-group love: Differentiating collective narcissism advances understanding of the relationship between in-group and out-group attitudes. *Journal of Personality, 81*, 16–28.

Groh, D. (1987). The temptation of conspiracy theory, or: Why do bad things happen to good people? In C. F. Graumann & S. Moscovici (Eds.), *Changing conceptions of conspiracy* (pp. 1–37). New York: Springer.

Haury, T. (2002). *Antisemitismus von links. Kommunistische ideologie, nationalismus und antizionismus in der frühen DDR.* Hamburg: Hamburger Edition.

Horkheimer, M., & Adorno, T. W. (1969). Elemente des Antisemitismus. In dies. Dialektik der Aufklärung (S. 177–217). Frankfurt am Main: Fischer.

Imhoff, R. (2010). Zwei Formen des modernen Antisemitismus? Eine Skala zur Messung primären und sekundären Antisemitismus. *Conflict and Communication Online, 9*. Retrieved April 17, 2010, from http://www.cco.regener-online.de/2010_1/pdf/imhoff.pdf

Imhoff, R. (2013a). Fragebogen zur Erfassung von Verschwörungsmentalität – Kurzform. In C. J. Kemper, E. Brähler, & M. Zenger (Eds.), *Psychologische und sozialwissenschaftliche Kurzskalen* (pp. 334–336). Berlin: Medizinisch Wissenschaftliche Verlagsgesellschaft.

Imhoff, R. (2013b). Skala zur Erfassung von Vorurteilen gegenüber dem Islam und säkularer Kritik am Islam – Kurzform. In C. J. Kemper, E. Brähler, & M. Zenger (Eds.), *Psychologische und sozialwissenschaftliche Kurzskalen* (pp. 279–282). Berlin: Medizinisch Wissenschaftliche Verlagsgesellschaft.

Imhoff, R. (2013c). Skala zur Messung von primärem und sekundärem Antisemitismus – Kurzform. In C. J. Kemper, E. Brähler, & M. Zenger (Eds.), *Psychologische und sozialwissenschaftliche Kurzskalen* (pp. 220–223). Berlin: Medizinisch Wissenschaft-liche Verlagsgesellschaft.

Imhoff, R., & Banse, R. (2009). Ongoing victim suffering increases prejudice: The case of secondary antisemitism. *Psychological Science, 20*, 1443–1447.

Imhoff, R., & Bruder, M. (2014). Speaking (un-)truth to power: Conspiracy mentality as a generalised political attitude. *European Journal of Personality, 28*, 25–43.

Imhoff, R., & Decker, O. (2013). Verschwörungsmentalität als Weltbild. In O. Decker, J. Kiess, & E. Brähler (Eds.), *Rechtsextremismus der Mitte* (pp. 130–145). Wiesbaden, Germany: Psychosozial Verlag.

Imhoff, R., & Recker, J. (2012). Differentiating Islamophobia: Introducing a new scale to measure Islamoprejudice and secular Islam critique. *Political Psychology, 33*, 811–824.

Inglehart, R. (1987). Extremist political positions and perceptions of conspiracy: Even par-anoids have real enemies. In C. F. Graumann & S. Moscovici (Eds.), *Changing conceptions of conspiracy* (pp. 231–244). New York: Springer.

Jolley, D., & Douglas, K. M. (2014). The social consequences of conspiracism: Exposure to conspiracy theories decreases the intention to engage in politics and to reduce one's carbon footprint. *British Journal of Psychology, 105*(1), 35–56.

Kofta, M., & Sedek, G. (2005). Conspiracy stereotypes of Jews during systemic transfor-mation in Poland. *International Journal of Sociology, 35*(1), 40–64.

Moscovici, S. (1987). The conspiracy mentality. In C. F. Graumann & S. Moscovici (Eds.), *Changing conceptions of conspiracy* (pp. 151–169). New York: Springer.

Paulhus, D. (1983). Sphere-specific measures of perceived control. *Journal of Personality and Social Psychology, 44*, 1253–1265.

Pittman, N. L., & Pittman, T. S. (1979). Effects of amount of helplessness training and internal–external locus of control on mood and performance. *Journal of Personality and Social Psychology, 37*, 39–47.

Popper, K. (1966). *The open society and its enemies* (5th ed.). Princeton, NJ: Princeton Uni-versity Press.

Postone, M. (1986). Antisemitism and National Socialism. In A. Rabinbach & J. Zipes (Eds.), *Germans and Jews since the Holocaust – The changing situation in West Germany* (pp. 302–314). New York: Holmes & Meier.

Pratto, F., Sidanius, J., Stallworth, L. M., & Malle, B. F. (1994). Social dominance orienta-tion: A personality variable predicting social and political attitudes. *Journal of Personality and Social Psychology, 67*, 741–763.

Roccas, S., Klar, Y., & Liviatan, I. (2006). The paradox of group-based guilt: Modes of national identification, conflict vehemence, and reactions to the in-group's moral vio-lations. *Journal of Personality and Social Psychology, 91*, 698–711.

Royston, J. P. (1982). An extension of Shapiro and Wilk's w test for normality to large samples. *Journal of the Royal Statistical Society. Series C (Applied Statistics), 31*, 115–124.

Schubert, T., & Otten, S. (2002). Overlap of self, ingroup, and outgroup: Pictorial measures of self-categorization. *Self & Identity, 1*, 535–576.

Steiner, J. M., & Fahrenberg, J. (1970). Die Ausprägung autoritärer Einstellung bei ehe-maligen Angehörigen der SS und der Wehrmacht – Eine Fragebogenstudie. *Kölner Zeitschrift für Soziologie und Sozialpsychologie, 22*, 551–566.

Stellmacher, J., & Petzel, T. (2005). Authoritarianism as a group phenomenon. *Political Psychology, 26*(2), 245–274.

Sullivan, D., Landau, M. J., & Rothschild, Z. K. (2010). An existential function of enemy-ship: Evidence that people attribute influence to personal and political enemies to com-pensate for threats to control. *Journal of Personality and Social Psychology, 98*, 434–494.

Tajfel, H., & Turner, J.C. (1986). The social identity theory of intergroup behavior. In S. Worchel & W.G. Austin (Eds.), *Psychology of intergroup relations* (pp. 7–24). Chicago: Nelson-Hall.

Turner, J.C., Hogg, M., Oakes, P., Reicher, S., & Wetherell, M. (1987). *Rediscovering the social group: A self-categorization theory.* Oxford: Blackwell.

Whitley, B.R. (1999). Right-wing authoritarianism, social dominance orientation, and prejudice. *Journal of Personality and Social Psychology, 77,* 126–134.

Whitson, J.A., & Galinsky, A.D. (2008). Lacking control increases illusory pattern perception. *Science, 322,* 115–117.

Wood, M.J., Douglas, K.M., & Sutton, R.M. (2012). Dead and alive: Beliefs in contradictory conspiracy theories. *Social Psychological and Personality Science, 3,* 767–773.

PART III

Conspiracy theories as explanatory structures

8

MOTIVATED ROOTS OF CONSPIRACIES

The role of certainty and control motives in conspiracy thinking

Małgorzata Kossowska and Marcin Bukowski

Conspiracies as motivationally fueled cognition

Nowadays it seems obvious that our cognition about the social world is at least partially motivated (e.g., Bruner, 1957; Duckitt, 2001; Dunning, 1999; Fiske & Taylor, 1991; Greenwald, 1980; Higgins, 1998; Kruglanski, 1996; Kunda, 1990). It means that nearly everyone is aware of the possibility that people are capable of believing what they want or need to believe (see Jost, Glaser, Kruglanski, & Sulloway, 2003). Thus, it seems probable that conspiracy beliefs that are used to explain how a group of individuals is covertly seeking to influence or cause certain events – like virtually all other belief systems – are adopted in part because they satisfy some psychological needs. Moreover, as conspiracy beliefs are usually activated when the surroundings are perceived as threatening, they can be conceptualized as a motivated response for reestablishing deprived basic social motives. Two such motives are recognized as having special significance in shaping the behavior of individuals and groups: the need for cognitive closure and the need for control (Kruglanski & Webster, 1996; Thompson & Schlehofer, 2008; White, 1959). Keeping in mind the assumption that "the same motives may underlie different beliefs and that different motives may underlie the same belief" (Jost et al., 2003, p. 341), we suggest that some people might adopt conspiracy beliefs out of a desire for certainty, whereas others adopt the same beliefs because of a threat to personal control. It is also possible that these two motives are intertwined. For example, low control and power usually also mean low certainty. Therefore, these two motives operating together may potentially lead to especially strong support for conspiracies. Finally, we propose that conspiracy thinking is a feature of the mind that is related to the search for explanations (meaning) when certainty, control, or power is lacking.

Uncertainty and conspiracies

Feeling discomfort in the face of uncertainty is an aversive state – when experienced it can constitute a threatening event to people (Jonas, McGregor, Klackl, Agroskin, Fritsche, Holbrook, et al., 2014; Kruglanski, 1989; Hogg, 2007; Van den Bos & Lind, 2002). All kinds of uncertainty (e.g., motivational, epistemic, or even perceptual) involve the experience of a discrepancy between an expectation or desire and the current circumstances (Jonas et al., 2014). This discrepancy is aversive because it deprives people's confidence in how to understand, what to expect from, and how to behave in the physical and social environment (e.g., Fiske & Taylor, 1991; Hogg, 2007; Sorrentino & Roney, 1986). Therefore, people generally feel a need either to eliminate uncertainty or to find some way to make it tolerable and cognitively manageable (Van den Bos, 2009; Greve & Strobl, 2004). In fact, resolving uncertainty seems to be the most important self-regulatory task for individuals and groups (see Harmon-Jones, 2000).

One way to efficiently reduce the feeling of uncertainty is to formulate clear and subjectively certain opinions or beliefs about reality (Kruglanski, 1989). Conspiracy theories that attribute significant unexplained events to a secret activity taken by powerful individuals, groups, or organizations may provide a sense of coherence, understanding, and reduction of ambiguity. For instance, it is much easier to attribute the financial crisis to the coordinated actions of greedy bankers rather than to systemic dynamics in a complex economy. Likewise, it is also comfortable for individuals to attribute the causes of a threat associated with a plane catastrophe, in which the president of the country died, to the intentional (although hidden) misconduct of politicians from the opposite side of the political scene, the government, or foreign secret agents. Such a way of thinking may easily reduce uncertainty about the cause of significant, unexplained, and sometimes threatening events because it provides simple answers for unanswered questions, points to an enemy that can be blamed for the problem, and helps to explain negative events. Thus, it allows people to retain a sense of safety and predictability. Indeed, some studies demonstrate that situationally induced threat or anxiety of a different kind (e.g., threat related to self-esteem, a belief system, or to the in-group) leads to an increased propensity for conspiracy thinking in general (Grzesiak-Feldman, 2013), as well as about a specific out-group, e.g., Jewish people (Grzesiak-Feldman, 2007).

Conspiracies may also buffer against uncertainty because, like any other firmly held convictions, they represent a mode of thinking that is closed, certain, and structured (Webster & Kruglanski, 1994). According to this explanation, conspiracy beliefs offer simple maps of meaning and attract people who prefer simple, structured solutions to life's complexity and uncertainty (Jost et al., 2003). Conspiracy beliefs, then, may be characterized by a need for certainty (e.g., need for closure) with a motivated denial of uncertainty.

Need for closure (Webster & Kruglanski, 1994) is described as the tendency to reduce the feeling of discomfort experienced in the face of cognitive uncertainty through quick formulation of a hypothesis regarding the situation, reluctance to abandon a crystallized hypothesis or judgment, and disregard for contrary evidence, which leads to a rapid validation of the hypothesis (Webster & Kruglanski, 1994). Thus, need for closure is associated with heuristic, simplistic, top-down information processing. This simplistic cognitive style results in reduced sensitivity to alternative hypotheses, greater resistance to persuasion, and reduced motivation to search for information, as well as increased uniformity of opinion and resistance to change (for an overview, see Kruglanski, 2004).

How does need for closure lead to increased conspiracy thinking? Various studies on need for closure have focused on its influence on authoritarianism or political conservatism (e.g., Kossowska & Van Hiel, 2003; Van Hiel, Pandelaere, & Duriez, 2004; Van den Bos, 2009). One possibility is that need for closure relates to conspiracy beliefs via right-wing political orientations. For example, right-wing authoritarianism (RWA; Altemeyer, 1996) helps people make sense of a world that contains evil forces beyond the control of individuals and offers a seemingly coherent yet narrow, distorted, and oversimplified explanation for complex social events. That is why RWA is so attractive for people with a high need for closure (Kossowska et al., 2011). On the other hand, a hallmark of authoritarianism is a need to have scapegoats to blame for the woes. The motivating force for beliefs in specific conspiracies may be a desire to blame others for negative events (Abalakina-Paap, Stephan, Craig, & Gregory, 1999). Indeed, Kossowska (2012) found that need for closure is related to conspiracy thinking through right-wing authoritarianism. The positive relations between RWA and conspiracy were also demonstrated in study of Abalakina-Paap and colleagues (1999) and Grzesiak-Feldman and Irzycka (2009).

However, McHoskey (1995) suggested that the relationship between RWA and conspiracy seems to be more complex. He found a negative relationship between authoritarian attitudes and endorsements of conspiracy theories. He argued that individuals with authoritarian attitudes are more likely to perceive government as legitimate and morally inscrutable. Indeed, in his study, high right-wing authoritarian individuals were more dismissive of possible conspiratorial explanations. Research by Kossowska (2012) and Grzesiak-Feldman and Irzycka (2009), however, was done in Poland where high right-wing authoritarianism is usually related to the delegitimization of the government and political system. Therefore, high right-wing authoritarian people in Poland are especially prone to commit to conspiracy beliefs related to government and politicians in power. These groups in particular are seen as being responsible for present and past crises, which may result in behavioral intentions to undermine the perceived conspiracy and therefore the groups' position in society.

It is also possible that conspiracy theories are the outcome of extremists' belief systems and not just right-wing or conservative beliefs. It is well established that seeking epistemic certainty motivates extremism (Hogg, Kruglanski, & van den Bos, 2013; Federico, Hunt, & Fisher, 2013). In the face of uncertainty, people may zealously cling to all-embracing ideologies and worldviews, engage in aggressive or disruptive behaviors aimed at protecting or promoting their worldview, and identify as true believers with rigidly and hierarchically structured social groups or categories that are ethnocentric and intolerant of dissent and diversity (Fiske, 2013). Blaming others for an uncertain world may be a part of all kind of extreme thinking (van Prooijen & Krouwel, this volume).

In sum, it seems that political orientation and beliefs may influence conspiracy beliefs in different ways and in different contexts (Leman & Cinnirella, 2013). Individuals may well pick and choose theories that fit with a particular political view or belief system (e.g., Leman, 2007; Swami & Furnham, 2012; Wood, Douglas, & Sutton, 2012). This belief system, however, is the exemplification of a perception of the world in ways that satisfy individual needs, values, and prior epistemic commitments.

Beliefs in conspiracy theories, as in many other theories or ideologies, also have much to do with the ways in which individuals interpret and contest the legitimacy of evidence (e.g., Harrison & Thomas, 1997; Leman, 2007). Despite their often-inherent implausibility, conspiracy theories appear not to play by the rules of rational inference. They can be acquired with brief exposure (Douglas & Sutton, 2008) and tend to resist disconfirming evidence (McHoskey, 1995; Sharp, 2008; Nyhan & Reifler, 2010). Even when their most basic claims go unverified, the lack of evidence itself may be construed as positive evidence that a conspiracy must have occurred (Bost & Prunier, 2013; Kramer & Gavrieli, 2005). Uncertainty should influence the motivational heuristics responsible for interpreting evidence. As need for closure affects all phases of information processing, it is probable that high need for closure individuals may be reluctant to consider or assimilate disconfirming evidence once conspiratorial beliefs have become established (confirmation bias, e.g., Klayman & Ha, 1987; Leman & Cinnirella, 2013; Kossowska & Bar-Tal, 2013). Moreover, evidence that is deemed to confirm a high need for closure individual's existing beliefs will tend to be unquestioned and accepted, whereas disconfirming evidence will often be critically evaluated and rejected (see Lord, Ross, & Lepper, 1979; Kruglanski, Dechesne, Orehek, & Pierro, 2009). It is well established that a high level of need for closure produces a reliance on confirmation heuristics (De Dreu, Koole, & Oldersma, 1999) that results in a strengthening of existing beliefs. Low level of need for closure induces systematic processing, resulting in greater scrutiny of information and evidence (Klein & Webster, 2002; Kruglanski et al., 2009). Thus, levels of need for closure determine how information may be processed, understood, and accepted when interpreting evidence. Indeed, Leman and Cinnirella (2013) were able to lower need for closure by increasing accountability and, hence giving participants a greater motivation to scrutinize the evidence and justify their rating. This finding also suggests that those who took a less systematic (more heuristic) approach to evaluating any evidence were more likely to end up with an account that was more consistent with their previous beliefs.

Soral, Kofta, & Szymanska (2014), however, found that under specific conditions (prolonged exposure to new conspiracy interpretations), low (but not high) need for closure people, who are also high in authoritarianism or collective narcissism, in fact are more likely to develop a conspiracy theory. Possibly, they are eager to encode – accumulating through the years – new information confirming their prejudiced beliefs. It is the tenet of social cognition that although people's attention is attracted by vivid and distinctive stimuli that stand out as different, people are often motivated to confirm their cognitive representations (schemas, stereotypes) about themselves, other people, and their world (see Fiske & Taylor, 2008). Uncertainty motivates confirmation bias, which requires a certain level of openness to process confirming information. Therefore, it may promote the impact of certainty-promising demagogues of various kinds, discouraging open-mindedness to a diversity of viewpoints and enhancing the appeal of rigidly simplistic, black/white ideologies, and fundamentalist belief systems and practices (e.g., Altemeyer, 2003; Baron, Crawley, & Paulina, 2003; Billig, 1982; Curtis & Curtis, 1993; Doty, Peterson, & Winter, 1991; Hoffer, 1951; Jost et al., 2003; Lambert, Burroughs, & Nguyen, 1999; Orehek et al., 2010).

In sum, conspiracy theories may provide an attractive way of restoring one's own sense of certainty by providing understanding of the causal relations in the environment. They may also be a byproduct of simple and biased information processing or of being open for information that confirms an individual's previous knowledge.

Uncontrollability and conspiracies

The other basic psychological motive that is related to the development of conspiracy thinking is personal agency and control over the environment (Bandura, 1977; DeCharms, 1968; White, 1959). Experiencing lack of personal control means to perceive lack of contingency between one's goals and the effects of actions taken and, thus, an inability to achieve desired and avoid undesired outcomes (Seligman, 1975; Skinner, 1996). Decades of research have consistently shown that a state of uncontrollability affects people's cognitive, emotional, and motivational aspects of functioning, leading to poorer cognitive abilities (e.g., problem solving, integration of information into meaningful mental models, etc.), more negative emotional states (i.e., depressive syndromes), and a lack of initiative (Hiroto & Seligman, 1975; Kofta & Sedek, 1989; Sedek & Kofta, 1990; von Hecker & Sedek, 1999). It is also well known, however, that people cope with those aversive states of uncontrollability by making attempts to restore the deprived sense of control and engage in attribution processes in order to make sense of the unpredictable environment (Pittman & Pittman, 1980; Wortman & Brehm, 1975).

More recently, Rothbaum, Weisz, and Snyder (1982) proposed that a common way of dealing with a lack of personal control (called also primary control, since it is related to the direct effectiveness of people's actions) is by trying to restore control, predictability, and order at a more symbolic and conceptual level (which is called secondary control, since it is a form of indirect or vicarious control, related to having some unique knowledge or by trusting powerful others). A natural candidate for such explanatory schemas are conspiracy theories, which provide a quick and simple way of restoring one's own feelings of control by understanding the causal relations in the environment. Conspiracy theories directly provide an answer to the question: Why do we not have control over many aspects of our lives? Recent research has shown that endorsing beliefs in conspiracies might help individuals to compensate for their perceived lack of control (Whitson & Galinsky, 2008). In this research, lack of control was experimentally manipulated, and later on participants were presented with ambiguous scenarios in which it was possible to interpret the behavior of other people that surrounded the protagonist as innocent or conspirational, causing negative or positive effects. Subsequently, participants were asked to assess to what extent they thought that there was a coordinated effort of other individuals to produce those outcomes, independently from the protagonist's efforts. The results revealed that lacking control made participants perceive greater probability of conspiracy, compared to those participants who were not deprived of control. Whitson and Galinsky (2008) interpret these results by suggesting that lacking control (but not experiencing any other type of psychological threat) leads to a general process of illusory pattern perception, which reveals itself also in the domain of endorsing conspiracy beliefs. This interpretation is in line with the notion that conspiracy beliefs provide causes and motives for outcomes and events that can be perceived as accidental (Pipes, 1997).

Threats and hazards to perceived control can arise from a wide range of potential causes that are often beyond the individual's capacities of control (catastrophes, natural disasters, economic crises, etc.). Becker (1969) argued that one potential way of dealing with multiple sources of uncontrollability is to narrow the scope of potential sources to one influential individual or group that can be effectively controlled or understood. Building on this idea, Sullivan, Landau, and Rothschild (2010) proposed that having enemies plays an important existential function, one of maintaining a sense of personal control by perceiving the environment as less random. This "need for having an enemy" was experimentally shown to increase in strength after being reminded of instances that render the participant without personal control. In fact, Sullivan and colleagues (2010) showed that a situational threat to control over external hazards augmented participants' conspiracy beliefs in the power of a potential political enemy. Additionally, they were especially likely to attribute a hidden impact of enemies on their lives when the surrounding social system was perceived as disordered. Kay, Gaucher, Napier, Callan, and Laurin (2008) demonstrated that lack of personal control might lead to greater support for sociopolitical institutions that offer control and predictability as a way to gain compensatory sense of control. Kosałka-Strutyńska and Bukowski (2013) replicated the result of Sullivan and colleagues (2010) in the context of the Polish sociopolitical scene. They showed that after activating a mindset related to lack of personal control, participants tend to explain situations in which a minority party or small company wins elections or obtains a contract by relying on conspiracy beliefs (i.e., supporting the idea that a hidden influence and not objective arguments and competencies must have been involved in the decision-making process). Additionally, after experiencing control threat, participants radicalized their political attitudes over time (relatively to a pre-measure of attitudes towards politicians representing specific ideological orientations), shifting the more positive attitudes towards right-wing and more negative attitudes towards left-wing politicians.

As shown by Fritsche and colleagues (2013), when personal control is threatened, membership in social groups can restore the global sense of control. In a set of studies they have shown that when lack of personal control is made salient, in-group bias and pro-organizational behavior increase (Fritsche et al., 2013). Also, blaming other groups for the negative outcomes (i.e., scapegoating) obtained by an individual or target group can have a function of maintaining or even restoring a deprived sense of control (e.g., by the economic crisis, unemployment, or environmental threat) by receiving a clear explanation of the negative outcomes (Bukowski, de Lemus, Rodriguez-Bailón, & Willis, 2014; Rothschild, Landau, Sullivan, & Keefer, 2012). The research described above indicates that control deprivation can lead to stronger mental rigidity, reliance on oversimplified attributions, and more radical social attitudes, which can serve as means to enhance or restore this particular motive of personal control. Belief in conspiracies seems to be an instance of the very same information processing style, which is guided by the motivation to deal with perceived uncontrollability of the surroundings.

Why would people stick to conspiracies when their sense of personal control is threatened? The answer to that question can be partly provided by laboratory studies on uncontrollability and powerlessness, which indicate that people who are exposed to such states show difficulties in performing tasks that require cognitive control and higher level, integrative information processing, such as reasoning or problem solving (Bukowski, Asanowicz, Marzecová, & Lupiáñez, 2015; Guinote, 2007; Kofta & Bukowski, 2011; Sedek & Kofta, 1990; Smith, Jostman, Galinsky, & van Dijk, 2008; von Hecker & Sedek, 1999). Those difficulties can lead to the preference for oversimplified explanations of how the social reality works, offered by a broad scope of conspiracy theories. Based on the reviewed literature, it could be argued that socially shared conspiracy theories that identify specific target groups as targets of conspiracies have a strong impact on the individual accessibility of such beliefs. However, it seems that the same mechanism of searching for patterns of hidden influence in the environment can be activated even when there are no existing conspiracy theories and can contribute to a development of new explanations. The question remains whether any group or institution that has the ability to exert control in the socioeconomic domain can be a target of conspiracy theories.

Conspiracy as a universal psychological mechanism of motivated cognition or as a phenomenon related to the attributes of specific social groups?

Until now we have argued that conspiracy beliefs may be easily adopted by people who feel uncertain about the social world or whose sense of control or power is threatened. A question arises, however, whether conspiracies need to be expressed towards any specific type of group in order to play their roles of control and/or certainty maintenance or restoration. In other words, is conspiracy thought of as an example of a more universal psychological mechanism of motivated information processing or is it a phenomenon related to the attributes of specific social groups? In general, it has been proposed that the tendency to hold conspiracy beliefs is linked to a threatened in-group identity (for a review, see Cichocka, Golec de Zavala, Marchlewska, & Olechowski, this volume). It then seems that the targets of conspiracies must be groups that can be easily blamed and accused for the misfortune of one's own group. But, are there any specific characteristics of such groups? According to Hofstadter (1966), conspiracy thinking is rooted in a general tendency to explain complex real-world phenomena by forming a coherent set of beliefs about the existence of a powerful and evil enemy. The power asymmetry between one's own group and the group that is the target of conspiracy seems a crucial element of conspiracy-based thinking – in such a conceptual system, there is a necessity for a clear external source of power that is responsible for the threatening lack of power, order, and predictability (Coady, 2006; Goertzel, 1994; Imhoff & Bruder, 2014; Popper, 1966).

The targets of conspiracies seem to resemble the targets of scapegoating in some ways. The classical research on scapegoating, however, did not at all emphasize the power asymmetry as a precondition for choosing a scapegoat target. On the contrary, Allport (1954) proposed that scapegoats serve as relatively weak and defenseless groups, towards which aggression could be justified and rationalized. Glick (2005) proposed an ideological model of scapegoating, which states that groups that historically were blamed and used as scapegoats are usually perceived as having (hidden) control over resources and, at the same time, a noncooperative, hostile approach to the in-group. Those groups, who are highly competent (smart, clever) but at the same time are cold and have harmful intentions, evoke envy and simultaneously tend to activate hostility and an exaggerated use of stereotypes and conspiracy theories. Such belief systems are reinforced by socially shared ideologies that indicate one group as a threatening and powerful agent, acting usually in a secret and hidden manner; in this way they resemble conspiracy beliefs (Kofta & Sedek, 2005). For example, the conspiracy theory regarding Jews provides a coherent explanation for such aversive experiences as recession, unemployment, loss of an in-group's power in society, decline of morality, and loss of national independence (Bilewicz & Krzeminski, 2010; Bilewicz, Winiewski, Kofta, & Wojcik, 2013). In fact, Bilewicz and Krzeminski (2010) found in samples of two posttransitional democracies (Poland and Ukraine) that relative deprivation (i.e., subjective perception of lower group status) experienced by the in-group influences the support for discriminatory policies towards Jews, but this relation is mediated by beliefs in Jewish control in the areas of politics, economy, and media (for a more detailed discussion, see Winiewski, Soral, & Bilewicz, this volume).

Conspiracy beliefs make sense of events that threaten the social order and bear large consequences for the in-group (Swami & Coles, 2010; van Prooijen, 2012). Cichocka and colleagues (this volume) suggest that collective narcissism, associated not only with chronic stereotyping of out-groups as prone for conspiring (Kofta & Sedek, 2005) but also with conspiratorial explanations of particular events or upheavals that concern the in-group, predicts blaming others for an in-group's misfortunes, and therefore is associated also with embracing explanations that involve intentional malevolent actions of threatening out-groups.

Powerful others are therefore often targets of scapegoating and conspiracy theories because they can be easily blamed for the in-group's loss of luck, influence, and control. Still, independently from the fact, whether the target of conspiracies is an ethnic minority (e.g., Jews) or any other type of group (e.g., pharmaceutics companies or bankers), the prerequisite for developing or sharing conspiracy beliefs seems to be an individual sense of uncertainty and confusion about reality, uncontrollability, or powerlessness. We discussed this issue above.

The important social consequences of conspiracy beliefs and the mediating role of powerlessness and uncertainty feelings was demonstrated also in a reduction of intentions to engage in politics and to take pro-environmental actions (Jolley & Douglas, 2014a). Feelings of powerlessness, disillusionment, and mistrust in authorities were also shown to be valid mediators of the relationship between antivaccine conspiracy beliefs and vaccination intentions (Jolley & Douglas, 2014b). This research shows that socially shared ideologies and beliefs regarding the hidden and malicious intentions of out-groups are fueled and supported by the individual's sense of lack of control, power, and predictability, leading eventually to disengagement from potential actions. In the field of health psychology, similar important effects of conspiracy beliefs and their justifying role for the prevention of risky health-related behaviors were found in the domain of AIDS research (Bird & Bogart, 2003). For example, conspiracy theories claim that birth control and AIDS are forms of genocide against African American people. Thus, AIDS denialism and generalized medical mistrust can be named as yet another example of the rapid development of conspiracy theories when epistemic, control, and power motives are threatened (Kalichman, 2014). This research leads to an intriguing idea, that control compensatory processes (i.e., restoration of a lacking personal control on a more symbolic, group level, for example, by embracing conspiracy theories) might lead to collective inaction, scapegoating, and support for radical ideologies. Still, recent research has shown that conspiracy beliefs can be associated with higher self-ratings of intentions to engage in different kinds of protest against nuclear power (Imhoff & Bruder, 2014). The authors of this research point to the facilitating role of conspiracy thinking for changing of the status quo. The question whether conspiracy thinking plays a social function of stimulating a sense of group efficacy and collective actions against powerful groups or, on the contrary, helps to restore feelings of control by targeting prejudice and blaming of specific groups, which in turn might lead to a decreased tendency to take actions against social inequality, seems an important and yet understudied one.

It seems that the targets of conspiracy theories can be also groups that have a diffused structure but yet can be characterized by a strong and obscured network of interconnections (like corporations, institutions, etc.). In fact, this type of structure that allows the group members to be hidden and dispersed across the entire globe serves only as additional proof for the conspiracy beliefs regarding their implicit and malicious intentions. The belief that there is an existing diffused network that has the features of a group (e.g., agency) but acts in an invisible manner seems to be a core aspect of many conspiracy beliefs. Therefore, control and power asymmetry seem to be the main defining attributes of the relationship type between the in-group and such groups that are accused of conspiracies.

Theoretical integration: How uncontrollability and uncertainty trigger and maintain conspiracy beliefs

In this chapter we focused on the motivational roots of conspiracy thinking, which seem to be deeply grounded in the needs for certainty and personal control. It is our impression that in the past, more effort has been devoted to debating differences between various needs and defensive reactions than to exploring commonalities. Thus, it is difficult to say how the need for certainty and control operate together. We think that the search for explanations, meaning, and predictability when certainty, control, or power motives are threatened or deprived is a universal psychological mechanism. It is also possible that the predictability aspect is present in control motivation as even when having control and power, a high need for certainty can potentially lead to support for conspiracies. However, the relation between certainty and control motives does not seem to be straightforward. For example, there is evidence that when control is deprived, high need for closure people tend to express more positive attitudes towards the out-group (Kossowska, Dragon, & Bukowski, 2015). This might be due to the fact that lack of control also decreases the ability to achieve certainty and therefore impairs the construction of cognitive schemas and their effective application. In sum, it seems that an interaction of both motives has to be taken into account when analyzing the effects of threat on social perception.

Still, it seems that in the case of conspiracies, these two motivational mechanisms of need for certainty (e.g., need for closure) and need for control or power act in the same direction; that is, when threatened, they enhance conspiracy thinking. Assuming that endorsement of conspiracy beliefs is a motivated process, its magnitude should be related to the value and expectancy (or attainability) of achieving certainty or personal control (Atkinson & Birch, 1970; Kruglanski, 1996). Additionally, the individual's capacity to engage in systematic and analytical thought also determines the intensity of motivation (the *driving force*, as proposed by Kruglanski, Belanger, Chen, Kopetz, Pierro, & Mannetti, 2012) and appears to be yet another important factor that influences the tendency to rely on conspiracy-based cognitive structures. Therefore, when the importance of the certainty and control motives is high, their attainability low, and the individual's propensity (or contextual demands, e.g., cognitive load) to engage in systematic thought impaired, then the magnitude of endorsement for conspiracy beliefs should grow. One could also imagine that a temporary experience of a lack of control or certainty, combined with a relatively high importance of those motives and demanding environmental conditions (e.g., demand to make a quick judgment), could lead to the formation of a conspiracy-based judgment (even if, in general, that particular person does not endorse conspiracy theories). However, chronic conditions of deprived control and certainty, combined with high value of those needs and low ability to engage in analytical thinking, might ultimately lead to the development of a relatively stable individual characteristic, named in literature as conspiracy mentality (i.e., general propensity towards conspirational thinking; Imhoff & Bruder, 2014; Wood et al., 2012). Therefore, we propose not to treat conspiracy thinking as a undifferentiated phenomenon or personality characteristic only, but rather as a cognitive activity that is both motivated (primarily by the need for certainty and control) and situated (context dependent). This preliminary framework, which includes an interaction of motivational (value and attainability) and cognitive (capacity) factors, could help to explain under what types of conditions the strength of support for conspiracy theories rises.

Additionally, it seems that conspiracy thinking does not have to be related to specific groups and form a coherent, uniform structure, but is rather a general phenomenon of motivated cognition. For example, it has been shown that the contents of various conspiracy theories do not have to be consistent with each other, as long as they serve the same motivational function (Wood et al., 2012). Additionally, a belief in a particular conspiracy theory is strongly predicted by belief in other conspiracies, even unrelated ones. Thus, conspiracy-based belief systems, regardless of whom is their target, may act as explanatory cognitive tools (Douglas & Sutton, 2008; Wood et al., 2012). The research of Whitson and Galinsky (2008) supports the idea that any type of cognitive structure (including also endorsement of a conspiracy theory) that helps to compensate for the experienced lack of certainty or control can be included in the individual's belief system.

Summing up, the last decades of research on the psychological underpinnings of conspiracy thinking revealed that its roots might have a motivational nature and, in this sense, the application of conspiracies in judgment and reasoning helps to cope with uncertainty and a sense of unpredictability and uncontrollability. Accordingly, conspiracy may be seen as any other defensive response that refers to commitments nested within social contexts, involve social support in interpersonal relations, or rely on social identities in group-related contexts. A remaining question for future research is the extent to which this kind of defense is merely palliative versus effective in dealing with uncertainty or uncontrollability. One possible prediction is that beliefs in conspiracies are an example of abstract defenses that refer to conceptual, identity-based, or idealistic commitments (see Jonas et al., 2014). In contrast, the concrete responses refer to the extent to which individuals respond to threats by focusing on concrete and immediate experiences and incentives in their physical environment. The abstract responses are usually more effective at reducing uncertainty than are the concrete ones (Jonas et al., 2014).

It is unclear, however, how effectively conspiracy beliefs might help to restore certainty and control. When addressing the question of effectiveness, the distinction between anxiety relief in the short term and uncertainty reduction or control restoration in the long term is important. Over the longer term, a criterion of effective coping may be that the threatening information can be integrated into the self and one's broader social life (e.g., relationships, values, group memberships, and worldviews). This would minimize the necessity of defensive reactions in upcoming threat situations because thoughts about the threats would already be linked with meaningful representations – that is, beliefs in conspiracy. This self-integrative process might buffer individuals against the stressful consequences of uncertainty and a lack of control in the future. Therefore, maybe people who believe in conspiracies cannot stop thinking that way. It is then probable that conspiracy thinking leads to effectively restore certainty and control and thus fulfills a defensive and immunizing function that must be integrated into self and social life.

Author note

Małgorzata Kossowska, Jagiellonian University, Marcin Bukowski, Jagiellonian University. The preparation of this paper was supported in part by a grant from the National Science Center DEC 2011/02/A/HS6/00155 awarded to Małgorzata Kossowska and partly by a grant from the National Science Center DEC 2011/01/D/HS6/00477 awarded to Marcin Bukowski. Correspondence regarding this chapter should be directed to Małgorzata Kossowska, Institute of Psychology, Jagiellonian University, al. Mickiewicza 3, 31–120 Krakow. E-mail: malgorzata. kossowska@uj.edu.pl

References

Abalakina-Paap, M., Stephan, W.G., Craig, T., & Gregory, W.L. (1999). Beliefs in conspiracies. *Political Psychology, 20*(3), 637–647.
Allport, G. W. (1954). *The nature of prejudice.* Reading, MA: Addison-Wesley.
Altemeyer, B. (2003). Why do religious fundamentalists tend to be prejudiced? *International Journal for the Psychology of Religion, 13*(1), 17–28.
Altemeyer, R. A. (1996). *The authoritarian specter.* Cambridge, MA: Harvard University Press.
Atkinson, J. W., & Birch, D. (1970). The dynamics of action. New York: Wiley.
Bandura, A. (1977). *Social learning theory.* New York: General Learning Press.
Baron, R.S., Crawley, K., & Paulina, D. (2003). Aberrations of power: Leadership in totalist groups. In D. van Knippenberg & M. Hogg (Eds.), *Leadership and power: Identity processes in groups and organizations* (pp. 169–183). London: Sage.
Becker, E. (1969). *Angel in armor.* New York: Free Press.
Bilewicz, M., & Krzeminski, I. (2010). Anti-Semitism in Poland and Ukraine: The belief in Jewish control as a mechanism of scapegoating. *International Journal of Conflict and Violence, 4*(2), 234–243.
Bilewicz, M., Winiewski, M., Kofta, M., & Wójcik, A. (2013). Harmful ideas, the structure and consequences of anti-Semitic beliefs in Poland. *Political Psychology, 34*(6), 821–839.
Billig, M. (1982). *Ideology and social psychology.* Oxford: Blackwell.

Bird, S. T., & Bogart, L. M. (2003). Birth control conspiracy beliefs, perceived discrimination, and contraception among African Americans. *Journal of Health Psychology, 8*, 263–276.

Bost, P. R., & Prunier, S. G. (2013). Rationality in conspiracy beliefs: The role of perceived motive. *Psychological Reports, 113*(1), 118–128.

Bruner, J. S. (1957). On perceptual readiness. *Psychological Review, 64*, 123–152.

Bukowski, M., Asanowicz, D., Marzecová, A., & Lupiáñez, J. (2015). Limits of control: The effects of uncontrollability experiences on the efficiency of attentional control. *Acta Psychologica, 154*, 43–53.

Bukowski, M., de Lemus, S., Rodriguez-Bailón, R., & Willis, G. B. (2014). *Who's to blame? Causal attributions of the economic crisis and personal control.* Manuscript under review.

Coady, D. (2006). *Conspiracy theories: The philosophical debate.* Hampshire, England: Ashgate.

Curtis, J. M., & Curtis, M. J. (1993). Factors related to susceptibility and recruitment by cults. *Psychological Reports, 73*(2), 451–460.

DeCharms, R. (1968). *Personal causation.* San Diego, CA: Academic Press.

De Dreu, C. K. W., Koole, S. L., & Oldersma, F. L. (1999). On the seizing and freezing of negotiator inferences: Need for cognitive closure moderates the use of heuristics in negotiation. *Personality and Social Psychology Bulletin, 25*, 348–362.

Doty, R. M., Peterson, B. E., & Winter, D. G. (1991). Threat and authoritarianism in the United States, 1978–1987. *Journal of Personality and Social Psychology, 61*(4), 629–640.

Douglas, K. M., & Sutton, R. M. (2008). The hidden impact of conspiracy theories: Perceived and actual influence of theories surrounding the death of Princess Diana. *Journal of Social Psychology, 148*, 210–222.

Duckitt, J. (2001). A dual-process cognitive-motivational theory of ideology and prejudice. *Advances in Experimental Social Psychology, 33*, 41–113.

Dunning, D. (1999). A newer look: Motivated social cognition and the schematic representation of social concepts. *Psychological Inquiry, 10*, 1–11.

Federico, C. M., Hunt, C. V., & Fisher, E. L. (2013). Uncertainty and status-based asymmetries in the distinction between the "good" us and the "bad" them: Evidence that group status strengthens the relationship between the need for cognitive closure and extremity in intergroup differentiation. *Journal of Social Issues, 69*(3), 473–494.

Fiske, S. T. (2013). A millennial challenge: Extremism in uncertain times. *Journal of Social Issues, 69*(3), 605–613.

Fiske, S. T., & Taylor, S. E. (1991). *Social cognition* (2nd ed.). New York: McGraw Hill.

Fiske, S. T., & Taylor, S. E. (2008). *Social cognition.* London: Sage.

Fritsche, I., Jonas, E., Ablasser, C., Beyer, M., Kuban, J., Manger, A.-M., & Schultz, M. (2013). The power of we: Evidence for group-based control restoration. *Journal of Experimental Social Psychology, 49*(1), 19–32.

Glick, P. (2005). Choice of scapegoats. In J. F. Dovidio, P. Glick, & L. A. Rudman (Eds.), *On the nature of prejudice: Fifty years after Allport* (pp. 244–261). Malden, MA: Blackwell Publishing.

Goertzel, T. (1994). Belief in conspiracy theories. *Political Psychology, 15*, 731–742.

Greenwald, A. G. (1980). The totalitarian ego: Fabrication and revision of personal history. *American Psychologist, 35*, 603–618.

Greve, W., & Strobl, R. (2004). Social and individual coping with threats: Outlines of an interdisciplinary approach. *Review of General Psychology, 8*, 194–207.

Grzesiak-Feldman, M. (2007). Conspiracy thinking and state-trait anxiety in young Polish adults. *Psychological Reports, 100*, 199–202.

Grzesiak-Feldman, M. (2013). The effect of high-anxiety situations on conspiracy thinking. *Current Psychology, 32*(1), 100–118.

Grzesiak-Feldman, M., & Irzycka, M. (2009). Right-wing authoritarianism and conspiracy thinking in a Polish sample. *Psychological Reports, 105*(2), 389–393.

Guinote, A. (2007). Power affects basic cognition: Increased attentional inhibition and flexibility. *Journal of Experimental Social Psychology, 43*, 685–697.

Harmon-Jones, E. (2000). Cognitive dissonance and experienced negative affect: Evidence that dissonance increases experienced negative affect even in the absence of aversive consequences. *Personality and Social Psychology Bulletin, 26*, 1490–1501.

Harrison, A., & Thomas, J. (1997). The Kennedy assassination, unidentified flying objects and other conspiracies: Psychological and organizational factors in the perception of "cover up." *Systems Research and Behavioral Science, 14*, 113–128.

Higgins, E. T. (1998). Promotion and prevention: Regulatory focus as a motivational principle. *Advances in Experimental Social Psychology, 30*, 1–45.

Hiroto, D. S., & Seligman, M. E. P. (1975). Generality of learned helplessness in man. *Journal of Personality and Social Psychology, 31*, 311–327.

Hoffer, E. (1951). *The true believer.* New York: Harper and Row.

Hofstadter, R. (1966). The paranoid style in American politics. In R. Hofstadter (Ed.), *The paranoid style in American politics and other essays* (pp. 3–40). New York: Knopf.

Hogg, M. A. (2007). Uncertainty–identity theory. *Advances in Experimental Social Psychology, 39*, 69–126.

Hogg, M. A., Kruglanski, A., & van den Bos, K. (2013). Uncertainty and the roots of extremism. *Journal of Social Issues, 69*(3), 407–418.

Imhoff, R., & Bruder, M. (2014). Speaking (un-)truth to power: Conspiracy mentality as a generalised political attitude. *European Journal of Personality, 28*, 25–43.

Jolley, D., & Douglas, K. M. (2014a). The social consequences of conspiracism: Exposure to conspiracy theories decreases the intention to engage in politics and to reduce one's carbon footprint. *British Journal of Psychology, 105*, 35–36.

Jolley, D., & Douglas, K. M. (2014b). The effects of anti-vaccine conspiracy theories on vaccination intentions. *PLOS ONE, 9*(2), e89177.

Jonas, E., McGregor, I., Klackl, J., Agroskin, D., Fritsche, I., Holbrook, C., . . . Quirin, M. (2014). Threat and defense: From anxiety to approach. *Advances in Experimental Social Psychology, 49*, 219–286.

Jost, J. T., Glaser, J., Kruglanski, A. W., & Sulloway, F. J. (2003). Political conservatism as motivated social cognition. *Psychological Bulletin, 129*, 339–375.

Kalichman, S. C. (2014). The psychology of AIDS denialism. Pseudoscience, conspiracy thinking, and medical mistrust. *European Psychologist, 19*, 13–22.

Kay, A. C., Gaucher, D., Napier, J. L., Callan, M. J., & Laurin, K. (2008). God and the government: Testing a compensatory control mechanism for the support of external systems. *Journal of Personality and Social Psychology, 95*, 18–35.

Klayman, J., & Ha, Y-W. (1987). Confirmation, disconfirmation and information in hypothesis testing. *Psychological Review, 94*, 211–228.

Klein, C., & Webster, D. (2002). Individual differences in argument scrutiny as motivated by need for cognitive closure. *Basic & Applied Social Psychology, 22*, 119–129.

Kofta, M., & Bukowski, M. (2011). Psychologia kontroli a psychologia władzy: Wzajemne relacje i możliwe obszary inspiracji [Psychology of control and psychology of power: Mutual relations and possible areas of inspiration]. In J. Czarnota Bojarska & I. Zinserling (Eds.), *W kręgu psychologii społecznej* [*Topics in Social Psychology*] (pp. 75–99). Warszawa: Wydawnictwo UW.

Kofta, M., & Sedek, G. (1989). Repeated failure: A source of helplessness, or a factor irrelevant to its emergence? *Journal of Experimental Psychology: General, 118*(1), 3–12.

Kofta, M., & Sedek, G. (2005). Conspiracy stereotypes of Jews during systemic transformation in Poland. *International Journal of Sociology, 35*(1), 40–64.

Kosałka-Strutyńska, J., & Bukowski, M. (2013). *Wpływ poczucia braku kontroli na radykalizację ocen i sądów społecznych* [*The influence of lack of control on the radicalization of social evaluations and judgments*]. Unpublished manuscript.

Kossowska, M. (2012). Motivational roots of conspiracy. Unpublished manuscript.

Kossowska, M., & Bar-Tal, Y. (2013). Need for closure and heuristic information processing: The moderating role of the ability to achieve the need for closure. *British Journal of Psychology, 104*, 457–480.

Kossowska, M., Dragon, P., & Bukowski, M. (2015). When need for closure leads to positive attitudes towards a negatively stereotyped outgroup. *Motivation and Emotion. 39*, 88–98 doi:10.1007/s11031-014-9414-5

Kossowska, M., Trejtowicz, M., de Lemus, S., Bukowski, M., Van Hiel, A., & Goodwin, R. (2011). Relationships between right-wing authoritarianism, terrorism threat, and attitudes towards restrictions of civil rights: A comparison among four European countries. *British Journal of Psychology, 102*, 245–259.

Kossowska, M., & Van Hiel, A. (2003). The relationship between need for closure and conservative beliefs in western and eastern Europe. *Political Psychology, 24*, 501–518.

Kramer, R. M., & Gavrieli, D. (2005). The perception of conspiracy: Leader paranoia as adaptive cognition. In D. M. Messick & R. M. Kramer (Eds.), *The psychology of leadership: New perspectives and research* (pp. 241–274). Mahwah, NJ: Lawrence Erlbaum Associates.

Kruglanski, A. W. (1989). *Lay epistemics and human knowledge: Cognitive and motivational bases.* New York: Plenum Press.

Kruglanski, A. W. (1996). Motivated social cognition: Principles of the interface. In E. T. Higgins & A. W. Kruglanski (Eds.), *Social psychology: Handbook of basic principles.* New York: Guilford Press.

Kruglanski, A. W. (2004). *The psychology of closed mindedness.* New York: Psychology Press.

Kruglanski, A. W., Belanger, J. J., Chen, X., Kopetz, C., Pierro, A., & Mannetti, L. (2012). The energetics of motivated cognition: A force-field analysis. *Psychological Review, 119*, 1–20.

Kruglanski, A. W., Dechesne, M., Orehek, E., & Pierro, A. (2009). Three decades of lay epistemics: The why, how, and who of knowledge formation. *European Review of Social Psychology, 20*, 146–191.

Kruglanski, A. W., & Webster, D. M. (1996). Motivated closing of the mind: "Seizing" and "freezing." *Psychological Review, 103*, 263–283.

Kunda, Z. (1990). The case for motivated reasoning. *Psychological Bulletin, 108*(3), 480–498.

Lambert, A. J., Burroughs, T., & Nguyen, T. (1999). Perceptions of risk and the buffering hypothesis: The role of just world beliefs and right-wing authoritarianism. *Personality and Social Psychology Bulletin, 25*(6), 643–656.

Leman, P. J. (2007). The born conspiracy. *New Scientist, 195*, 35–38.

Leman, P. J., & Cinnirella, M. (2013). Beliefs in conspiracy theories and the need for cognitive closure. *Frontiers in Psychology, 4*, 378.

Lord, C., Ross, L., & Lepper, M. (1979). Biased assimilation and attitude polarization: The effects of prior theories on subsequently considered evidence. *Journal of Personality & Social Psychology Bulletin, 37*, 2098–2109.

McHoskey, J. W. (1995). Case closed? On the John F. Kennedy assassination: Biased assimilation of evidence and attitude polarization. *Basic and Applied Social Psychology, 17*(3), 395–409.

Nyhan, B., & Reifler, J. (2010). When corrections fail: The persistence of political misperceptions. *Political Behavior, 32*(2), 303–330.

Orehek, E., Fishman, S., Dechesne, M., Doosje, B., Kruglanski, A. W., Cole, A. P., . . . Jackson, T. (2010). Need for closure and the social response to terrorism. *Basic and Applied Social Psychology, 32*(4), 279–290.

Pipes, D. (1997). *Conspiracy: How the paranoid style flourishes and where it comes from.* New York: Simon & Schuster.

Pittman, T. S., & Pittman, N. L. (1980). Deprivation of control and the attribution process. *Journal of Personality and Social Psychology, 39,* 377–389.

Popper, K. (1966). *The open society and its enemies* (5th ed.). Princeton, NJ: Princeton University Press.

Rothbaum, F., Weisz, J. R., & Snyder, S. S. (1982). Changing the world and changing the self: A two-process model of perceived control. *Journal of Personality and Social Psychology, 42,* 5–37.

Rothschild, Z. K., Landau, M. J., Sullivan, D., & Keefer, L. A. (2012). A dual-motive model of the motives underlying scapegoating: Displacing blame to reduce guilt or increase control. *Journal of Personality and Social Psychology, 102,* 1148–1163.

Sedek, G., & Kofta, M. (1990). When cognitive exertion does not yield cognitive gain: Toward an informational explanation of learned helplessness. *Journal of Personality and Social Psychology, 58,* 729–743.

Seligman, M. E. P. (1975). *Helplessness: On depression, development, and death.* San Francisco: Freeman.

Sharp, D. (2008). Advances in conspiracy theory. *Lancet, 372*(9647), 1371–1372.

Skinner, E. A. (1996). A guide to constructs of control. *Journal of Personality and Social Psychology, 71,* 549–570.

Smith, P. K., Jostman, N., Galinsky, A. D., & van Dijk, W. W. (2008). Lacking power impairs executive functions. *Psychological Science, 19,* 441–447.

Soral, W., Kofta, M., & Szymanska, J. (2014, June). *The role of collective narcissism and the need for cognitive closure in acquiring conspiracy beliefs about Smolensk catastrophe.* Paper presented at 5th Annual Tajfel Seminar Social Identities in Conflict in Warsaw, Poland.

Sorrentino, R. M., & Roney, C. J. R. (1986). Uncertainty orientation, achievement-related motivation, and task diagnosticity as determinants of task performance. *Social Cognition, 4,* 420–436.

Sullivan, D., Landau, M. J., & Rothschild, Z. K. (2010). An existential function of enemyship: Evidence that people attribute influence to personal and political enemies to compensate for threats to control. *Journal of Personality and Social Psychology, 98*(3), 434–449.

Swami, V., & Coles, R. (2010). The truth is out there: Belief in conspiracy theories. *The Psychologist, 23,* 560–563.

Swami, V., & Furnham, A. (2012). Examining conspiracist beliefs about the disappearance of Amelia Earhart. *Journal of General Psychology, 139,* 244–259.

Thompson, S. C., & Schlehofer, M. M. (2008). The many sides of control motivation: Motives for high, low, and illusory control. In J. Y. Shah & W. L. Gardner (Eds.), *Handbook of motivation science* (pp. 41–56). New York: Guilford.

Van den Bos, K. (2009). Making sense of life: The existential self trying to deal with personal uncertainty. *Psychological Inquiry, 20,* 197–217.

Van den Bos, K., & Lind, E. A. (2002). Uncertainty management by means of fairness judgments. In M. P. Zanna (Ed.), *Advances in experimental social psychology* (Vol. 34, pp. 1–60). San Diego, CA: Academic Press.

Van Hiel, A., Pandelaere, M., & Duriez, B. (2004). The impact of need for closure on conservative beliefs and racism: Differential mediation by authoritarian submission and authoritarian dominance. *Personality and Social Psychology Bulletin, 30,* 824–837.

van Prooijen, J. W. (2012). Suspicions of injustice: The sense-making function of belief in conspiracy theory. In E. Kals & J. Maes (Eds.), *Justice and conflict: Theoretical and empirical contributions* (pp. 121–132). Berlin: Springer-Verlag.

von Hecker, U., & Sedek, G. (1999). Uncontrollability, depression, and the construction of mental models. *Journal of Personality and Social Psychology, 77,* 833–850.

Webster, D. M., & Kruglanski, A. W. (1994). Individual differences in need for cognitive closure. *Journal of Personality and Social Psychology, 67,* 1049–1062.

White, R. (1959). Motivation reconsidered: The concept of competence. *Psychological Review, 66,* 297–330.

Whitson, J. A., & Galinsky, A. D. (2008). Lacking control increases illusory pattern perception. *Science, 322,* 115–117, 268.

Wood, M. J., Douglas, K. M., & Sutton, R. M. (2012). Dead and alive: Beliefs in contradictory conspiracy theories. *Social Psychological and Personality Science, 3,* 767–773.

Wortman, C. B., & Brehm, J. W. (1975). Reponses to uncontrollable outcomes: An integration of reactance theory and the learned helplessness model. In L. Berkowitz (Ed.), *Advances in experimental social psychology* (Vol. 8, pp. 277–336). New York: Academic Press.

9

BEHIND THE SCREEN CONSPIRATORS

Paranoid social cognition in an online age

Olivier Klein, Nicolas Van der Linden,
Myrto Pantazi, and Mikhail Kissine

> We are so constituted that we believe incredible things, and once they are engraved
> upon the memory, woe to him who would endeavor to erase them.
>
> *Goethe (1774/2009, August 15, 1771)*

Conspiracy theories are often viewed with skepticism. In our recent study conducted via the online software AMAZON MTurk, 96 U.S. participants were asked to indicate on a scale from 1 to 5 whether a series of 21 traits applied more to people who believed in conspiracy theories or to people who did not believe in them. The traits roughly tapped the two main dimensions of social judgment (Fiske, Cuddy, & Glick, 2007): competence on the one hand, warmth on the other. As shown in Figure 9.1, believers were perceived, in decreasing order of importance, as more gullible, crazy, easily influenced, stupid, naïve, manipulative, dishonest, assertive, and selfish than nonbelievers. By contrast, nonbelievers were perceived to be more rational, trustworthy, likeable, intelligent, honest, sociable, lucid, warm, and nice. Thus, believers are perceived more negatively on both warmth and competence. They are also viewed as suffering from mental disorders.

Thus, designating an account of social events as a conspiracy theory renders it illegitimate. Such a qualification amounts to denying any pretense of authenticity to the proposed explanation. It comes from a skeptic who rebels against the irrational believer. By debunking the conspiracy theory, skeptics affirm their clairvoyance and stigmatize the obscurantism of their opponent. In the same sample, we found that, indeed, 74% of participants defined themselves as more rational than the average person in their country. This tendency was moderately correlated ($r = .34$, $p < .001$) with a self-definition as a nonbeliever (vs. believer) in conspiracy theories.

To affirm their rationality, skeptics put forward empirical data questioning the plausibility of the conspiracy theory. They affirm their adhesion to a Cartesian

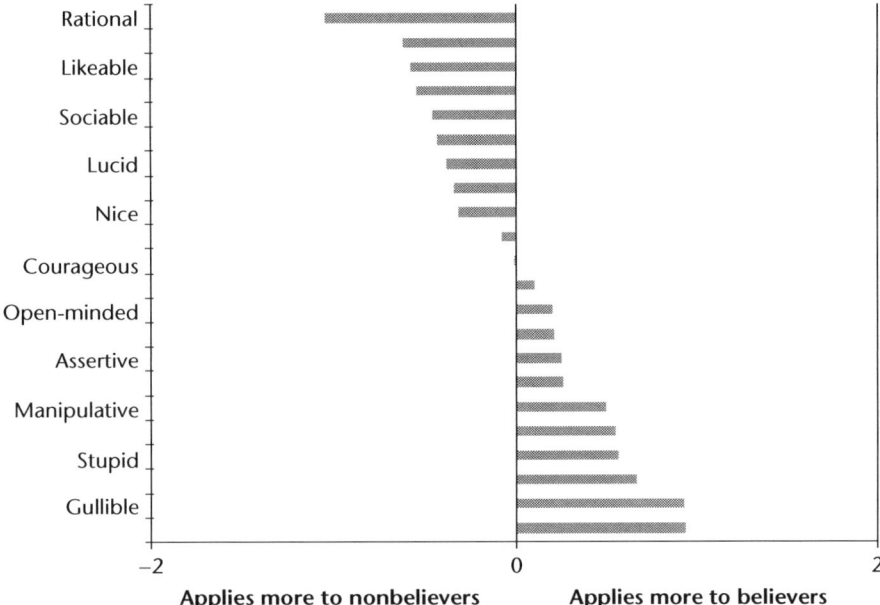

FIGURE 9.1 Perceived applicability of psychological traits to nonbelievers and believers in conspiracy theories.

ideal (i.e., their conclusions are logical deductions) and positivism (i.e., the deductions are based on objectively appraised facts).

In spite of these aspirations, belief in conspiracy theories remains widespread in developed countries. For example, Oliver and Wood (in press) found that 19 percent of Americans agree with the statement that "the U.S. invasion of Iraq was not part of a campaign to fight terrorism but driven by oil companies and Jews in the U.S. and Israel," and that 24 percent believe that "President Barack Obama was not really born in the United States and does not have an authentic Hawaiian birth certificate." How can aspirations to rationality coexist with such a vast endorsement of conspiracy theories? In this paper, we purport to address this paradox by considering the cognitive underpinnings of conspiracy theories.

We will first suggest that conspiracy theories are not perversions of rationality. To the contrary, we shall argue that general processes of causal explanation are likely to account for their formation and resistance to attacks against them.

Second, we will propose that the pathological view of conspiracy theories is not only misguided but that it may facilitate their endorsement by reducing vigilance towards dubious information.

Third, digital technologies may exacerbate the influence of the cognitive processes involved in the endorsement of conspiracy theories. Thus, rather than being a simple channel for the diffusion of such theories, the Internet may provide a social context facilitating their endorsement.

Before considering each of these points in detail, we will turn to terminological clarifications.

What is a conspiracy theory?

Keeley (1999, p. 116) defines a conspiracy theory as a "proposed explanation of some historical event (or events) in terms of the significant causal agency of a relatively small group of persons, the conspirators acting in secret."

Note first that the above definition does not have any bearing on the plausibility of the theory. In addition, according to this definition, a conspiracy theory necessarily possesses the following attributes:

- It involves causal reasoning.
- It implies a form of social categorization.
- It presumes intentionality on the part of members of the group.

To consider a group of individuals as possessing a joint intentionality and a capacity to act collectively presumes that this group is not only perceived as a set of distinct individuals, what Lorenzi-Cioldi (2002) calls a "collection group" (e.g., as one could categorize the owners of electric razors), but rather as an entity with an internal organization or "aggregate group" (see also Kofta & Sedek, 2005). This claim echoes work on entitativity (Yzerbyt, Judd, & Corneille, 2004), a term coined by Campbell (1958) to refer to the degree to which a group of individuals are (perceived as being) bonded together in a homogeneous entity. Lickel and colleagues (2000) indeed demonstrated that different kinds of groups are perceived at different levels of entitativity. Furthermore, Grzesiak-Feldman and Suszek (2008) observed that perceived entitativity predicted the degree to which their participants believed that members of different groups were engaged in conspiracies, whereas Kofta and Sedek (2005) also showed the role played by essentialism (i.e., a mode of category representation in which group members are seen as sharing deep, nonobvious, and immutable properties) in the endorsement of conspiracy theories.

The conspiring group is therefore not selected arbitrarily. We further contend that the members of such a group must be perceived as sharing motivations that justify the organization of a conspiracy and as capable of implementing it. This competence and these motivations are embedded in social stereotypes regarding the conspiring group. Hence, the existence of mixed stereotypes describing Jews as ethnocentric but also as powerful and clever may have facilitated the emergence of conspiracy theories about Jewish domination (Glick, 2002; see also Winiewski, Soral, & Bilewicz, this volume). Thus, conspiracy theories presuppose stereotypes. Moreover, not any stereotype will do. In order for a group to be the target of a conspiracy theory, its members need to be perceived as malevolent and in a position to put their plan into action.

Cognitive processes promoting the endorsement of conspiracy theories

In social psychology, conspiracy theories are often approached in terms of their motivational underpinnings: For example, they can be considered as geared at finding a convenient scapegoat (Rothschild, Landau, Sullivan, & Keefer, 2012), at legitimizing one's prejudice against the "conspiring group" (or a surrogate, cf. Swami, 2012), at restoring predictability in an uncertain world (van Prooijen & Jostmann, 2013), or at compensating for perceptions of reduced control over one's environment (Sullivan, Landau, & Rothschild, 2010). In this section, we depart from this motivational approach and consider several cognitive processes that may facilitate the endorsement of conspiracy theories. Below we consider four of them.

Conspiracy theories and conceptions of chance

At the source of any conspiracy theory, one can always find an array of "facts," real or assumed, that are subsequently organized into a coherent narrative. When a theory can account for many disparate events, it is often tempting to overestimate how necessary the co-occurrence, or *conjunction*, of these events is to produce the effect. This reflects a well-known bias, the *conjunction fallacy* (Tversky & Kahneman, 1983). This bias precisely consists in estimating the likelihood of two joint events as higher than that of any of these events considered separately. For example, let us adopt the perspective of a believer in a Bush-led conspiracy of the 9/11 attacks to justify a subsequent war in Iraq. How would such a person appraise some of the observations related to these events, such as "finding melted steel in the remains of the Twin Towers" or "absence of reaction from the Bush government to information indicating that supporters of Al Qaida were training in U.S. flight schools." Post hoc, the conjunction of these events may seem as more probable than any of these events taken separately because an alternate theory accounting for their co-occurrence is available. Precisely, research on the conjunction fallacy (Ahn & Bailenson, 1996) suggests that this bias is more likely to occur when a mechanistic explanation is available that allows one to weave these events into a tight, coherent narrative.

People's difficulties in assessing chance may be another contributor to belief in conspiracy theories. Thus, due to the representativeness heuristic (Tversky & Kahneman, 1974), people tend to view chance as more orderly than it is. For example, people typically underestimate the likelihood that a random process may produce the same outcome successively (e.g., a series of tails when flipping a coin). This may lead to view real coincidences as produced by nonrandom cause (because such coincidences are not representative of the sort of outcomes chance should produce). This problem becomes particularly acute when ignoring sample size. Thus, the occurrence of such series is obviously more likely when considering a large sample of events than when considering a small sample. But, when appraising "strange patterns," people often ignore the number of possible events of which they are part. For example, that two former CIA agents did not go to the World Trade Center (WTC) on 9/11 can only be appraised by considering the larger sample of employees who did not go the WTC on that day (and especially of the number of current or former agents of the CIA who went to the WTC).

Conspiracy theories and attributions of intentionality

Every event is the product of a wide array of conditions, some of which are granted the status of causes, whereas others will only be perceived as intermediary mechanisms. Law theorists Hart and Honoré (1959) argue that, in a judicial context, we tend to give the status of cause to a preceding event if it involves an intentional behavior. Social psychologists (McClure, Hilton, & Sutton, 2007) have supported this claim empirically by presenting their participants with long chains leading to a critical event (for instance, the derailment of a train or a house fire). They experimentally varied certain preceding events involved in the causal chain depending on whether they were intentional (e.g., an individual throwing a cigarette butt) or not (e.g., sunshine). They were thus able to demonstrate that their participants (college students) more often granted the status of cause to intentional behaviors. If we limit ourselves to the explanation of behaviors, other authors even suggest that an intentional explanation is chosen by default (Rosset, 2008). In other words, one of the central features of conspiracy theories, intentionality, seems to stem from an automatically triggered explanatory mode.

Stereotyping and causal power

Other aspects contribute to the perceived causal power of an antecedent. Among these, the role of typicality seems particularly relevant to the understanding of conspiracy theories. When an antecedent is typical of an agent, it is more likely to be considered an important cause even if, in practice, it is not more predictive of the outcome than a nontypical antecedent. Imagine that, in order to explain the massacre of American soldiers on November 5, 2009, in Fort Hood (Texas) by a psychiatrist of Palestinian descent, Nidal Malik Hassan, we could select from two potential causes: "Hassan was upset at his colleagues" versus "Hassan was depressed." Further, consider that these causes are equally likely to lead to the observed effect (when the psychiatrist is upset, he is as likely to behave aggressively as when he is depressed). In other words, the conditional probability of an aggression is similar irrespective of whether Hassan is depressed or upset. It appears that, in such a situation, individuals show a preference for what they believe to be the more typical or frequent cause (Johnson, Long, & Robinson, 2001). That is, if we believe that Hassan is often (seldom) upset at his colleagues, we will more (less) often use this cause in our explanation. This finding bears important implications for the understanding of conspiracy theories, because it suggests that the way agents are socially categorized is likely to influence the perceived causal power of an antecedent. In our example, knowing that Hassan is of Palestinian descent, one could rely on this information to estimate the typicality or frequency of the antecedent, "He must often be irritated by native-born Americans," and consequently use this cause in his or her explanation. This mechanism can potentially explain why stereotype-consistent behaviors easily find their way into conspiracy theories.

It thus appears that antecedents of behaviors performed by one or more members of a group are more likely to be selected for inclusion in a causal explanation when these antecedents are (stereo-)typically associated with this group. As a result, they will generally be perceived as consequences of internal dispositions shared by members of this group. In this psychology, intentions can link up the disposition with the behavior. For instance, imperialism (a general disposition that may be viewed as typical of Americans' orientations towards the rest of the world) can be used to explain the attack on the Twin Towers (behavior) – the collapse of which has been attributed to an explosion organized and camouflaged by the American administration – by invoking the will of the American authorities to dominate the Middle East (intention). Note that this example presumes that the conspiracy theorists consider imperialism to be typical of Americans (and a more potent cause than Islamic fanaticism).

Outcomes and causes

Another attributional process that may favor the endorsement of conspiracy theories is the tendency to prefer single-factor explanations: It is often much more satisfying, and less cognitively demanding, to identify an all-encompassing factor that can singly explain an outcome (Fischhoff, 1980).

Similarly, people generally engage in causal explanation of events that have a high social or personal significance. In doing so, they may often be motivated to seek explanations that are proportional to the outcome (Fiedler, Freytag, & Unkelbach, 2011). Yet, as we well know, even the most dramatic outcomes may be caused by trivial events. This is particularly evident when loved ones disappear: The extent of the grief experienced by loss may make it difficult to accept that a simple ordinary cause may have produced it. In the same vein, the shock generated by the assassination of JFK was so strong that the "single shooter theory" may have seemed difficult to accept. Coping with such a momentous event may demand a narrative that is paramount to the significance of the event to be explained. This assumption that causes should be proportional to their effects may reflect cognitive constraints as well. Thus, Heider (1944) posited the existence of a causal schema stipulating that a good cause should match an effect in magnitude. Recent experimental research (Fiedler et al., 2011) indeed suggests that people tend to consider a large effect as more likely to ensue from a given factor when the magnitude of the "cause" is large rather than small. This pattern contradicts logic (i.e., if a weak cause produces a strong effect, the cause must be powerful indeed!). This may contribute to the popularity of conspiracy theories, which offer grand explanations of significant events (for an illustration, see Licata & Klein, 2000).

In sum, this overview of cognitive processes promoting adhesion to conspiracy theories suggests that skeptics may be right in arguing that conspiracy theories do not conform to Cartesian standards of logic and rationality. The use of judgmental heuristics based on faulty reasoning may facilitate the endorsement of such theories. However, the use of such heuristics, far from being the preserve of lunatics, seems to characterize the way most people ordinarily perform judgments and decisions, even when they can sometimes rely on more sophisticated strategies (Kahneman, 2011).

Skepticism and conspiracy theories

So far we considered several factors that facilitate the endorsement of conspiracy theories as opposed to other kinds of explanations. Let us now look at the effect that a conspiracy theory has on someone who is exposed to it. We consider two possible receivers: the naïf, who adheres to the theory once exposed to it, and the skeptic, who refuses to endorse it unless he or she is offered strong evidence of its validity. The posture of the latter is grounded on the Cartesian assumption that it is possible to be exposed to a conspiracy theory without, yet, believing it. In his fourth metaphysical meditation, Descartes (1641/2010) contemplates the possibility of forming a "true" idea. "How can we know that we are not misled?" he wonders. In his view, people must suspend their will before deciding to affirm an idea. Once this idea is known well enough, one can attribute to it the status of truthfulness:

> The reason for fallacies and errors: When I hold back my will enough in the bounds of my knowledge, so that it only makes judgments about the things that are clearly and distinctly represented by comprehension, I cannot be mistaken; because every clear and distinct conception is undoubtedly something real and positive, and thus, it cannot originate from nothing.
>
> *(p. 62, our translation)*

In the Cartesian approach, one can thus envision an idea before considering it as true. Once we have comprehended this idea well enough, so as to have constructed a satisfactory representation of it, we are able to adhere to it or, to the contrary, consider it false or unfounded. Descartes thus makes a fundamental distinction between representation on the one hand and conviction on the other. He encourages us to be skeptical about every theory and to examine the different facts in favor or against it before making a decision.

Contrary to this skeptical view, adherence to conspiracy theories often seems to be guided by motivations – for example, anti-Semitic or racist – rather than by a cold-blooded quest for accuracy. In the adherence of conspiracy theories, comprehension often seems subordinate to the will, rather than preceding it. In this way, adherents of conspiracy theories do not refrain from selecting among the available facts those that best match their theory and even deploy their high imagination skills in order to assimilate those facts that seem to challenge it. They thus make great usage of explanations that are complex and unparsimonious (Bronner, 2013). In the case of 9/11, for example, the idea that the airplane collisions were just a decoy, explicitly or implicitly, assumes the collusion of two agents (the American government and the terrorists) and implicates the formulation of peripheral explanations instead of *prima facie* and more economical explanations involving only one agent, i.e., Al Qaida. This ad hoc and unparsimonious character may explain the contempt for conspiracy theories. The Cartesian intellect appears as an ideal that designates the functioning of "my" intellect as a denunciator, as opposed to that of the credulous who is enslaved by his ideology and formulates less elegant explanations. In our study, the more people defined themselves as nonbelievers, the more they characterized believers as "crazier" than nonbelievers ($r = .37$, $p < .001$). Note that the lack of parsimony of many conspiracy theories may seem to be at odds with the predilection for single-factor explanations that we highlighted above. It is possible to reconcile them, however, if we assume that, from the conspirator's perspective, a chief dominant cause (such as, for example, American imperialism or a Jewish quest for world dominance) explains a large set of events. Specific conspiracy theories are then crafted to accommodate these explanations, with the addition of peripheral, ad hoc causes, thereby deteriorating the overall elegance of the explanation.

However, the opposition between the intellect and the will proposed by Descartes is not endorsed by everyone. Spinoza (1677/2003) in particular rejects this opposition and views beliefs as cognitive products of stimuli. In this view of the mind, we have the tendency to "believe everything we know," and only through the force of will can we reject some representations, which initially exact our conviction unavoidably. If this is the case, then a conspiracy theory would become plausible just because it exists. Hence, contrary to the Cartesian view, distancing oneself from it would require more effort than adhering to it.

Can we solve such a debate? When we are confronted with unverified affirmations about the world, do we behave in a Cartesian or a Spinozan way? Gilbert, Tafarodi, and Malone (1993) have tried to answer this question. They put their participants (psychology students) in the shoes of a trial judge and asked them to read two reports about two different offenses. The researchers told the participants, however, that part of the information contained in the two reports was false. They manipulated the truthfulness of the information by varying the font color: The true information was presented in black font and the false information was presented in red font and was, thus, easily identifiable. For one report, the false information exacerbated the severity of the crime, and for the other, it mitigated the severity by presenting attenuating circumstances. Independently, half of the participants were asked to perform a concurrent digit-search task when reading the two reports. After doing so, participants were asked to play the role of judges and propose a prison term for the two perpetrators on the basis of the information they had just read. Gilbert and colleagues assumed that if people are "Cartesian," they should be able to disregard the false information printed in red before making their judgments. Thus, the judgments of the two perpetrators – who only differed between them with respect to the *false* information presented in the reports – should not differ, regardless of whether participants were in the "distracted" or in the control group. On the contrary, if they are "Spinozan," a difference between the two groups should show up, as distracted participants, due to their restricted cognitive resources, should be unable to proceed to the rejection of the false information, which would be unavoidably endorsed upon reading. As a matter of fact, the authors found exactly this difference between the two groups: The difference in prison terms in the "attenuated" and "exacerbated" conditions was bigger for the distracted participants than for the control group. The conclusion of this experiment is simple: When lacking sufficient cognitive resources, all affirmations seem true. Although subsequent research (e.g., Hasson, Simmons, & Todorov, 2005; Richter, Schroeder, & Wöhrmann, 2009) has suggested boundary conditions for such a "gullibility," it remains the case that not believing statements seems often much more taxing than believing them (see Kissine & Klein, 2013, for an extended discussion).

With respect to conspiracy theories and the two kinds of receivers we mentioned above, this study suggests that it is difficult to behave in a skeptical way when confronted with such constructions. In other words, a Cartesian stance towards any type of information – and hence, conspiracy theories – is an illusion; when lacking sufficient cognitive resources, we are likely to take new information for granted, without even realizing the shortcomings of our critical sense. This, obviously, may be of particular significance when confronted by novel information supporting conspiracy theories at the expense of more conventional accounts of events. A Spinozan mind would be expected to assimilate such information much more easily than a Cartesian mind.

Does our self-proclaimed rationality make us more vulnerable to conspiracy theories?

A somehow paradoxical picture emerges from the previous sections. On the one hand, people tend to define themselves as skeptics and to decry conspiracy theories, which presupposes a default critical stance; on the other hand, experimental research shows that rejection of false information requires cognitive effort. Depletion of cognitive resources thus considerably increases the likelihood of being influenced. In the present section, we shall consider how these two phenomena may interact.

In view of the foregoing, one may expect that mere exposure to a conspiracy theory, even a completely imaginary one, is sufficient to elicit at least some degree of adherence to it. Douglas and Sutton (2008) tested exactly this hypothesis. The participants in their study read several pieces of information, each supporting a different conspiracy theory concerning the "murder" of Lady Diana. For example, in support of the theory that rogue cells in the British secret services organized the murder, participants read that witnesses report having heard gunshots just before the accident. After that, participants were asked to indicate the extent to which they endorse each of the conspiracy theories supported by the information they had read, as well as the extent to which they thought they endorsed the theories before reading the evidence (retrospective judgments). Crucially, the subjects thought that their judgments had not changed after reading the information, although they actually adhered to the conspiracy theories more than did a control group, which had not been previously exposed to the evidence. Moreover, the subjects believed that the other participants in the study, in contrast to themselves, had been influenced by the information. This is an effect widely known as the "third person effect" (Davison, 1983), referring to a tendency for people to believe that others are more credulous or more powerless than themselves against persuasive media.

This study demonstrates the susceptibility of our judgments to "empirical" evidence – in our case, facts supporting a conspiracy theory. What is more, we are, apparently, unconscious of this susceptibility of our judgments, which also goes against a Cartesian approach. We are then always prone to overestimate our immunity to conspiracy theories.

Being under the spell of this "Cartesian illusion" – namely, perceiving oneself as rationally resistant to conspiracy theories – may render us even more vulnerable to them, as our vigilance decreases. Consistent with this proposition, studies have found that beliefs in one's own objectivity or rationality could lead to more biased judgment of applicants in a job selection context (Uhlmann & Cohen, 2007). Thus, our misguided adhesion to the Cartesian ideal – that is, to the belief that we are Cartesian when we are actually Spinozan beings – may exacerbate this tendency. We precisely considered the validity of this hypothesis, as applied to conspiracy theories, in a preliminary experiment (Pantazi, Klein, Douglas, & Kissine, 2014). In the study, we exposed student participants to information consistent with conspiracy theories regarding education reform. For example, the information that the Minister of Higher Education was also the Minister of Economy could suggest that the government was secretly reforming higher education to profit businesses (while its overt goal was to improve access to higher education). Two experimental manipulations were introduced. First, prior to receiving the information regarding the education reform, a third of participants were asked to generate 10 situations in which they had behaved rationally, whereas a second third only had to generate 5 instances. The last (control) group was not asked to generate any behavior. This manipulation, inspired by Schwarz et al. (1991), was intended to manipulate self-perceptions as rational. Thus, we expected that participants would experience more difficulties retrieving a large than a small number of instances. Due to the accessibility heuristic (Tversky & Kahneman, 1974), they should utilize information about ease of retrieval to form judgments about their own rationality and, therefore, perceive themselves as less rational in the 10 behaviors than in the 5 behaviors condition. Independently, for half the participants, we introduced the information presented to them as "supporting a conspiracy theory," whereas for the other half, the information was presented as "facts."

Two hours later, we evaluated participants' adhesion to conspiracy theories regarding the educational reform and uncovered an interesting pattern of results: There was a marginally significant interaction between the rationality manipulation and labeling ($p < .08$). In the condition in which participants had to retrieve few instances of their rationality as well as in the control group especially, endorsement of the conspiracy theories was (descriptively) higher when the information was labeled as supporting a conspiracy theory than when it was not. Only when participants generated many instances of rational behavior did the opposite tendency appear (although it did not reach statistical significance). Thus, assuming that the manipulation of self-perceived rationality had the intended effect, these findings suggest that perceiving oneself as more rational leads to a greater, rather than to a lesser, endorsement of information explicitly labeled as supporting a conspiracy theory. This is consistent with our hypothesis that by overestimating one's immunity to conspiracy theories, one becomes more vulnerable to them. Decrying conspiracy theories as "crazy," while trusting one's own rationality, may thus not only be unfounded, but make us even more vulnerable to such beliefs.

In the two experiments just described, participants were exposed to information that was consistent with conspiracy theories. Another way to test the limits of our rationality involves considering how people respond to facts when those contradict a conspiracy theory. After all, self-proclaimed skeptics should be sensitive to such facts and, like good Bayesians, adjust their beliefs accordingly. To this assumption we now turn.

Empiricism: An antidote?
"A firm belief atthracts facts. They come out iv holes in th' ground an' cracks in th' wall to support belief, but they run away fr'm doubt."
Dunne (1910/2005, "Things spiritual")

We saw that a conspiracy theory is grounded on some "facts." Naturally, this empirical invocation presupposes that the interpretation of a fact is univocal. Yet, even when the authenticity of facts cannot be denied, people adhering to a theory may be immune to facts that blatantly contradict the theory. Consider, for example, a study by Redelmeier and Tversky (1996) on the (unfounded) belief that there is a correlation between atmospheric pressure and arthritis pain. These authors presented their subjects (students) with made-up graphs showing the evolution of the two variables in a 30-day period. It is noteworthy that even when in the graphs arthritic pain and atmospheric pressure were not correlated, the subjects (influenced by the false belief) perceived a relation between the two variables.

This study is a typical example of motivated reasoning (Kunda, 1990), indicating that people will tend to interpret facts in line with their preexisting beliefs. A rational response to a conspiracy theory would involve showcasing evidence that is incompatible with the conspiracy theory – that is, to challenge the facts that lead to its emergence. For example, during his first presidential campaign, Barack Obama was confronted with allegations that his nationality was not really American, but rather Kenyan (or Indonesian) and that he was a Muslim. In response to these allegations, his campaign team set up a website displaying the documents that proved his citizenship, his Christian faith, etc. This strategy is based on the assumption that the supporters of conspiracy theories are capable of correcting their theories once they are confronted with facts that contradict them. However, ample evidence suggests that even when new facts do not conform to an existing theory, they can be assimilated and thus help keep intact its perceived plausibility (cf. Lewandowsky, Ecker, Seifert, Schwarz, & Cook, 2012; Wyer, 1974). The same holds for conspiracy theories. All facts, even those seemingly challenging a conspiracy theory, can be integrated, for example, by evoking a "camouflage attempt" or a "will to divert attention," which renders the theory irrefutable. For example, endorsers of the above mentioned theory concerning Obama argued that the certificate put forth by his team, even though authentic, was not valid because it did not have a stamp.

Belief perseverance

Despite these assimilatory tendencies, adherents to conspiracy theories relish data. As we have already said, a theory emerges because it explains the contingency of some facts. The skeptic can thus expect an adherent to the theory to doubt his or her beliefs in the face of evidence questioning these initial data. Consider, for example, that in the light of newly discovered archives, it is found out that the substance identified as melted steel is compatible with the "airplane collision theory" of the 9/11 bombings. We would expect the theory according to which the two airplanes were a mere diversion to hide a real explosion set up by the Pentagon not to be endorsed anymore. But are we capable of correcting inferences once the facts generating them prove to be wrong a posteriori?

Research on belief perseverance (Anderson, Lepper, & Ross, 1980) undermines this hope. In such studies, people are presented with a finding (e.g., that firefighters have a more risky temperament than others) and asked to explain it. Half of the subjects are subsequently informed that the effect to be explained was actually absent (e.g., there is no correlation between being a firefighter and being risky). In spite of such a debriefing, participants keep believing more in the presence of the effect than a control group (that has not been exposed to the effect).

These results suggest that merely formulating an explanation about an empirically induced relation strengthens the observer's feeling that this relation is true, even if the evidence inducing this relation proves to be false *post hoc*. Such belief perseverance seems to depend in a large part on our tendency to draw inferences from the initial (false) information (Greitemeyer, 2014). When correcting the misinformation, one rarely succeeds in deleting all the inferences that were drawn from it. With respect to conspiracy theories, people who initially formulate conspiracy theories to account for unexpected phenomena may stick to them even in the face of contradictory evidence. For example, in a study by Lewandowsky, Stritzke, Oberauer, and Morales (2005), Americans, who had generally supported the U.S. intervention in Iraq in 2003, still held on to the belief that

Saddam possessed hidden weapons of mass destruction after this information was retracted (and although they knew it had been). Thus, in line with the Spinozan hypothesis, being exposed to information makes people believe it.

The mille-feuilles

Another problem facing skeptics of conspiracy theories resides in the level of expertise often needed to debunk one. The relation between facts and theories is not self-evident. Understanding the relevance of one to the other often demands a level of expertise that few can achieve. For example, the conspiracy theories surrounding 9/11 were backed up by knowledge in the domain of construction, aeronautics, counterintelligence, politics, etc. A single skeptic could hardly master the evidentiary quality of the facts harbored in each of these domains to support the theory. Bronner (2014) has suggested that believers rely on the *mille-feuilles*[1] strategy, which involves relying on a wealth of weak arguments from very different domains. An expert in each of these domains could easily debunk the arguments relevant to her field, but she could not engage with all of them.

To conclude this section, although strategies may be available to correct false conspiracy theories (Lewandowsky et al., 2012), doing so demands overcoming mighty cognitive and motivational barriers that may prove insurmountable.

Paranoid social cognition

In this chapter, we have considered conspiracy theories as reflecting an ordinary mode of reasoning. We highlighted several cognitive processes that may facilitate the elaboration of such theories, especially preferences for explanations featuring intentional factors and stereotyping. Such factors involve data that are immediately available in the believer's environment. We have also alluded to motivational factors that may facilitate adhesion to conspiracy theories. Nevertheless, beyond such purely psychological perspectives, social psychology has done little to shed light on the emergence of conspiracy theories in larger social institutions. A notable exception comes from a model developed by Kramer (1998) in organizational contexts. The model is based on the assumption that beliefs proceed from the interaction between ordinary (and therefore nonpathological) cognitive processes in specific social conditions. He especially considers three factors that may facilitate the development of a "paranoid" social cognition: the perception that the self is "different" from the other members of the organization (e.g., being "new" or belonging to a minority group), uncertainty regarding one's status in the organization, and finally, the perception that one is evaluated within this system. These three factors are thought to produce a form of defiance towards the organization and a state of hypervigilance. The latter results in a tendency to overly detect and interpret ambiguous behavior on the part of colleagues.

Kramer's work constitutes an attempt to approach the emergence of conspiracy beliefs within organizations. He did not consider how such paranoid cognition may develop more broadly across all layers of society. In the next section, we precisely consider how, in the past decades, the development of digital technologies may have facilitated the diffusion of conspiracy theories by exploiting the type of ordinary cognitive functioning we have considered in the previous sections. In doing so, we echo the analyses proposed by the French sociologist Gerald Bronner (2013) that have been widely reported in the French-speaking world, but are not yet available to English-speaking audiences.

How digital information technologies may exacerbate conspiracy theories

Digital technologies may contribute to the endorsement of conspiracy theories in several ways. First, they may facilitate the production and diffusion of unverified information. Second, they may remove barriers to belief in conspiracy theories Third, they may facilitate surveillance by large organizations or states (what we call the "Snowden effect").

The current interests for conspiracy theories stems to a great extent from the expansion of the Internet, which facilitates the diffusion of knowledge. With Internet access, people can easily publicize their thoughts and interpretations about current events and access an almost unlimited store of knowledge about these same events. The number of individuals with Internet access has multiplied nine-fold between 2008 and 2013 (Carlson & Shontell, cited by Sparrow & Chatman, 2013) and the amount of information available on the World Wide Web is gigantic. In line with a situated social cognition perspective (Smith & Semin, 2007), we should consider the "ecology" of the processes we investigate. In this regard, we suggest that the Internet enhances the impact of some of the processes that facilitate the adhesion to conspiracy theories. Let us now consider how.

Availability

The abundance of information available on the Internet may facilitate the endorsement of conspiracy theories in several respects. Thus, Bronner (2013) has shown that pseudoscientific accounts are often more easily available than orthodox explanations of events (e.g., as revealed by a tabulation of Google page ranks). For example, websites about creationism or skeptical about the reality of global warming are more likely to be featured in the top Google search results than are those, respectively, favoring the evolutionary account and the existence of global warming. Bronner has not examined the frequency of conspiracy theories but, if his analysis applies to them as well, the sheer overrepresentation of information consistent with such "theories" may make Internet users more likely to be influenced by them. They are indeed strongly represented on the Internet. For example, when searching for "9/11" on Google,[2] two sites advocating conspiracy theories on the attacks[3] appear in the top 10 searches. Thus, the sheer overrepresentation of information consistent with conspiracy theories may make Internet users more likely to be influenced by them.

We should also consider the influence of digital technology on information processing. This can be considered from the production or the reception side.

On the reception side

Consider a (literate) New Yorker in the early 20th century: Such a person may primarily access information via the print media. At best, information could be updated on a daily basis. Purchasing a newspaper would demand a financial investment and, typically, the amount of information presented in the newspaper would be quite limited, maximizing the likelihood that it will be processed in depth.

Compare this experience with that of a contemporary New Yorker: Information from a vast number of media sources is available instantaneously. Besides, when such information is found, reading it on a screen rather than on paper may lead to more shallow processing (e.g., Mangen, Walgermo, & Bronnick, 2013). In addition, readers will be faced with competing stimuli: images, videos, and advertisements, but also information from other websites or applications. These factors may constitute a formidable challenge for readers' attentional skills. Further, information is likely to be updated much more frequently, further increasing the difficulty of processing it thoroughly.

On the production side

For our imaginary reader of the early 20th century, information was most likely to be provided by professional journalists. Although such information could very well be incorrect, influenced by propaganda, etc., the journalist – materially – had time to verify the information.

Today, the frequent update of information means that the producers of the information often have less time to double check information before broadcasting it. Also, outside of professional journalists, anyone with Internet access may post unverified information.

As Bronner argues, for many producers of information, there may be more rewards to posting interesting information than to posting accurate information. These rewards may be social (e.g., others may enjoy the company of those who communicate information with high entertainment value) or financial (sites with "juicy" information may be more profitable due to advertisement revenue). In this respect, it is important to consider the many intermediaries between the producers and the consumers of information. More and more people are reading newspapers via social networking sites (e.g., "friends" who recommend reading a specific article or share it via their Facebook page). This was possible in a purely offline world (e.g., acquaintances could recommend an article), but we surmise that the expansion of online social networks and the sheer facility of sharing information online considerably accentuates this phenomenon (Bakshy, Rosenn, Marlow, & Adamic, 2012). For these "friends," again, transmitting accurate information may not be a chief concern. Contrary to the actual producers of information, they are not accountable for its content and may therefore convey it with less concern for its accuracy, sometimes even transmitting an article without having read it, just on the basis of its title.

In an environment in which so much information is freely available, the increased pressure on commercial producers of information to gain an edge on their competitors may also facilitate the spreading of unverified information. Besides, there are financial incentives to diverting readers' attentional resources from the core of the story to the advertisements that surround it in the hope of generating more "clicks" and thereby revenue. Although this may reduce the likelihood that people assimilate false information for lack of attention, it may also lead to more shallow, and less critical, processing of such information, and hence to more assimilation. This prediction would be consistent with a Spinozan model and lead to greater endorsement of false information. Thus, this diversion can result in greater gullibility or in greater reliance on causal explanations featuring a single factor (such as a grand conspiracy), because critical thinking and more elaborate explanations demand more cognitive resources.

What is more, Internet users tend to overestimate their Internet literacy (Sparrow & Chatman, 2013). Thus, they tend to believe that they are more competent Internet users than they actually are. Also, people tend to believe that the information they receive on the Internet, such as search engine results, is more objective and reliable than it actually is (Jansen et al., cited by Sparrow & Chatman, 2013). They also tend to believe that online information is more credible than traditional sources (Johnson & Kaye, 1998), when it is not. Based on the analysis we have presented in the previous sections, such overconfidence may render people more likely to be influenced by inaccurate information. The belief that one is a competent Internet user may make her or him less vigilant to possible biases.

The "Snowden effect"

While digital technology may be an efficient channel for the dissemination of conspiracy theories, it is also possible that the very structure of the Internet may contribute to producing, rather than simply broadcasting, such theories. Indeed, as more people are interconnected, collecting data about individuals becomes much easier. When you buy a book at an online bookstore, this bookstore often has much more information on you than the typical offline bookseller does. Private companies, but also governments, actively collect such information. The perception that one is under surveillance from companies and governments, while it may seem paranoid, is actually true (Ball, Borger, & Greenwald, 2013). There is a leap from holding such a belief to espousing conspiracy theories, but not a great one. When companies or governments actively monitor users' activity, it is easy to attribute to them malicious intentions for doing so and secret plans. Conspiracy theories may easily shape up.

On the one hand, by creating the conditions for such surveillance, these technological advances may paradoxically increase skepticism towards any information and therefore make people *less* gullible. After all, shouldn't the realization that the media collects information about individuals result in less trust towards content posted on the Internet, including questionable conspiracy theories?

While this inference may be logically appropriate, a generalized distrust of information communicated on the Internet may not lead people to become more skeptical of conspiracy theories. On the contrary, it may fuel a tendency to disbelieve information that comes from easily accessible and mainstream sources more than anything else and therefore contribute to conspiracy thinking: "The truth must be hidden somewhere," far from our eyes. The increasing distrust towards the media, which predates the Snowden case (Gallup, 2013), provides a fertile ground for such tendencies. Such distrust indeed predicts a tendency to turn towards nonmainstream media sources (Tsfati & Cappella, 2003) – that is, those that are most likely to advocate conspiracy theories.

Further, distrust in government and official discourse is one of the main drivers of adhesion to conspiracy theories (Douglas & Sutton, 2008). To the extent that official accounts of events coincide with the mainstream media (as is the case, for example, for global warming or the 9/11 terrorist attacks), Internet users may easily confuse both.

These, admittedly speculative, conjectures suggest that the Internet provides an ideal environment for promoting the form of paranoid cognition highlighted by Kramer (1998), and, by extension, adhesion to conspiracy theories, not only because it may serve as a channel for broadcasting such theories, but because it creates favorable conditions for the development of a generalized distrust of (official) institutions.

Conclusion

We began this chapter by showing that people generally define themselves as rational and mentally sane individuals as opposed to the deluded believers in conspiracy theories. We have then suggested that, contrary to this belief, the cognitive processes driving adhesion to conspiracy theories were perfectly ordinary and did not depend on pathological tendencies.

Based on a Spinozan model, we suggested that extra effort is demanded to "unbelieve" information that, by default, is considered as true. This may render people particularly vulnerable to conspiracy theories. Combined with self-perceptions as "rational" and "not easily influenced," it may result in an underestimation of one's own gullibility as well. This, we suggested, may not be without consequences, as self-inflated beliefs in one's rationality may foreclose the effortful "epistemic vigilance" necessary to discard information that is consistent with conspiracy theories.

In view of this analysis, we suggested that digital media may constitute an ideal breeding ground for the emergence of conspiracy theories for several reasons. First, because by providing an immense amount of information, the cost of engaging in effortful disbelieving of questionable information is higher. Second, because the Internet can be viewed as a competitive "ideas market" (Bronner, 2011), which rewards the production of entertaining information at the expense of accuracy. Third, because it enables a mass surveillance of citizens, which may fuel suspicion and encourage paranoid social cognition.

Author note

This chapter is partially based on a text previously published in French (Klein & Van der Linden, 2010). This work was conducted within the framework of COST Action IS1205 "Social psychological dynamics of historical representations in the enlarged European Union." Correspondence regarding this chapter should be addressed to Olivier Klein. E-mail: oklein@ulb.ac.be

Notes

1 A *mille-feuilles* is a multi-layered cake traditional in French pastry.
2 On June 30, 2014.
3 911Truth.org and www.reopen911.info

References

Ahn, W. K., & Bailenson, J. (1996). Causal attribution as a search for underlying mechanisms: An explanation of the conjunction fallacy and the discounting principle. *Cognitive Psychology, 31*, 82–123.

Anderson, C. A., Lepper, M. R., & Ross, L. (1980). Perseverance of social theories: The role of explanation in the persistence of discredited information. *Journal of Personality and Social Psychology, 39*, 1037–1049.

Bakshy, E., Rosenn, I., Marlow, C., & Adamic, L. (2012, April). The role of social networks in information diffusion. In Proceedings of the 21st International Conference on World Wide Web (pp. 519–528).

Ball, J., Borger, J., & Greenwald, G. (2013, September 6). Revealed: How US and UK spy agencies defeat internet privacy and security. *The Guardian*. Retrieved from http://www.theguardian.com/world/2013/sep/05/nsa-gchq-encryption-codes-security

Bronner, G. (2011). *The future of collective beliefs*. Oxford: Bardwell Press.

Bronner, G. (2013). *La démocratie des crédules* [The democracy of the Credulous]. Paris: Presses Universitaires de France.

Bronner, G. (2014). *La planète des hommes. Réenchanter le risque* [Planet of men. Reenchant risk]. Paris: Presses Universitaires de France.

Campbell, D. T. (1958). Common fate, similarity, and other indices of the status of aggregates of person as social entities. *Behavioural Science, 3*, 14–25.

Davison, W. P. (1983). The third-person effect in communication. *Public Opinion Quarterly, 47*, 1–15.

Descartes, R. (2010). *Metaphysical mediations*. Grenoble, France: PhiloSophie. Retrieved June 30, 2014, from http://www.ac-grenoble.fr/PhiloSophie/file/descartes_mediations.pdf (Original work published in 1641.)

Douglas, K. M., & Sutton, R. M. (2008). The hidden impact of conspiracy theories: Perceived and actual influence of theories surrounding the death of Princess Diana. *Journal of Social Psychology, 148*, 210–222.

Dunne, F. P. (2005). *Mr. Dooley says*. Retrieved from http://www.gutenberg.org/files/ 14684/14684-h/14684-h.htm (Original work published 1910.)

Fiedler, K., Freytag, P., & Unkelbach, C. (2011). Great oaks from giant acorns grow: How causal-impact judgments depend on the strength of a cause. *European Journal of Social Psychology, 41*, 162–172.

Fischhoff, B. (1980). For those condemned to study the past: Reflections on historical judgment. *New Directions for Methodology of Social and Behavioral Sciences, 4*, 79–93.

Fiske, S. T., Cuddy, A. J., & Glick, P. (2007). Universal dimensions of social cognition: Warmth and competence. *Trends in Cognitive Sciences, 11*, 77–83.

Gallup. (2013). *Global states of mind*. Retrieved from http://www.gallup.com/poll/165497/ global-states-mind-2013.aspx

Gilbert, D. T., Tafarodi, R. W., & Malone, P. S. (1993). You can't not believe everything you read. *Journal of Personality and Social Psychology, 65*, 221–233.

Glick, P. (2002). Sacrificial lambs dressed in wolves' clothing: Envious prejudice, ideology, and the scapegoating of Jews. In L. S. Newman & R. Erber (Eds.), *Understanding genocide: The social psychology of the Holocaust* (pp. 113–142). London: Oxford University Press.

Goethe, J. W. (2009). *The sorrows of Young Werther*. Retrieved from http://www.gutenberg. org/files/2527/2527-h/2527-h.htm (Original work published 1774.)

Greitemeyer, T. (2014). Article retracted, but the message lives on. *Psychonomic Bulletin & Review, 21*(2), 557–561.

Grzesiak-Feldman, M., & Suszek, H. (2008). Conspiracy stereotyping and perceptions of group entitativity of Jews, Germans, Arabs and Homosexuals by Polish students. *Psychological Reports, 102*, 755–758.

Hart, H. L. A., & Honoré, T. (1959). *Causation in the law*. Oxford: Clarendon Press.

Hasson, U., Simmons, J. P., & Todorov, A. (2005). Believe it or not: On the possibility of suspending belief. *Psychological Science, 16*, 566–571.

Heider, F. (1944). Social perception and phenomenal causality. *Psychological Review, 51*(6), 358–374.

Johnson, J. T., & Kaye, B. K. (1998). Cruising is believing? Comparing internet and traditional sources on media credibility measures. *Journalism & Mass Communication Quarterly, 75*, 325–340.

Johnson, J. T., Long, D. L., & Robinson, M. D. (2001). Is a cause conceptualized as a generative force? Evidence from a recognition memory paradigm. *Journal of Experimental Social Psychology, 37*, 398–412.

Kahneman, D. (2011). *Thinking, fast and slow*. New York: Macmillan.

Keeley, B. L. (1999). Of conspiracy theories. *Journal of Philosophy, 96*, 109–126.

Kissine, M., & Klein, O. (2013). Models of epistemic communication, epistemic trust and epistemic vigilance. In J. Forgas, J. Laslzo, & O. Vincze (Eds.), *Sydney symposium on social psychology: Social cognition and communication* (Vol. 14, pp. 139–154). New York: Psychology Press.

Klein, O., & Van Der Linden, N. (2010). *Lorsque la cognition sociale devient paranoïde ou les aléas du scepticisme face aux théories du complot* [When social cognition becomes paranoid: The hazards of skepticism towards conspiracy theories]. In E. Danblon & L. Nicolas (Eds.), *Les rhétoriques de la conspiration* (pp. 133–152). Paris: CNRS.

Kofta, M., & Sedek, G. (2005). Conspiracy stereotypes of Jews during systemic transformation in Poland. *International Journal of Sociology, 35*(1), 40–64.

Kramer, R. M. (1998). Paranoid cognition in social systems: Thinking and acting in the shadow of doubt. *Personality and Social Psychology Review, 2*, 251–275.

Kunda, Z. (1990). The case for motivated reasoning. *Psychological Bulletin, 108*(3), 480–498.

Lewandowsky, S., Ecker, U. K. H., Seifert, C. M., Schwarz, N., & Cook, J. (2012). Misinformation and its correction: Continued influence and successful debiasing. *Psychological Science in the Public Interest, 13*(3), 106–131.

Lewandowsky, S., Stritzke, W. G., Oberauer, K., & Morales, M. (2005). Memory for fact, fiction, and misinformation: The Iraq war 2003. *Psychological Science, 16,* 190–195.

Licata, L., & Klein, O. (2000). *Situation de crise, explications profanes et citoyenneté: L'affaire Dutroux* [Crisis situations, lay explanations and citizenship: The Dutroux case]. *Cahiers Internationaux de Psychologie Sociale, 47–48,* 155–174.

Lickel, B., Hamilton, D. L., Wieczorkowska, G., Lewis, A., Sherman, S. J., & Uhles, A. N. (2000). Varieties of groups and the perception of group entitativity. *Journal of Personality and Social Psychology, 78*(2), 223.

Lorenzi-Cioldi, F. (2002). *Les représentations des groups dominés: collections et agrégats* [Representations of subordinate groups: Collections and aggregates]. Grenoble, France: Presses Universitaires de Grenoble.

Mangen, A., Walgermo, B. R., & Brønnick, K. (2013). Reading linear texts on paper versus computer screen: Effects on reading comprehension. *International Journal of Educational Research, 58,* 61–68.

McClure, J., Hilton, D. J., & Sutton, R. M. (2007). Judgments of voluntary and physical causes in causal chains: Probabilistic and social functionalist criteria for attributions. *European Journal of Social Psychology, 37,* 879–901.

Oliver, J. E., & Wood, T. J. (in press). Conspiracy theories and the paranoid style(s) of mass opinion. *American Journal of Political Science.*

Pantazi, M., Klein, O., Douglas, K., & Kissine, M. (2014). The influence of self-perceptions as rational on the endorsement of conspiracy theories. Manuscript in preparation.

Redelmeier, D. A., & Tversky, A. (1996). On the belief that arthritis pain is related to the weather. *Proceedings of the National Academy of Sciences, 93,* 2895–2896.

Richter, T., Schroeder, S., & Wöhrmann, B. (2009). You don't have to believe everything you read: Background knowledge permits fast and efficient validation of information. *Journal of Personality and Social Psychology, 96,* 538–558.

Rosset, E. (2008). It's no accident: Our bias for intentional explanations. *Cognition, 108,* 771–780.

Rothschild, Z. K., Landau, M. J., Sullivan, D., & Keefer, L. A. (2012). A dual-motive model of the motives underlying scapegoating: Displacing blame to reduce guilt or increase control. *Journal of Personality and Social Psychology, 102*(6), 1148–1163.

Schwarz, N., Bless, H., Strack, F., Klumpp, G., Rittenauer-Schatka, H., & Simons, A. (1991). Ease of retrieval as information: Another look at the availability heuristic. *Journal of Personality and Social Psychology, 61,* 195–202.

Smith, E. R., & Semin, G. R. (2007). Situated social cognition. *Current Directions in Psychological Science, 16,* 132–135.

Sparrow, B., & Chatman, L. (2013). Social cognition in the internet age: Same as it ever was? *Psychological Inquiry, 24*(4), 273–292.

Spinoza, B. (2003). *Ethics* (R. H. M. Elwes, Trans). Project Gutenberg. Retrieved June 30, 2014, from http://www.gutenberg.org/files/3800/3800-h/3800-h.htm (Original work published in 1677.)

Sullivan, D., Landau, M. J., & Rothschild, Z. K. (2010). An existential function of enemyship: Evidence that people attribute influence to personal and political enemies to compensate for threats to control. *Journal of Personality and Social Psychology, 98,* 434–449.

Swami, V. (2012). Social psychological origins of conspiracy theories: The case of the Jewish conspiracy theory in Malaysia. *Frontiers in Psychology, 3,* 280.

Tsfati, Y., & Cappella, J. (2003). Do people watch what they do not trust? Exploring the association between news media skepticism and exposure. *Communication Research, 30,* 504–529.

Tversky, A., & Kahneman, D. (1974). Judgment under uncertainty: Heuristics and biases. *Science, 185*(4157), 1124–1131.

Tversky, A., & Kahneman, D. (1983). Extensional versus intuitive reasoning: The conjunction fallacy in probability judgment. *Psychological Review, 90,* 293.

Uhlmann, E. L., & Cohen, G. L. (2007). "I think it, therefore it's true": Effects of self-perceived objectivity on hiring discrimination. *Organizational Behavior and Human Decision Processes.*

van Prooijen, J.-W., & Jostmann, N. B. (2013). Belief in conspiracy theories: The influence of uncertainty and perceived morality. *European Journal of Social Psychology, 43*(1), 109–115.

Wyer, R. S. (1974). *Cognitive organization and change: An information processing approach.* Hillsdale, NJ: Erlbaum.

Yzerbyt, V., Judd, C. M., & Corneille, O. (Eds.). (2004). *The psychology of group perception: Perceived variability, entitativity, and essentialism.* London: Psychology Press.

10

THE SOCIAL, POLITICAL, ENVIRONMENTAL, AND HEALTH-RELATED CONSEQUENCES OF CONSPIRACY THEORIES

Problems and potential solutions

Karen M. Douglas, Robbie M. Sutton, Daniel Jolley, and Michael J. Wood

CBS News recently reported how one unvaccinated child may have sparked an outbreak of measles in the U.S. state of Minnesota, sickening 19 children and 2 adults (CBS News, 2014). The outbreak reportedly began when an unvaccinated two-year-old boy was taken to Kenya, where he contracted the measles virus. On returning to the United States the child became ill, but prior to being diagnosed he had passed on the virus to three children in a childcare center and to one household member. When contacts then multiplied, over 3,000 people had been exposed to the virus. While nine of the children who were ultimately infected were of an age to receive the combined measles–mumps–rubella (MMR) vaccination that would have prevented infection, they had not received it. According to researchers at the Minnesota Department of Health, the majority of parents of the unvaccinated children feared that the MMR vaccine could cause autism (CBS News, 2014).

Although the link between the MMR vaccine and autism – made by former British physician Andrew Wakefield – has since been thoroughly discredited (Demicheli, Rivetti, Debalini, & Di Pietrantoni, 2012), doubts still remain in the popular imagination about the safety of the MMR vaccine. Indeed, a highly visible antivaccine movement has done much to promote public suspicion not only about the safety and efficacy of the MMR vaccine, but of childhood vaccinations in general. This movement is characterized by accusations of conspiracy, deceit, and cover-ups on the part of the medical establishment. A senior U.S. pediatrician argued that outbreaks like the one in Minnesota point to the "power of bad information," arguing further that "the first infection that spread in the community was misinformation. The second was measles" (CBS News, 2014).

This case suggests that once they have reached public awareness, unfounded conspiracy allegations may be a powerful source of influence, swaying people's attitudes, intentions, and behaviors, with potentially damaging consequences not only for individuals, but also for the broader society. In the case of vaccination, it only takes a small number of refusals to compromise herd immunity and see the return of diseases long thought to have been eliminated. In this chapter, we explore the potential consequences of conspiracy theories such as this in some detail, focusing on the potential effects of social, political, and health-related conspiracy theories on people's attitudes, intentions, and behaviors. We then outline the existing research in this area and outline some suggestions that have been made by scholars for dealing with the influence of conspiracy theories. Finally, we make some suggestions for future research.

Conspiracy theories

As discussed throughout this volume, conspiracy theories can be defined as explanations for significant political and social events that place responsibility on secret and malevolent forces (e.g., Douglas & Sutton, 2008; 2011; Goertzel, 1994; McCauley & Jacques, 1979; Sunstein & Vermeule, 2009; Wood, Douglas, & Sutton, 2012). For example, popular conspiracy theories allege that Princess Diana was murdered by elements within the British government or the royal family and that the 9/11 attacks were deliberately organized by the United States government as a "false flag" terrorist attack to justify the war on terror. Conspiracy theories are a prominent feature of contemporary culture, facilitated by the ease of sharing information across digital channels (Coady, 2006). They are often viewed as contagious, capturing public interest and drawing attention from logical explanations in favor of nebulous plots, plans, and intrigue (Swami & Coles, 2010; Huffington Post, 2014). Goertzel (2010) pointed out that while they are easy to propagate, they are difficult to refute, for reasons that will become clear in this chapter.

In recent years, psychologists have made good ground in understanding the psychological factors that are associated with the tendency to believe in conspiracy theories. One of the most powerful predictors of belief in conspiracy theories turns out to be belief in other conspiracy theories. That is, people are likely to believe in a particular conspiracy theory if they also believe in others (Goertzel, 1994). Remarkably, this phenomenon may be observed even when conspiracy theories contradict each other. For example, Princess Diana could not possibly have faked her own death and also have been murdered by the royal family, and yet people who believe the "alive" conspiracy theory are also likely to believe that she was murdered (Sutton & Douglas, 2014; Wood et al., 2012).

The tendency for people who believe some conspiracy theories to also believe others has often been interpreted as evidence that belief in such theories is part and parcel of a *monological mindset* (Goertzel, 1994; Wood et al., 2012). This mindset is closed to specific facts and new ideas that threaten to undermine belief in other conspiracy theories. Thus, an adherent of established conspiracy theories will be highly receptive to conspiracy theories about a new event, since these are coherent with his or her worldview and will tend not to avoid or attempt to explain away specific facts about the new event that might disconfirm a conspiracy. However, as Sutton and Douglas (2014) argue, this account suffers from several problems. There is little evidence to suggest that conspiracy theorists are less sensitive to specific facts, and there is even some evidence that they are more, rather than less, open to new ideas and experiences. Indeed there is some evidence that nonadherents of conspiracy theories are rather more vituperative in the defense of their ideas and rejection of alternative explanations (Wood & Douglas, 2013). Although it is clear that belief in some conspiracy theories provokes distrust in authority (Jolley & Douglas, 2014a) and therefore facilitates the adoption of new conspiracy beliefs (Swami et al., 2013), this does not mean that conspiracy beliefs, together, form a closed and internally consistent belief system.

Although conspiracy beliefs may not comprise a monological belief system, it remains true that they tend to be correlated with each other, and this may be due to the fact that, in general, conspiracy beliefs are predicted by much the same variables (Sutton & Douglas, 2014; see also Kossowska & Bukowski, this volume). Various cognitive factors have also been found to be associated with conspiracy beliefs, such as beliefs in the paranormal (Darwin, Neave, & Holmes, 2011; Lobato, Mendoza, Sims, & Chin, in press; Newheiser, Farias, & Tausch, 2011; Stieger, Gumhalter, Tran, Voracek, & Swami, 2013), feelings of uncertainty (van Prooijen & Jostmann, 2013), ambivalence (van Harreveld, Rutjens, Schneider, Nohlen, & Keskinis, in press), and the tendency to overestimate the likelihood of co-occurring events (Brotherton & French, 2014). Conspiracy beliefs may also reflect a tendency to attribute insignificant events to mundane causes and larger causes to more significant events (Leman & Cinnerella, 2007; McCauley & Jacques, 1979), as well as the tendency to project one's own moral leanings onto the alleged conspirators (Douglas & Sutton, 2011).

Conspiracy beliefs have also been found to be associated with individual differences variables such as Machiavellianism (Douglas & Sutton, 2011), schizotypy (Darwin et al., 2011), anomie, distrust in authority, political cynicism, and powerlessness (Abalakina-Paap, Stephan, Craig, & Gregory, 1999; Goertzel, 1994). Some studies have shown that conspiracy belief is positively associated with openness to experience (Swami et al., 2011; Swami et al., 2013), though others have failed to replicate this correlation (Brotherton, French, & Pickering, 2013; Swami & Furnham, 2012). Further, some scholars argue that conspiracy theories may appeal to creative (e.g., Carson, Peterson, & Higgins, 2005), curious (e.g., Flegg & Hukins, 1973), or sensitive (e.g., Guarino, Roger, & Olason, 2007) individuals, although no research to date supports these claims.

Finally, various demographic factors have been found to be associated with conspiracy beliefs, such as age (Swami, 2012), education level (Bird & Bogart, 2003; Oliver & Wood, 2014), annual income (Bird & Bogart, 2003), perceived importance of religion (Oliver & Wood, 2014), religiosity (Furnham, 2013), ethnic minority status (Crocker, Luhtanen, Broadnax, & Blaine, 1999), and political orientation (Furnham, 2013; Inglehart, 1987; Oliver & Wood, 2014). Researchers have therefore made significant progress in understanding the characteristics and thought patterns of people who are likely to believe in conspiracy theories.

Much less is known, however, about the consequences of believing in, or being exposed to, conspiracy narratives. Researchers may have largely overlooked this issue because conspiracy theories are commonly thought to be harmless, trivial notions held by people only on the outer fringes of society (Bratich, 2008; Sunstein & Vermeule, 2009). If people perceive that only the most paranoid and distrustful individuals entertain conspiracy theories, they may also perceive that conspiracy theories will have little or no influence on the more rational majority of society. Further, the term "conspiracy theory" itself tends to be viewed negatively, and people who believe them are often characterized as deluded, crazy "conspiracy theorists," disconnected from logic and reason (Bratich, 2008; Husting & Orr, 2007).

Of course, making such general assumptions about conspiracy theories and their adherents overlooks the heterogeneity of both. Specifically, it is one thing to assume certain characteristics of individuals who believe that the world is run by lizard people and that Bigfoot is real, but quite another to assume that everyone who endorses antivaccine conspiracy theories is detached from reality. We think that this may be another reason why people dismiss the potential consequences of conspiracy theories. By characterizing all conspiracy theories as ridiculous regardless of what they are about, those that can be easily dismissed are not differentiated from those that are plausible. Further, those that are trivial are not distinguished from those that may have socially important consequences, as may be the case for antivaccine conspiracy theories and those concerning anthropogenic global warming. Indeed, people attempting to debunk conspiracy theories often compare them to seemingly outlandish theories such as those involving alien abduction, Bigfoot, and Elvis Presley (Wood & Douglas, 2013). Drawing a connection between these highly esoteric conspiracy theories and more mundane ones concerning assassinations, wars, and medicine implicitly dismisses the latter theories as trivial speculation or the product of mental illness.

When sharing information with others on the Internet is so quick and effortless, it is also important to consider the possible consequences of everyday exposure to conspiracy theories. As Goertzel (2010) puts it, conspiracy theories may be best characterized as "memes" that pass from one mind to another and either survive or die out via processes similar to natural selection (Dawkins, 1976). Goertzel (2010) argues that such memes may be dangerous if they are used to discredit information for which there is clear scientific or legal confirmation.

There is already empirical evidence to suggest that exposure to some conspiracy theories may indeed change the way people think about social events. For example, Douglas and Sutton (2008) asked participants to read a paragraph that highlighted conspiracy theories surrounding the death of Princess Diana. Participants were then asked to rate how much they agreed with a series of conspiracy-related statements about her death (e.g., "There was an official campaign by MI6 to assassinate Princess Diana, sanctioned by elements of the establishment") and were also asked to rate what they thought their attitudes were before they read the material. Compared to controls, participants who had read about the conspiracy

theories were more likely to agree with the conspiracy-related statements. Exposure to the conspiracy theories therefore changed participants' attitudes concerning the death of Princess Diana. However, these participants did not perceive that
their attitudes had changed. Specifically, they did not rate their retrospective attitudes as significantly different to their attitudes after having read the conspiracy
material. Further, Butler, Koopman, and Zimbardo (1995) found that people who
had viewed the film *JFK* – which explores several popular conspiracy theories
surrounding the assassination of President John F. Kennedy – disbelieved official
explanations more than those who had not seen the film. Douglas and Sutton
(2008) argued that conspiracy theories may therefore have a "hidden impact"
(p. 217) on people's attitudes and beliefs about significant events, altering their
attitudes potentially without their awareness.

If conspiracy theories indeed have the power to change people's attitudes about
significant social and political events, then they have the potential to change
people's social and political behavior. If conspiracy theories are able to influence
people without their awareness, then their political and social consequences may
fairly be described as not only hidden but also as insidious. It is therefore necessary
to consider how intentions and behaviors can change when people are convinced
by conspiracy theories. Researchers have suggested that there may be both benefits
and costs, and we highlight these in the following sections.

Potential benefits of conspiracy theories

First, researchers have pointed to some of the potential positive consequences of
conspiracy theories. For example, belief in 9/11 conspiracy theories tends to be
associated with greater support for democratic principles (Swami, Chamorro-
Premuzic, & Furnham, 2010), though as with much of the research on the subject,
which to date has been correlational, it is not clear which one causes the other or
if there is a causal relationship at all.

It has also been argued that conspiracy theories may allow individuals to challenge
social hierarchies and question the actions of those in power. In doing so, accusations
of conspiracy may result in increased government transparency (e.g., Clarke, 2002;
Fenster, 1999; Swami & Coles, 2010). In line with this characterization, Freedom of
Information requests by conspiracist individuals or organizations have resulted in the
declassification of a variety of official documents. For example, requests from UFO
enthusiast groups resulted in the declassification of Project Blue Book, the U.S. Air
Force's own internal investigation into UFO sightings (Clark, 1998).

Conspiracy theories can also reveal inconsistencies in official accounts of events
(e.g., Clarke, 2002) and may open up possibilities for political debate (Miller, 2002).
Indeed, some conspiracy theories reveal genuine anomalies in official explanations
and may even uncover actual conspiracies. One example was the U.S. Department
of Defense's plans to coordinate terrorist actions and pin the blame on Cuba in
the 1960s (Swami & Coles, 2010). Such theories may therefore encourage political
powers to provide solid evidence for their claims.

Potential costs of conspiracy theories

On the negative side, beliefs in conspiracy theories have been found to be weakly associated with negative attitudes towards human rights and civil liberties (Swami et al., 2012), and also racist attitudes (Swami, 2012; see also Imhoff, this volume). For example, Golec de Zavala and Cichocka (2012) found that belief in conspiracy theories about Jewish domination of the world (e.g., Kofta & Sędek, 2005) were associated with anti-Semitic attitudes (see also Bilewicz & Sędek, this volume; Cichocka, Golec de Zavala, Marchlewska, & Olechowski, this volume). Imhoff and Bruder (2014) found that conspiracy beliefs were a significant predictor of prejudice against a variety of high-power groups (e.g., Jews, Americans, and capitalists). Further, in a sample of White Americans, reports of negative contact with Black Americans was found to be associated with expressed doubts about Barack Obama's American citizenship and his eligibility to be president of the United States (Barlow et al., 2012). This conspiracy theory may at least in part be racially motivated (Barlow et al., 2012) and suggests that some conspiracy theories may be a way of expressing prejudice towards particular groups.

Conspiracy theories may not only worsen poisoned intergroup relations but may contribute to mass illness and mortality. One prominent conspiracy theory proposes that birth control and HIV/AIDS are a form of genocide against African Americans (Bird & Bogart, 2003). Among African Americans, including HIV-positive individuals, endorsement of this conspiracy theory is associated with increased engagement in risky behaviors, such as avoiding treatment programs and not using condoms (Bogart & Thorburn, 2006; Bogart, Wagner, Galvan, & Banks, 2010; Bogart, Galvan, Wagner, & Klein, 2011; Hoyt et al., 2012). Also, negative attitudes towards condoms have been shown to partially mediate the relationship between conspiracy beliefs and condom use (Bogart & Thorburn, 2006). Further, it has been estimated that over 330,000 South Africans died between 2000 and 2005, arguably at least in part due to a government statement that HIV is not the cause of AIDS and that antiretroviral (ARV) drugs are not useful in controlling HIV infection (Chigwedere, Seage, Gruskin, Lee, & Essex, 2008). The South African government also declined to accept donations of ARV medication. This work points to the harmful influence that conspiracy theories may therefore have on people's health decisions and behaviors.

Goertzel (2010) further argued that conspiracy theories targeting scientific research can have drastic and often tragic consequences. Citing anecdotal examples from medicine and research on global warming, Goertzel argued that the conspiracy meme can powerfully influence how people engage with social issues, resulting ultimately in harmful consequences such as refusals to vaccinate and exercise birth control. By arousing a strong fear and suspicion of science (see also Lewandowsky, Oberauer, & Gignac, 2013), conspiracy theories may lead people to a state of inaction and disengagement.

To provide a concrete example of this potentially negative effect, Oliver and Wood (2014) have shown that over half of the U.S. population endorses medical conspiracy theories, such as the vaccine–autism link. They also found that people who endorse such conspiracy theories are less likely to engage with medical professionals (e.g., getting regular checkups), are more likely than nonbelievers to trust medical advice from nonmedical people such as family, friends, and celebrities, and are more likely to choose alternative medicines to cure illness rather than to use tested medical vaccines.

Finally, some theorists have argued that conspiracy theories may be a catalyst for radicalized and extremist behavior (Bartlett & Miller, 2010; see also van Prooijen & Krouwel, this volume). In an analysis of a broad range of extremist groups, Bartlett and Miller demonstrated that conspiracy theories are widely prevalent and that there is a great deal of overlap between many of the conspiracies, even across groups that are at opposite ends of the ideological spectrum. For example, both extreme right- and extreme left-wing groups tend to endorse anti-Jewish capitalist conspiracy theories. According to Bartlett and Miller (2010), conspiracy theories play an important social and functional role for extremist groups. Although it is not possible to demonstrate direct causal effects of conspiracy theories on extremist behavior, Bartlett and Miller (2010) argue that conspiracy theories may be a "radicalizing multiplier" (p. 4) that contributes to the ideologies and psychological processes within the group. For example, it may contribute to a siege mentality in which the group is surrounded by devious and sophisticated enemies and lead to hostile attributions for the innocent or at least ambiguous actions of other groups. Ultimately, this may lead to more extreme and violent behavior. Bartlett and Miller argue that in fighting the ideology of extremist groups, counterterrorism strategists must address the misinformation associated with conspiracy theories.

Experimental research on the potential costs of conspiracy theories

Research and theorizing to date suggest that conspiracy theories may have some benefits, but that the costs may be more significant and may therefore be more worthy of researchers' attention. Conspiracy theories may indeed encourage government transparency, but if enough people refuse to have their children vaccinated, then the impact on regional, national, and possibly international health may be catastrophic. Scholars are recognizing the potential barriers and opportunities presented by conspiracy theories. However, one significant limitation of existing research is that it has been based on either anecdotal evidence or correlational data investigating relationships between conspiracy beliefs and various attitudes and behavioral intentions. To date, therefore, it has not been possible to establish whether conspiracy theories have specific consequences, or whether what we view as consequences (e.g., racist attitudes, vaccine refusal) are themselves causes of greater belief in conspiracy theories. Research has therefore not yet explicitly addressed whether conspiracy theories make things happen. In our research, we have therefore set out to examine experimentally whether or not exposure to conspiracy theories has direct consequences on attitudes and intentions.

First, we examined the effects of being persuaded of the merits of conspiracy theories on political engagement (Jolley & Douglas, 2014a). As mentioned earlier, some scholars have argued that conspiracy theories may open up debate about the actions of governments and thus spark political action (e.g., Miller, 2002). However, we hypothesized that conspiracy theories may in fact discourage political action by inducing feelings of powerlessness and mistrust. Specifically, people may not be inclined to engage with a political system that deceives and misleads them. Conspiracy theories may therefore discourage people from voting and taking other forms of political action. To test this idea, we manipulated exposure to pro- and anti-conspiracy arguments and examined their impact on behavioral intentions (Jolley & Douglas, 2014a). In Study 1, we focused on governmental conspiracy theories. Participants were presented with one of two articles, arguing either in favor of theories that the government is involved in secret plots and schemes (e.g., 9/11, death of Princess Diana), or arguing against such theories. Participants also reported feelings of mistrust, powerlessness, uncertainty, and disillusionment towards the government, which were measured as potential mediators. Participants' intended political behavior (e.g., to vote, to engage in legitimate protests) formed the dependent variable. Results revealed that participants who had been exposed to conspiracy theories showed less intention to engage in politics than those who had read anticonspiracy arguments. This effect was mediated by feelings of political powerlessness.

The second study used a similar approach to examine the impact of climate change conspiracy theories. In this important domain, conspiracy theories downplay or discredit the scientific evidence for anthropogenic global warming. We argue that such conspiracy theories are likely to discourage people from taking action to reduce their carbon footprint. Specifically, if people believe that climate change is a hoax, then they will also be likely to believe that nothing needs to be done about it. Our study revealed that exposure to several such theories reduced intentions to engage in climate-friendly behaviors in comparison to participants exposed to anticonspiracy information and controls. This effect was mediated by feelings of uncertainty, disillusionment, and powerlessness associated with climate change.

Second, we examined the effects of being persuaded to accept conspiracy theories on intended health behavior. Specifically, we examined the effects of being exposed to antivaccine conspiracy theories, arguing that such theories would sway people against the important decision to vaccinate their children. Jolley and Douglas (2014b, Study 2) used a similar experimental method after demonstrating a correlation between belief in antivaccine conspiracy theories and intentions to have a fictitious child vaccinated against a made-up disease. In this study, participants were exposed to common conspiracy theories surrounding vaccines (e.g., that they harm more than they help and that this fact is covered up), an anticonspiracy counterargument, or no argument (control). It was found that vaccination intentions were significantly lower in the proconspiracy condition than in the anticonspiracy condition and control. Overall, it appeared that participants in the proconspiracy condition were reluctant to vaccinate compared to the other two conditions, because the conspiracy information aroused suspicion concerning the perceived dangers of vaccines and made people feel powerless, disillusioned, and mistrustful.

As we mentioned earlier, psychologists have made significant ground in understanding the individual traits associated with beliefs in conspiracy theories, but there has been limited research concerning what these beliefs entail. Our research program to date experimentally demonstrates that conspiracy theories may be an important source of a disengagement with politics (by reducing intentions to vote), a lack of concern about the environment (by reducing intentions to engage in climate-friendly behaviors), and a disengagement with important health recommendations (by reducing intentions to engage in child vaccination regimes). These findings demonstrate that conspiracy theories may therefore have potentially disastrous consequences for politics, the environment, and health-related behaviors. One question remains, therefore. If conspiracy theories do indeed have potentially negative consequences, what, if anything, should be done about them?

Addressing the consequences of conspiracy theories

Researchers have suggested various ways of dealing with the potential impact of conspiracy theories. Sunstein and Vermeule (2009) focused specifically on conspiracy theories related to terrorism – especially those that postdate the 9/11 attacks – arguing that such conspiracy theories pose risks to government antiterrorist efforts. Sunstein and Vermeule put forward various ways in which conspiracy theories may be undermined by governments to ensure public safety. First, it may be possible to ban conspiracy theorizing altogether, although this suggestion is of course undemocratic, unreasonable, and impractical. Second, governments may be able to impose a financial disincentive (e.g., a tax) for people who disseminate conspiracy theories – a solution that seems a softer but no less undemocratic version of the first. Third, governments themselves may engage in counterspeech, arguing against conspiracy theories. Fourth, credible private parties may be hired to engage in counterspeech. Fifth, governments may informally communicate with credible private parties and enlist their help. However, Sunstein and Vermeule assert that engaging in "cognitive infiltration" – a combination of the third, fourth, and fifth elements above – will be the most effective. By entering conspiracist groups and planting ideas to undermine the "crippled epistemology" (p. 15) of individuals who subscribe to conspiracy theories, a broader diversity of ideas can tempt people away from conspiratorial thinking.

Sunstein and Vermeule (2009) also note, however, that conspiracy theories may be extremely resistant to correction, and "contrary evidence can usually be shown to be a product of the conspiracy itself" (p. 210). In other words, conspiracy theory believers may feel that by providing an alternative account, the conspirators are deliberately planting an alternative account to cover their tracks (Sunstein & Vermeule, 2009). Jolley and Douglas's (2014b) results support this suggestion. While exposure to proconspiracy information (arguing in favor of antivaccine conspiracy theories) reduced intentions to vaccinate a fictional child in comparison to a control condition where no information was presented, anticonspiracy information (refuting antivaccine conspiracy theories) had no effect relative to control. This suggests that conspiracy theories may indeed be resistant to correction. Jolley and Douglas further suggest that "once the very idea of a conspiracy has been mentioned and taken root, even strong counter-arguments may be unable to lead to behavioural action" (Jolley & Douglas, 2014b, p. 8).

However, the success of counterspeech may be enhanced if the misinformation is explicitly retracted (Lewandowsky, Ecker, Seifert, Schwarz, & Cook, 2012). For example, Ecker, Lewandowsky, Fenton, and Martin (in press, Experiment 1) asked participants to read a fictitious report about a crime, which consisted of 14 statements including one about the suspects' race (i.e., "police . . . believed the three suspects were Caucasian"). In the no-misinformation condition, participants read the information about the suspects' race and then a neutral piece of information that "police . . . confirmed that the owner of the store was the sole person in the store." In both the retraction and no-retraction conditions, misinformation was introduced, stating that "police . . . believed the three suspects were Aboriginal." In the retraction condition, it was further stated that "police . . . no longer believed the suspects were . . . Aboriginal," whereas the no-retraction condition contained the neutral piece of information. It was found that retraction significantly reduced references to the misinformation. However, reliance on misinformation was not completely eliminated. Repeatedly presenting a correction may help alleviate the impact of incorrect information (Ecker, Lewandowsky, & Apai, 2011), but by repeating corrections, one runs the risk of appearing to "protest too much," therefore reducing confidence in the correction (Bush, Johnson, & Seifert, 1994). In a similar vein, Eakin, Schreiber, and Sergent-Marshall (2003) showed that when participants were given an immediate warning about the lasting effects of misinformation (i.e., that people tend to rely on it even when it has been corrected), participants were more able to resist the misinformation, but only when it was presented once. It therefore appears that combining correcting messages with a warning may be a successful avenue to intervention, but only if the misinformation was not very prominent.

In general, however, warnings seem to be more effective when they are administered before misinformation than afterwards (e.g., Lewandowsky et al., 2012). Loftus (2005) argued that this occurs because the misinformation has already been incorporated into memory before the warning or correction is received. People have an expectation that the information they will be presented with will be valid, but by being given a warning, this expectation can be altered (Lewandowsky et al., 2012). Receiving warnings may therefore induce a temporary state of skepticism and prompt the recipient to become more vigilant, and they may then suppress the misinformation that has been presented to them (Lewandowsky et al., 2012; Eakin et al., 2003; Loftus, 2005). Schul (1993) found evidence for this assertion, showing that people took longer to process misinformation when they were warned about it, suggesting greater vigilance in processing the information. The type of warning presented has also been examined. For example, Ecker et al. (2011) found that for pre-misinformation warnings, specific warnings explaining how people continue to rely on misinformation even when it has been corrected were more effective than general warnings designed to induce alertness. Research therefore shows that using a specific pre-warning alongside refuting information can be an effective way to reduce reliance on misinformation. This may also be a method worth testing to address people's reliance on conspiracy versus official or mainstream information.

Both practical and ethical issues, however, complicate such techniques. For instance, one option put forward by Sunstein and Vermeule (2009) is for authoritative public bodies, such as governments or scientific organizations, to openly publish corrective information that debunks harmful conspiracy theories. As noted by Sunstein and Vermeule, this could have a paradoxical backlash effect, in that arguing against a claim may work as an implicit acknowledgement that it is at least worth considering. As reviewed above, there are many potential pitfalls in countering misinformation, conspiratorial or otherwise (e.g., Bush et al., 1994). Moreover, public debunking of conspiracy theories by officials may increase exposure to and interest in conspiracy theories, which is associated with increased conspiracy belief (Douglas & Sutton, 2008; Swami, Furnham, Haubner, Stieger, & Voracek, 2009).

A second option proposed by Sunstein and Vermeule (2009) that we mentioned earlier is to engage in cognitive infiltration – to send covert agents into conspiracist communities with the goal of creating some epistemological diversity. However, there may be problems with this approach, not the least of which concern the ethics of such an enterprise. In particular, government agents infiltrating private discussion groups in order to align citizens' opinions with an ideologically accepted norm could seem like propaganda. It also bears an uncomfortable resemblance to COINTELPRO, an infamous FBI domestic counterintelligence program that involved illegal infiltration, disruption, and surveillance of domestic political movements (Weiner, 2012). Conspiracy theories may produce cynicism about the political system, promote mistrust, and decrease engagement with society, but programs like COINTELPRO (or, indeed, a hypothetical cognitive infiltration campaign) would perhaps make that mistrust, cynicism, and disengagement justified. It is certainly arguable whether a cure such as this would be any better than the disease.

Even putting those issues aside, cognitive infiltration might not work as well as suggested. As acknowledged by Sunstein and Vermeule (2009), it could poison the well for legitimate discourse. That is, the knowledge that dissenting opinions might be planted by governments or other large-scale organizations could encourage even further mistrust of nonconspiracist narratives and the people who believe them, resulting in an even greater drive towards ideological purity in conspiracist communities. People within conspiracist movements such as the 9/11 Truth Movement are aware of the Sunstein and Vermeule paper, and many suspect that such a program is already in place (e.g., Griffin, 2011). Cognitive infiltration may introduce dissenting opinions where none existed before, but it may also cultivate suspicion about the legitimacy of dissenting opinions and prevent actual dissent within communities from being taken seriously.

Further, an important limitation of all of the approaches we have reviewed thus far is that they are essentially reactive. That is, all of these approaches suggest responses to conspiracy theories that are already circulating. Their aim is to reduce the degree to which people are influenced by existing conspiracy theories by obstructing their dissemination, or by disseminating warnings and counterinformation. As we have seen, such approaches face profound challenges. One is that, ironically, they may require officials to conspire in order to counteract the spread of conspiracy theories. Another is that conspiracy theories are in themselves a type of counterinformation, arming people with skepticism and doubt when they encounter official attempts to change their minds.

A proactive approach to counteracting conspiracy theories

We would like to advocate an alternative – or at least complementary – method of allaying the harmful consequences of conspiracy theories. In contrast to the essentially *reactive* stance of cognitive infiltration, counterinformation, and other currently advocated approaches, it is possible take a *proactive* stance by addressing the underlying conditions that allow conspiracy beliefs to prosper. It is useful at this point to draw on an analogy from medicine, which is divided into branches of practice including curative and preventive medicine. Curative medicine seeks to treat or cure an existing illness. Preventive medicine – and in particular a branch of preventive medicine known as primary prevention – seeks to prevent or reduce the occurrence of the illness in the first place (Leavell & Clark, 1965).

Both types of medicine are properly based on evidence about the factors that cause disease. However, curative medicine is often informed by evidence identifying a specific disease agent or pathogen and how it may be disabled or eliminated. In contrast, preventive medicine is typically informed by evidence identifying contributory factors that place individuals or communities at risk of being exposed to the disease agent or on the severity of their illness when they are exposed.

In the case of conspiracy belief, preventive approaches would draw on research into the antecedents of conspiracy theorizing and concentrate on contributory factors that are mutable. Of course, many of the known predictors of conspiracy belief include demographic and personality factors that may not be subject to change. However, and as we saw earlier in this chapter, several alterable social psychological variables also influence susceptibility to conspiracy belief. These include feelings of uncertainty (van Prooijen & Jostmann, 2013), feelings of powerlessness (Abalakina-Paap et al., 1999), political cynicism (Swami et al., 2010), magical thinking (Barron, Morgan, Towell, Altemeyer, & Swami, 2014), and errors in logical and probabilistic reasoning (Brotherton & French, 2014). This implies that by intervening on these factors, it is possible, in principle, to attenuate conspiracy theorizing and the harm that follows from it. For example, since a lack of control has been found to increase belief in conspiracy theories (Whitson & Galinsky, 2008), it may be the case that inducing instead a strong sense of personal control may reduce belief in conspiracy theories. However, such interventions do not have to be tailored to particular conspiracy theories. If effective, they will reduce harm from conspiracy theories that has yet to be formulated and regardless of their particular content.

An important potential advantage of preventive approaches to conspiracy theorizing is their collateral benefits. The mutable psychological predictors of conspiracy belief that research has uncovered are generally viewed as adverse and undesirable in their own right. So, we might wish that even if there were no such thing as conspiracy theories, our educational and political institutions would help people become critical and rational thinkers, help them feel that their lives are meaningful and controllable, and help them feel that they can place a reasonable degree of trust in their leaders to represent their interests. Further, the predictors of conspiracy belief have been linked to a range of undesirable outcomes. For example, adverse appraisals such as uncertainty, powerlessness, and anomie are linked not just to conspiracy beliefs but to impaired mental health, physical health, and decision making (Hirsh, Mar, & Peterson, 2012). So, intervening on such factors is likely to be of value in itself and to bring about reductions not just in conspiracy belief but also in social and psychological ills more generally.

What, then, would preventive approaches to the harm of conspiracy theorizing look like in practice? Each preventive factor may require different kinds of intervention, delivered via policy and practice and in education, politics, or economics. Uncertainty, powerlessness, and political cynicism together form a cluster of adverse appraisals of the world and one's place in it. They all respond to objective sociopolitical conditions, such as relative deprivation and political transparency (Rogers & Pilgrim, 2010). This means that policies that increase equality and political transparency have a reasonable prospect of making people appraise the world in a less adverse way – and so be less susceptible to influence by conspiracy theories.

For their part, magical and fallacious thinking comprise a predisposition to appraise the world in an irrational way. It is not clear whether they are attenuated by normal formal education programs (Eckblad & Chapman, 1983; Peltzer, 2003), but there is strong evidence that they are reduced by training in logic and probability specifically (e.g., Agnoli & Krantz, 1989; Sedlmeier & Gigerenzer, 2001). Thus, they lend themselves to educational interventions such as training in logical and critical thought, run in the context of schools and other educational institutions (see Swami et al., 2013, for a similar suggestion in relation to conspiracy theories). An advantage of this educational approach is that it does not necessarily encourage blanket rejection of conspiracy theories – some of which are plausible, turn out to be true, and play an important role in holding authorities to account. Rather, it would allow people to critically consider the evidence and logic underpinning conspiracy theories and make informed, coherent judgments about them.

Ultimately, the choice of intervention strategy depends on a variety of factors. If conspiracy theories are perceived to have few or no consequences, or mostly positive consequences, there is no need to intervene. Such theories can be seen as a by product of healthy skepticism about official narratives, or simply as the natural background noise of an ideologically pluralistic society. Widespread theories with immediately harmful consequences, such as antivaccine conspiracy theories, deserve closer attention and would probably merit some open and transparent antimisinformation efforts by scientific and academic organizations. As long as the theories are well-known and widely repeated (Lewandowsky et al., 2012), corrective information could potentially be effective, although conspiracy theories seem to be particularly resistant to disconfirmation efforts (Jolley & Douglas, 2014b). This is an area of much research interest, and our knowledge of techniques for countering conspiracist misinformation will undoubtedly progress further in the next few years.

Conclusion

We believe that research exploring the potential consequences of conspiracy theories is timely. Despite claims that they may be harmful for individuals, groups, and society, especially in raising suspicion concerning scientific claims (e.g., Goertzel, 2010; Sunstein & Vermeule, 2009) or facilitating terrorist acts (Bartlett & Miller, 2010), there has been very little evidence supporting these claims. In this chapter, and in our research to date, we have demonstrated that some wariness about the effects of conspiracy theories may indeed be warranted. Specifically, exposure to conspiracy theories may have a negative impact on intentions to engage in politics, engage in environmentally friendly initiatives, and vaccinate children against harmful diseases. Further research should attempt to identify other potential consequences of conspiracy theories, but researchers should also pay more attention to the benefits, for which there is no empirical evidence at present. Researchers should also carefully consider the ethical, legal, and practical implications of intervening on conspiracy theories.

From emerging evidence we know that it is often inaccurate to characterize conspiracy theories as trivial views that are held by paranoid and deluded individuals who separate themselves from broader society. They should therefore not be dismissed out of hand as harmless or of little importance. Governments and environmental and health professionals should be aware that conspiracy theories may be detrimental to their efforts to increase prosocial, proenvironmental, and healthy behaviors. A future challenge for researchers will be to identify possible ways in which the effects of conspiracy theories may be further evaluated and responsibly addressed.

Author note

Address correspondence to Karen Douglas, School of Psychology, University of Kent, Canterbury, CT2 7NP, U.K. E-mail: k.douglas@kent.ac.uk

References

Abalakina-Paap, M., Stephan, W.G., Craig, T., & Gregory, W.L. (1999). Beliefs in conspiracies. *Political Psychology, 20*, 637–647.

Agnoli, F., & Krantz, D.H. (1989). Suppressing natural heuristics by formal instruction: The case of the conjunction fallacy. *Cognitive Psychology, 21*, 515–550.

Barlow, F.K., Paolini, S., Pedersen, A., Hornsey, M.J., Radke, H.R., Harwood, J., . . . Sibley, C.G. (2012). The contact caveat: Negative contact predicts increased prejudice more than positive contact predicts reduced prejudice. *Personality and Social Psychology Bulletin, 38*, 1629–1643.

Barron, D., Morgan, K., Towell, T., Altemeyer, B., & Swami, V. (2014). Associations between schizotypy and belief in conspiracist ideation. *Personality and Individual Differences, 70*, 156–159.

Bartlett, J., & Miller, C. (2010). *The power of unreason: Conspiracy theories, extremism and counter-terrorism.* London: Demos.

Bird, S.T., & Bogart, L.M. (2003). Birth control conspiracy beliefs, perceived discrimination, and contraception among African Americans. *Journal of Health Psychology, 8*, 263–276.

Bogart, L.M., Galvan, F.H., Wagner, G.J., & Klein, D.J. (2011). Longitudinal association of HIV conspiracy beliefs with sexual risk among Black males living with HIV. *AIDS and Behavior, 15*, 1180–1186.

Bogart, L.M., & Thorburn, S.T. (2006). Relationship of African Americans' sociodemographic characteristics to belief in conspiracies about HIV/AIDS and birth control. *Journal of the National Medical Association, 98*, 1144–1150.

Bogart, L.M., Wagner, G., Galvan, F.H., & Banks, D. (2010). Conspiracy beliefs about HIV are related to antiretroviral treatment nonadherence among African American men with HIV. *Journal of Acquired Immune Deficiency Syndromes, 53*(5), 648–655.

Bratich, J.Z. (2008). *Conspiracy panics: Political rationality and popular culture.* New York: State University of New York Press.

Brotherton, R., & French, C.C. (2014). Belief in conspiracy theories and susceptibility to the conjunction fallacy. *Applied Cognitive Psychology, 28*, 238–248.

Brotherton, R., French, C.C., & Pickering, A.D. (2013). Measuring belief in conspiracy theories: The generic conspiracist beliefs scale. *Frontiers in Psychology, 4*, 279.

Bush, J.G., Johnson, H.M., & Seifert, C.M. (1994). The implications of corrections: Then why did you mention it? In A. Ram & K. Eiselt (Eds.), *Proceedings of the sixteenth annual conference of the cognitive science society* (pp. 112–117). Hillsdale, NJ: Erlbaum.

Butler, L.D., Koopman, C., & Zimbardo, P.G. (1995). The psychological impact of viewing the film *JFK*: Emotions, beliefs, and political behavioral intentions. *Political Psychology, 16*, 237–257.

Carson, S., Peterson, J.B., & Higgins, D.M. (2005). Reliability, validity and factor structure of the creative achievement questionnaire. *Creativity Research Journal, 17*, 37–50.

CBS News. (2014). How one unvaccinated child sparked Minnesota measles outbreak. Retrieved from http://www.cbsnews.com/news/how-one-unvaccinated-child-sparked-minnesota-measles-outbreak/

Chigwedere, P., Seage, G.R., III, Gruskin, S., Lee, T.H., & Essex, M. (2008). Estimating the lost benefits of antiretroviral drug use in South Africa. *Journal of Acquired Immune Deficiency Syndromes, 49*, 410–415.

Clark, J. (1998). *The UFO book: Encyclopedia of the extraterrestrial.* Detroit, MI: Visible Ink Press.

Clarke, S. (2002). Conspiracy theories and conspiracy theorizing. *Philosophy of the Social Sciences, 32*, 131–150.

Coady, D. (2006). *Conspiracy theories: The philosophical debate*. Hampshire, England: Ashgate.

Crocker, J., Luhtanen, R., Broadnax, S., & Blaine, B. E. (1999). Belief in U.S. government conspiracies against Blacks among Black and White college students: Powerlessness or system blame? *Personality and Social Psychology Bulletin, 25*, 941–953.

Darwin, H., Neave, N., & Holmes, J. (2011). Belief in conspiracy theories. The role of paranormal belief, paranoid ideation and schizotypy. *Personality and Individual Differences, 50*, 1289–1293.

Dawkins, R. (1976). *The selfish gene*. Oxford: Oxford University Press.

Demicheli, V., Rivetti, A., Debalini, M. G., & Di Pietrantoni, C. (2012). Vaccines for measles, mumps, and rubella in children. *Cochrane Database of Systematic Reviews, 2*, CD004407.

Douglas, K. M., & Sutton, R. M. (2008). The hidden impact of conspiracy theories: Perceived and actual influence of theories surrounding the death of Princess Diana. *Journal of Social Psychology, 148*, 210–222.

Douglas, K. M., & Sutton, R. M. (2011). Does it take one to know one? Endorsement of conspiracy theories is influenced by personal willingness to conspire. *British Journal of Social Psychology, 50*, 544–552.

Eakin, D. K., Schreiber, T. A., & Sergent-Marshall, S. (2003). Misinformation effects in eyewitness memory: The presence and absence of memory impairment as a function of warning and misinformation accessibility. *Journal of Experimental Psychology: Learning Memory and Cognition, 29*, 813–825.

Eckblad, M., & Chapman, L. J. (1983). Magical ideation as an indicator of schizotypy. *Journal of Consulting and Clinical Psychology, 51*, 215–225.

Ecker, U. K. H., Lewandowsky, S., & Apai, J. (2011). Terrorists brought down the plane! —No, actually it was a technical fault: Processing corrections of emotive information. *Quarterly Journal of Experimental Psychology, 64*, 283–310.

Ecker, U. K. H., Lewandowsky, S., Fenton, O., & Martin, K. (in press). Do people keep believing because they want to? Pre-existing attitudes and the continued influence of misinformation. *Memory and Cognition*.

Fenster, M. (1999). *Conspiracy theories: Secrecy and power in American culture*. Minneapolis: University of Minnesota Press.

Flegg, R. B., & Hukins, A. A. (1973). The measurement of a scientific attitude-curiosity. *Research in Science Education, 3*, 69–74.

Furnham, A. (2013). Commercial conspiracy theories: A pilot study. *Frontiers in Psychology, 4*, 379.

Goertzel, T. (1994). Belief in conspiracy theories. *Political Psychology, 15*, 731–742.

Goertzel, T. (2010). Conspiracy theories in science. *EMBO Reports, 11*, 493–499.

Golec de Zavala, A., & Cichocka, A. (2012). Collective narcissism and anti-Semitism in Poland: The mediating role of siege beliefs and the conspiracy stereotype of Jews. *Group Processes and Intergroup Relations, 15*, 213–229.

Griffin, D. R. (2011). *Cognitive infiltration: An Obama appointee's plan to undermine the 9/11 conspiracy theory*. Northampton, MA: Olive Branch Press.

Guarino, L., Roger, D., & Olason, D. T. (2007). Reconstructing N: A new approach to measuring emotional sensitivity. *Current Psychology, 26*, 37–45.

Hirsh, J. B., Mar, R. A., & Peterson, J. B. (2012). Psychological entropy: A framework for understanding uncertainty-related anxiety. *Psychological Review, 119*, 304–320.

Hoyt, M. A., Rubin, L. R., Nemero, C. J., Lee, J., Huebner, D. M., & Proeschold-Bell, R. J. (2012). HIV/AIDS-related institutional mistrust among multiethnic men who have sex with men: Effects on HIV testing and risk behaviors. *Health Psychology, 31*, 269–277.

Huffington Post. (2014). Flight MH370 – theories . . . theories . . . and yet more theories (but no facts). Retrieved from http://www.huffingtonpost.co.uk/navjot-singh/post_7222_b_5056524.html

Husting, G., & Orr, M. (2007). Dangerous machinery: "Conspiracy theorist" as a transpersonal strategy of exclusion. *Symbolic Interaction, 30,* 127–150.

Imhoff, R., & Bruder, M. (2014). Speaking (un-)truth to power: Conspiracy mentality as a generalised political attitude. *European Journal of Personality, 28*(1), 25–43.

Inglehart, R. (1987). Extremist political positions and perceptions of conspiracy: Even paranoids have real enemies. In C. F. Graumann & S. Moscovici (Eds.), *Changing conceptions of conspiracy* (pp. 231–244). New York: Springer.

Jolley, D., & Douglas, K. M. (2014a). The social consequences of conspiracism: Exposure to conspiracy theories decreases the intention to engage in politics and to reduce one's carbon footprint. *British Journal of Psychology, 105,* 35–56.

Jolley, D., & Douglas, K. M. (2014b). The effects of anti-vaccine conspiracy theories on vaccination intentions. *PLOS ONE, 9*(2): e89177.

Kofta, M., & Sędek, G. (2005). Conspiracy stereotypes of Jews during systemic transformation in Poland. *International Journal of Sociology, 35,* 40–64.

Leavell, H. R., & Clark, E. G. (1965). *Preventive medicine for the doctor in his community* (3rd ed.). New York: McGraw-Hill.

Leman, P. J., & Cinnirella, M. (2007). A major event has a major cause: Evidence for the role of heuristics in reasoning about conspiracy theories. *Social Psychological Review, 9,* 18–28.

Lewandowsky, S., Ecker, U. K. H., Seifert, C. M., Schwarz, N., & Cook, J. (2012). Misinformation and its correction: Continued influence and successful debiasing. *Psychological Science in the Public Interest, 13,* 106–131.

Lewandowsky, S., Oberauer, K., & Gignac, G. E. (2013). NASA faked the moon landing – Therefore (climate) science is a hoax: An anatomy of the motivated rejection of science. *Psychological Science, 24,* 622–633.

Lobato, E., Mendoza, J., Sims, V., & Chin, M. (in press). Examining the relationship between conspiracy theories, paranormal beliefs, and pseudoscience acceptance among a university population. *Applied Cognitive Psychology.*

Loftus, E. F. (2005). Planting misinformation in the human mind: A 30-year investigation of the malleability of memory. *Learning Memory, 12,* 361–366.

McCauley, C., & Jacques, S. (1979). The popularity of conspiracy theories of presidential assassination: A Bayesian analysis. *Journal of Personality and Social Psychology, 37,* 637–644.

Miller, S. (2002). Conspiracy theories. *Argumentation & Advocacy, 39,* 40–56.

Newheiser, A.-K., Farias, M., & Tausch, N. (2011). The functional nature of conspiracy beliefs: Examining the underpinnings of belief in the *Da Vinci Code* conspiracy. *Personality and Individual Differences, 58,* 1007–1011.

Oliver, J. E., & Wood, T. J. (2014). Medical conspiracy theories and health behaviors in the United States. *JAMA Internal Medicine, 174,* 817–818.

Peltzer, K. (2003). Magical thinking and paranormal beliefs among secondary and university students in South Africa. *Personality and Individual Differences, 35,* 1419–1426.

Rogers, A., & Pilgrim, D. (2010). *A sociology of mental health and illness* (4th ed.). New York: McGraw-Hill.

Schul, Y. (1993). When warning succeeds: The effect of warning on success in ignoring invalid information. *Journal of Experimental Social Psychology, 29,* 42–62.

Sedlmeier, P., & Gigerenzer, G. (2001). Teaching Bayesian reasoning in less than two hours. *Journal of Experimental Psychology: General, 130,* 380–400.

Stieger, S., Gumhalter, N., Tran, U. S., Voracek, M., & Swami, V. (2013). Girl in the cellar: A repeated cross-sectional investigation of belief in conspiracy theories about the kidnapping of Natascha Kampusch. *Frontiers in Psychology, 4*, 297.

Sunstein, C. R., & Vermeule, A. (2009). Conspiracy theories: Causes and cures. *Journal of Political Philosophy, 17*, 202–227.

Sutton, R. M., & Douglas, K. M. (2014). Examining the monological nature of conspiracy theories. In J-W. van Prooijen & P. A. M. van Lange (Eds.), *Power, politics and paranoia: Why people are suspicious of their leaders* (pp. 254–272). Cambridge: Cambridge University Press.

Swami, V. (2012). Social psychological origins of conspiracy theories: The case of the Jewish conspiracy theory in Malaysia. *Frontiers in Psychology, 3*, 280.

Swami, V., Chamorro-Premuzic, T., & Furnham, A. (2010). Unanswered questions: A preliminary investigation of personality and individual difference predictors of 9/11 conspiracist beliefs. *Applied Cognitive Psychology, 24*, 749–761.

Swami, V., & Coles, R. (2010). The truth is out there: Belief in conspiracy theories. *Psychologist, 23*, 560–563.

Swami, V., Coles, R., Stieger, S., Pietschnig, J., Furnham, A., Rehim, S., & Voracek, M. (2011). Conspiracist ideation in Britain and Austria: Evidence of a monological belief system and associations between individual psychological differences and real-world and fictitious conspiracy theories. *British Journal of Psychology, 102*, 443–463.

Swami, V., & Furnham, A. (2012). Examining conspiracist beliefs about the disappearance of Amelia Earhart. *Journal of General Psychology, 139*, 244–259.

Swami, V., Furnham, A., Haubner, T., Stieger, S., & Voracek, M. (2009). The truth is out there: The structure of beliefs about extraterrestrial life among Austrian and British respondents. *Journal of Social Psychology, 149*, 29–43.

Swami, V., Nader, I. W., Pietschnig, J., Stieger, S., Tran, U., & Voracek, M. (2012). Personality and individual difference correlates of attitudes toward human rights and civil liberties. *Personality and Individual Differences, 53*, 443–447.

Swami, V., Pietschnig, J., Tran, U. S., Nader, I. W., Stieger, S., & Voracek, M. (2013). Lunar lies: The impact of informational framing and individual differences in shaping conspiracist beliefs about the moon landings. *Applied Cognitive Psychology, 27*, 71–80.

van Harreveld, F., Rutjens, B. T., Schneider, I. K., Nohlen, H. U., & Keskinis, K. (in press). In doubt and disorderly: Ambivalence promoted compensatory perceptions of order. *Journal of Experimental Psychology: General.*

van Prooijen, J.-W., & Jostmann, N. B. (2013). Belief in conspiracy theories: The influence of uncertainty and perceived morality. *European Journal of Social Psychology, 43*, 109–115.

Weiner, T. (2012). *Enemies: A history of the FBI.* New York: Random House.

Whitson, J. A., & Galinsky, A. D. (2008). Lacking control increases illusory pattern perception. *Science, 322*, 115–117.

Wood, M. J., & Douglas, K. M. (2013). "What about building 7?" A social psychological study of online discussion of 9/11 conspiracy theories. *Frontiers in Psychology, 4*, 409.

Wood, M. J., Douglas, K. M., & Sutton, R. M. (2012). Dead and alive: Beliefs in contradictory conspiracy theories. *Social Psychological and Personality Science, 3*, 767–773.

INDEX

Printed in Great Britain
by Amazon

56648619R00127